"How wonderful it is, [ ] the DNA our Founder us that we were founded to be a multicultural tapestry of collaborative risk takers for the sake of seeing the Kingdom advanced. Let's recapture our DNA with every page and continue to exalt Jesus as our Savior, Sanctifier, Healer and Coming King!"

—Kelvin Walker
Vice Chair of the C&MA Board of Directors and Superintendent of the Metropolitan District of the C&MA

Jones beautifully unveils the man behind the legend who was one of church history's most influential leaders, giving us a front row seat to witness Simpson's remarkable journey, igniting a vision that grew to a global movement.

—Aaron Shust
Christian Music Artist

David Jones' grasp of the details of the story of A. B. Simpson is both wide and deep. But more than the details he has been able to capture the heart of this visionary leader who called the church out of lethargy and irrelevance and helped to launch the great missionary movement of the 20th century—a movement which in the end transcended him and The Christian and Missionary Alliance but which in so many aspects continued to resonate with both his heart and his insights. I was vividly challenged to renew again my commitment to the worldwide proclamation of the gospel.

—Franklin Pyles
Former President, The Christian and Missionary Alliance in Canada

A. B. weaves the story of Simpson's life with pertinent quotes which help us get to know this great man of God. Every Alliance family member should read this book.

—Amy Roedding
Director for Candidate Recruitment & Development, U.S. C&MA

David Jones has provided the Alliance family, and its extended family, with a long-overdue biography of the movement's founder, Rev. A. B. Simpson. It is eminently readable, thoughtful, and engaging—a rare bird, indeed. This book will undoubtedly play a significant role in reacquainting the family not only with the complex and dynamic figure who is its father but also, therefore, with its own identity.

—BERNIE VAN DE WALLE
Chair of the Canadian C&MA Board of Directors and of the Alliance World Fellowship International Commission for Theological Education

Compelling and insightful. I appreciated the author's candor and thoughtful commentary interlaced throughout this retelling of our Alliance story. I was especially intrigued by the attention given to the spiritual journeys of A. B. Simpson, his wife Margaret, and, to a lesser extent, their children. I was reminded that each life is uniquely shaped by family dynamics, historical and cultural contexts, and can be transformed by God's faithful provision. Definitely a worthy addition to my library.

—JEN VOGEL
National Director, Alliance Women

As I read David Jones' manuscript, I was thoroughly impressed. Although I had taught the life of Simpson and done considerable original research into his life, I learned a great deal from this analysis.

—DAVID HUTTAR
Professor Emeritus of Bible and Greek, Nyack College

Having wandered the C&MA Archives countless times over the past few decades, I assumed I knew just about everything there was to know about Albert Benjamin Simpson. I was wrong. Dave Jones has unearthed not only some hidden gems about this uniquely equipped man of God but also some of the earthly weaknesses and adversities that compelled him to tap into the presence, power, and fullness of the Holy Spirit that so characterized his life and fueled his ministry—and are equally available to us.

—PETER BURGO
Editor, Alliance Life Magazine

A.B.

THE UNLIKELY FOUNDER
OF A GLOBAL MOVEMENT

DAVID P. JONES

CONTENTS

INTRODUCTION vii
DEDICATION ix
ACKNOWLEDGMENTS xi

PREFACE		xv
CHAPTER 1	Raise up a Child	1
CHAPTER 2	When the Bough Breaks	11
CHAPTER 3	Following the Call	23
CHAPTER 4	The Regular Pastor	37
CHAPTER 5	Letters to Maggie	45
CHAPTER 6	Blessed Are the Peacemakers	57
CHAPTER 7	Sealed Orders	75
CHAPTER 8	The Wandering Gospel Tabernacle: 1881 to 1887	93
CHAPTER 9	Two Are Better than One: 1887 to 1897	115
CHAPTER 10	Growing Pains: 1897 to 1912	131
CHAPTER 11	Lengthening Shadows	151
CHAPTER 12	The Measure of the Man	177
Appendix 1	Margaret Simpson— A Mother in Israel	195
Appendix 2	Preacher's Kids	203
Appendix 3	Transition	217
Appendix 4	Covenants and Vows	225

NOTES 229
ANNOTATED BIBLIOGRAPHY 247

A. B.: The unlikely founder of a global movement
Copyright © 2019 (1st printing), The Christian and Missionary Alliance
David P. Jones

All scripture passages are from the King James Version (KJV) unless otherwise indicated.

Scripture quotations marked (NIV) are taken from the Holy Bible, New International Version®, NIV®. Copyright © 1973, 1978, 1984, 2011 by Biblica, Inc.™ Used by permission of Zondervan. All rights reserved worldwide. www.zondervan.com The "NIV" and "New International Version" are trademarks registered in the United States Patent and Trademark Office by Biblica, Inc.™

Cover Illustration: Kenneth Crane
Interior and Cover Design: Pamela Fogle
Editors: Joan Phillips, Peter Burgo, Cathy Ellis
Author Photo: David P. Jones

All rights reserved. No part of this publication may be reproduced, stored in a retrieval system, or transmitted in any form or by any means—electronic, mechanical, photocopying, recording, scanning, or otherwise—without the prior written permission of the publisher and copyright owners.

Published by The Christian and Missionary Alliance
P.O. Box 35000, Colorado Springs, CO 80935-3500

ISBN: 978-0-9892622-6-2

First Edition

Printed in the United States of America.

INTRODUCTION

IRRELEVANT TO INTRIGUING

One of my personal goals in life was to visit the Gospel Tabernacle, the church that A. B. Simpson planted when he launched a new movement for God. The church, located just off Times Square in New York City, is now known as John's Pizzeria, a popular restaurant. Upon entering the building, one is immediately impressed by the historic architecture and unique features of the original church. One of the key Alliance elements in the building is the stained-glass windows, which still carry the symbols of the Fourfold Gospel. My wife and I had the thrill of visiting John's Pizzeria recently and were inspired by the majestic ambiance and the delicious pizza. Once we were seated at our table, I immediately made a beeline for the balcony where I could see the windows up close. I took multiple pictures of the Fourfold Gospel symbols and imagined myself sitting in the congregation as A. B. Simpson preached one of his stirring sermons on the deeper life and missions.

Upon returning to my seat, I engaged in conversation with our waitress, who was in her early twenties and had been working at the restaurant for a few years. I asked her if she knew what this building used to be. She had no idea, and when I told her it was a church, she smiled and was somewhat shocked. Then I asked her if she had seen the symbols in the stained-glass windows. Again, she was bewildered but became very intrigued as I showed her the pictures on my camera. "What do they mean?" she asked. For the next few moments, I was able to share the marvelous truth of Christ our Savior, Sanctifier, Healer, and Coming King in language she could understand. In an instant, her workplace took on a whole new perspective.

The old was no longer irrelevant but actually intriguing. The historic was not insignificant but inspiring. She looked up at the windows that had encircled her for the past two years and realized in that moment that she was no longer just serving pizza in a restaurant but was surrounded by a rich heritage of eternal significance.

Isn't this what we would desire for our kids and grandkids—that somehow the old story of A. B. Simpson and Alliance beginnings would inspire a new movement within our next generation, and they would see that they are encircled by a heritage of faith-filled vision, dynamic passion, and fearless risk?

—Dr. David Hearn
President, The Christian and Missionary Alliance in Canada

DEDICATION

This book is dedicated to the memory of two men who worked quietly and alone for decades, collecting information, anecdotes, and biographical resources on the life of Dr. A. B. Simpson.

DR. C. DONALD MCKAIG, longtime professor and eventual vice president at Nyack Missionary College (now Nyack College) and founder of the Simpson Memorial Church in Nyack (now Living Christ Church), collected and preserved important historical accounts about Simpson from his daughter, Margaret, as well as Simpson's longtime secretary, Miss Emma Beere. Additionally, McKaig preserved assorted stories and a wealth of "Simpsonalia," that provide color and context to this book. His collection, *The Simpson Scrapbook,* is a treasure trove of little-known "nuggets" to share. As McKaig's student at Nyack, I was inspired, and often entertained, by the Simpson stories that "Doc McKaig" shared in class.

DR. JOHN S. SAWIN, former Alliance pastor and missionary to Vietnam (1947–63), returned to the United States and became the archivist at the Simpson Historical Library in Nyack, New York, now known as the National Office Archives in Colorado Springs, Colorado. Through years of investigation and research, Sawin produced a massive amount of material on the life and ministry of Simpson, handwritten on hundreds of 4X6 cards. He turned the whole collection over to the Archibald Foundation Library of the Canadian Bible College/Canadian Theological Seminary (now Ambrose University) for transcription and preservation. The result of this "John Sawin File Project" is *The Life and Times of A. B. Simpson,* available online as a PDF file. His extensive research work was a primary source of information while writing this volume.

For this reason, the memory of these men, who recognized the historic importance of A. B. Simpson, merits the dedication of the book:

Honor to whom honor is owed.

ACKNOWLEDGMENTS

I have always enjoyed reading Apostle Paul's final words found in his letters. In them, he greets friends, sends personal messages, asks for scrolls and forgotten cloaks, encourages, reprimands, instructs, and laments those who abandoned him. Even Tertius, his scribe who penned Romans, is given a bow. Paul's remarks acknowledged that he had collaborators, that he did not generate his enormous New Testament literary production without a "little bit of help from his friends."

Such is the case regarding this life story of Dr. A. B. Simpson. When I first began to see the need for a new biography of the founder of The Christian and Missionary Alliance (C&MA) a few years ago, it came from my interest in history. *The Life of A. B. Simpson*, the first official biography, was written by Rev. A. E. Thompson just a year after Simpson's death. A little more than two decades later, a Centenary Edition commemorating Simpson's birth, *Wingspread—A. B. Simpson: A Study in Spiritual Altitude*, was written by Rev. A. W. Tozer in 1943. This year, 2019, is the centennial year of Simpson's death in Nyack, New York, on October 29, 1919. Thus, 75 years have passed since publication of Tozer's slim volume.

Over the years, valuable research on Simpson's life and ministry has been published in books like *The Birth of a Vision*, edited by Dr. David F. Hartzfeld and Dr. Charles Nienkirchen in the centennial year of the C&MA of Canada and the United States. In addition, *All for Jesus* was produced in 1986 by Rev. Robert L. Niklaus, Rev. John S. Sawin, and Dr. Samuel J. Stoesz, with a revised 125th anniversary edition in 2013. Many excellent books have been written regarding Simpson's theology: *Genuine Gold* by Dr. Paul L. King, *The Heart of the Gospel* by Dr. Bernie Van De Walle, and *The Whole Gospel for the Whole World* by Dr. Franklin Pyles and Dr. Lee Beach. Dr. Michael G. Yount's *A. B. Simpson—His Message and Impact on the Third Great Awakening* frames Simpson's life in the historical context of the evangelical movement in North America. *Relentless Spirituality—Embracing the Spiritual Disciplines of A. B. Simpson* by Dr. Gary Keisling shines a light on Simpson's spiritual disciplines. Dr. Daniel J. Evearitt's *Body and Soul—Evangelism and The Social Concern of A. B. Simpson* highlights his interest and involvement in social issues as the C&MA developed. Dr. Lindsay Reynolds' *Footprints* recounts the early years of The Alliance in Canada. These books all provide valuable snapshots of little-known aspects of Simpson, his family, and the founding and early years of the C&MA.

A relatively unknown booklet of 31 pages, *Mrs. A. B. Simpson—The Wife or Love Stands* by granddaughter Katherine Alberta Brennen, was written about the same time as Tozer's book. It recounts remembrances of Simpson's wife, Margaret, who died on January 1, 1924. Fascinating family stories, unknown facts about the Simpsons and early Alliance, and a dimension of the couple from Katherine's perspective provides insight on their marriage.

Another important source of information comes from academia. In the last 50 years or so, many scholarly papers have been written about Simpson's life, ministry, theology, missiology, social concerns, spiritual development and practices, even his emotional life! Two Ph.D. dissertations in particular, *Jesus Only: The Early Life and Presbyterian Ministry of Albert Benjamin Simpson, 1843–1881* by Dr. Darrel Robert Reid, and *A Larger Christian Life: A. B. Simpson and the Early Years of the Christian and Missionary Alliance* by Dr. William Boyd Bedford, Jr., have provided historical detail not found in either of the official biographies or most other sources.

The above-mentioned as well as a wealth of material found in Simpson's books, early missions publications (*The Gospel in All Lands*, and *The Word, The Work and The World*), and the various iterations of what became known as *The Alliance Weekly* published during his lifetime provide bits and pieces of Alliance lore, family stories, struggles and victories, heartbreaks, and history that I have endeavored to weave into a narrative of the life of this amazing man of God. A. B. Simpson scaled the heights of spiritual experience and plumbed the depths of depression. This volume seeks to present a balanced portrait of a real person, admired around the world for his vision and drive to take the "whole gospel to the whole world." A hagiography of an idealized "Saint Simpson," immune to the "world, the flesh, and the devil," would produce a cardboard saint not relatable or credible. The goal of this book is to present Albert Benjamin Simpson as a man gifted by God—not only intelligent and multi-talented but also a true-to-life person, subject to error, occasional questionable judgment, as well as a husband and father who struggled to find balance in those roles.

It should also be noted that the challenge in portraying a well-rounded view of a man as complex as A. B. Simpson is deciding which stories warrant telling within a reasonably-sized and engaging narrative and which ones to leave for future discovery. Especially as his fame increased, much interest was paid to his every movement, sermon, writing—in short, his life. This produced an abundance of insightful glimpses into what made him who he was—as well as more than a few colorful tales, humorous anecdotes, and deeply personal accounts. I have endeavored here to thoughtfully select the stories that remain true to his "whole" person—and even so, there is much left to tell.

This project would have not materialized without the aid of many friends. After recognizing that the centennial year of Simpson's death was approaching, I contacted two Alliance pastors/writers, Drs. Paul King and James Snyder, to see if they were working on a new Simpson biography. Both answered in the negative, begging lack of time and previous commitments, but both encouraged me to tackle the project. The biggest boost came from Dr. Ronald Brown, District Missions Coach for the Western Canadian District of the C&MA. He had helped me previously publish a history of Simpson's first missionary initiative in Cabinda, *So Being Sent, They Went*. He told me to "take a crack at it." Mr. H. D. (Sandy) Ayer, chief archivist of Ambrose University in Calgary, Canada, also proved to be an invaluable source of information, files, and tips to track down.

I owe much to the staff of The Christian and Missionary Alliance National Office in Colorado Springs. Mrs. Kristin Rollins, managing archivist, gave unstintingly of her time and expertise, helping me find documents, digging deep into the files and discovering hitherto-unpublished historical material filed in the Archives. Mrs. Joan Phillips, former National Office staff writer, did the bulk of the editing before passing it on to Mr. Peter Burgo, *Alliance Life* editor, and Mrs. Cathy Ellis, *Alliance Life* managing editor, who prepared the final draft for publication. Mr. Matthew DeCoste, director for the Alliance design team, provided his expertise for the book's copy and cover design. Dr. John Stumbo, C&MA president, also gave great encouragement and backing for the project.

Additional help and editorial suggestions were made by several "readers," including Dr. David Huttar, member the original editorial committee of the 1986 edition of *All for Jesus,* as well as Dr. David Reese and Dr. Jarvis Crosby of Toccoa Falls College. Dr. Kenneth Draper of Ambrose University also collaborated on the project along with Dr. Franklin Pyles, former president of The Christian and Missionary Alliance of Canada. Longtime friend Rev. Abraham Sandler gave important historical perspective in relation to Simpson's commitment to the reaching of "the Jew first and also to the Greek." And once again, my long-suffering wife, Judy, spent hours proofreading, giving valuable suggestions and encouragement over the long life of this project.

My sincere hope is that this book will provide an authentic picture of Simpson to a new generation of Alliance leaders and members worldwide, seeing Simpson as not only an historic figure but also as an example of a man committed to fulfilling his life's mission to reach the "neglected masses" everywhere, while relentlessly pursuing the "Christ-in-me" relationship as his own living reality.

PREFACE

Why read a biography of one who passed 100 years ago? What could possibly be new for us today in someone's old story? One could say it depends on the story.

If a chronicle of a rebel—a radical who shook up the Church and challenged society's view of the "neglected masses" and in so doing helped shape the world of modern evangelism—is of interest, look no further than the life journey of A. B. Simpson.

A. B. Simpson was one of the major figures of the English-speaking evangelical world in the late 1800s and early 1900s. Not only does The Christian and Missionary Alliance count him as its founding father but also The Assemblies of God, The Foursquare Church, and other Pentecostal movements that follow his "fourfold" gospel format in their theology. He is often better known among those bodies than in many Alliance churches. This book takes a fresh look at this great man of God.

Dr. Albert Benjamin Simpson, or A. B., as he is often referred to in The Alliance, was born on December 15, 1843, on Prince Edward Island, Canada, and died October 29, 1919, in Nyack, New York. In 1920, the "official biography" of A. B. Simpson was written by Rev. A. E. Thompson, Canadian C&MA missionary to Israel and longtime disciple of Simpson. The book was published by the C&MA's Christian Publications, Inc. To paraphrase a clever quote, "Biographies [like vengeance] are best served cold." By that is meant that an account of a person's life written just one year after said person's death is premature. Barely had a year passed and Simpson's remains been buried next to Pardington Hall at the Missionary Training Institute, now known as Nyack College, that an instant Alliance bestseller on Dr. Simpson's life had been published. The extent and effects of Simpson's life and ministry worldwide were yet to be tested by time. While factually true and reverentially rendered, Thompson's chronicle often feels more like a hagiography than a biography.

Alliance pastor, author, magazine editor, and spiritual mentor A. W. Tozer said it well in his introduction of *Wingspread, A. B. Simpson: A Study in Spiritual Altitude,* also published by Christian Publications, Inc. in 1943: "Any man who has reason to hope (or to fear) that someone may someday write the story of his life would do well to pray that he may not fall into the hand of an enemy, a disciple, a rival, or a relative. Of all men, these make the poorest biographers." Thompson was an associate of Simpson. To "paint in the warts and moles" of Simpson's amazing life was too much to ask of a disciple. As Tozer wryly put it: "True disciples never see warts, or if one is called to their attention, they will argue that it is only a callous anyway, caused by a halo that had slipped down." Consequently, Tozer's rendering of Simpson's life, including warts and moles, likely scandalized many Alliance pastors, missionaries, and the faithful of "the Society," as it was known in those days. This author's father, a local Alliance pastor, did not appreciate Tozer's attempt to humanize and "humorize" the life of Dr. Simpson. It is a little-known fact that eventually Brother Tozer had second thoughts regarding his biography of Simpson. "According to Alliance historian John Sawin, Tozer told him he wanted to withdraw *Wingspread* from circulation because it was an 'interpretation, not a biography of Simpson.'"[1]

On the occasion of the Centennial Celebration of The Christian and Missionary Alliance in 1987, a book celebrating 100 years of Alliance history and ministry, *All for Jesus,* was published by Christian Publications, Inc. The editors, Robert Niklaus, John Sawin, and Samuel Stoesz, all contributed to the writing of three chapters that trace the life of Simpson. While their treatment was a condensed account of the life and times of Simpson, it did contain some new source material and valuable insights. However, it fell far short of being considered a new official biography of Simpson. Any of those three godly men, all historians in their own right, could have written an excellent new biography of the founder. However, such was not the case.

It is my intention to tell the story of Simpson's life with as much clarity and detail necessary to provide a clear picture of the man. Since *Wingspread,* no biographical work on the life of A. B. Simpson has been written. However, many academic theses have been written on his theology, missiology, hymnology, educational philosophy, and much more. Two in particular stand out: One written by Dr. Darrell Robert Reid, "Jesus Only: The Early Life and Presbyterian Ministry of Albert

Benjamin Simpson, 1843–1881," provides an invaluable in-depth look at Simpson's early years. Reid's thesis clearly reveals Simpson's formative years that led to his becoming a Presbyterian clergyman until he set out on his own in late 1881. The second dissertation by Dr. William Boyd Bedford, longtime Alliance pastor, is entitled "A Larger Christian Life: A. B. Simpson and the Early Years of the Christian and Missionary Alliance."

Birth of a Vision, the excellent Canadian Alliance centennial *Festschrift* (festival of writings), edited by Hartzfeld and Neinkirchen, focused on the life and work of this great man of God, who was Canada's gift to the world. Van de Walle's *The Heart of the Gospel* contains biographical material and zeros in on the development of Simpson's experiential theology known as the Fourfold Gospel. Additionally, many other books have been written over the years by writers in and out of The Alliance that present Simpson's story, his missiology, eschatology, pneumatology, education philosophy, mystic bent, his treatment of the Fourfold Gospel, and his effect on the Pentecostal movement. All have proven to be helpful.

New biographical material on Simpson is hard to find. Simpson's critics were hard on him and are largely forgotten today. Simpson's granddaughter, Katherine Alberta Brennen, wrote an intriguing little booklet about the same time as Tozer's biography. Brennen's memoir, *Mrs. A. B. Simpson—The Wife or Love Stands,* introduces a fascinating family perspective from A. B.'s wife, Margaret Simpson, as well as anecdotes that give additional color and contour to the portrait and make A. B. more believable and relatable to today's generation of Alliance leaders and believers.

This biography's purpose is to introduce today's worldwide Alliance family to Albert Benjamin Simpson, not as an iconic, bearded evangelical giant of the late 19th and early 20th century but as a man of God—a kind of Elijah, "with a nature like ours." A. B. Simpson has cast a long and lasting shadow across the world. Most of the younger generation of those born into the Kingdom of God because of his broad vision and focused mission in life do not know, nor can they identify with, this "great man."

Charles Colson, former White House Counsel under President Richard Nixon and founder of Prison Fellowship, once said, "Our faith is rooted in history."[2] This certainly is a true statement. I paraphrase

Colson's quote: Our C&MA history is rooted in one man's faith journey. I think it could be fairly said about the worldwide Alliance movement that our future as a movement of God depends on the depth of those roots of faith. A pastor friend of mine made a simple but pertinent comment: "If you don't understand A. B. Simpson, then you can't really understand The Christian and Missionary Alliance."[3] Amen!

It is my hope that this story of Simpson's life and legacy will encourage others to live "all-for-Jesus" lives. I seek to place Simpson in the context of his age, within the perspective of events and personalities that impacted his world and times. The narrative "thread" that will give the book coherence and continuity is the story of the man behind the Acts 1:8 movement that emerged from his life experiences and evolution as a Christian leader of his day.

The future pulpiteer would transform the kitchen table into his "sacred desk," gather his "brethren" around, and preach to the captive congregation.

CHAPTER 1
RAISE UP A CHILD

*W*HILE STRUGGLING TO KEEP THE PAIN and disappointment from his bearded face, the lanky Presbyterian pastor, still young looking at 37, despaired for his ministry at 13th Street Presbyterian Church. Rev. Albert Benjamin Simpson had accepted the call from the well-to-do New York congregation after they agreed with his stated goal of reaching the "neglected masses" of the city. Thus, he began a concentrated effort to reach the "neglected," the unchurched multitudes of the city.

Simpson's new pastorate was located on 13th Street, near the corner of 7th Avenue. Vaguely resembling a Roman temple with its six Doric columns, it was surrounded by brownstones. He noted in his November 1879 diary: "Led to survey my field today, extending especially from 14th Street to 17th, and 6th Avenue to the West side, and my soul filled with joy to find it so great and full of the plain people—whom I love. It is all our own, this field, and God is with us and will bless."[1] Hundreds of thousands of city dwellers lived in that "field," most untouched by the gospel.

Soon after getting settled in New York with his wife and four children, Simpson held three weeks of evangelistic services at his new charge, with many decisions for salvation. Some weeks later, 37 new members were received, and the church leaders were pleased. But Simpson wasn't satisfied. So, he began to preach on the streets, accompanied by a few hardy souls from 13th Street Presbyterian. This experience was somewhat threatening to the affluent parishioners, who rarely ventured to Little Italy, Mulberry Street, or farther south to the notorious Five Points slum.

As a result, Simpson and his evangelistic team preached to hundreds of recent arrivals, some fresh off the boat and others already working on the docks at the street markets. Most of them had a poor grasp of English, and almost all claimed to be Roman Catholic. Simpson's warm preaching and simple explanation of God's grace brought many to realize that good works and the Church would not save their souls.

By spring 1881, Simpson started to see 13th Street Presbyterian Church become a place where people of all classes, colors, and creeds could come together to worship Jesus Christ as Lord and Savior. This was what he had "signed up for" and what the church had agreed to previously. However, despite the church's original promise to support his vision, he found that "they had no desire for aggressive urban evangelism of the unchurched masses, nor did they welcome attempts to turn the church itself into a home for all comers."[2] Soon, a group of 100 Italian immigrants, recently converted through Simpson's street evangelism, were presented by Simpson to the church leadership to become members, but the church leaders refused to allow them into membership at 13th Street Presbyterian Church. This deep disappointment, coupled with his depleted energies, poor health, and growing disillusionment with the affluent congregation that loved him and his family, but not the "neglected masses," broke his heart and his health. After months of pouring out his energy on the marginalized immigrants, the leadership's abrupt decision led to a serious break in Simpson's physical and emotional health, requiring him to take an extended vacation during the summer of 1881. A short time later, Simpson resigned from 13th Street Presbyterian due to differing visions of the church's mission. In November 1881, the first service of what would later become the Gospel Tabernacle of New York City was held in the Caldonian Club Hall with seven people. Within a year, this small congregation had grown to almost 300 people.[3]

New York was more than a magnet for Europe's "tired and the poor" who yearned for freedom and a chance at a better life. Young women, with little or no prospect in their hometowns in rural America, came to the Big City after hearing about the well-paying jobs for ambitious girls looking to move up in the world. However, their hoped-for dreams soon faded before the stark reality of a cruel, cold city waiting to devour them. Thousands rapidly discovered that the job market was limited and demanding. However, other opportunities for "work" were abundant in the saloons, dance halls, gambling dens, and eventually, the brothels. Quickly, the promise of a better life became a faint memory, while the daily struggle to survive led them on a downward path of exploitation and abuse.

Many affluent New Yorkers were attracted to Simpson's newly opened Gospel Tabernacle and its outreach efforts directed toward the "neglected." Simpson was a booster of the rescue mission movement. In his preaching and practice, he championed a unique blend of evangelism and compassion ministries. As a result, several of the wealthy members of the Tabernacle opened rescue missions with the blessing of their pastor. Orphanages, healing homes, and other services directed toward those in need received open encouragement by their pastor. Simpson was a motivator and mobilizer. He was not a social reformer

> "A church that wants the poor, misses them, seeks them, will always find them, feed them and be filled with them."

but a soul winner. However, he felt that the gospel was best shared by words backed up by deeds. "There is room not only for the worship of God, the teaching of sacred truth and the evangelization of the lost, but also for every phase of practical philanthropy and usefulness."[4] He went on to enumerate different compassion ministries: charitable relief for the poor, training for the unemployed, orphan shelters for the helpless, refuges for alcoholics, and a safe harbor for those washed up on the shores of society.

A. B. Simpson often quoted Acts 1:8, one of his favorite Scripture passages and the theme of many sermons. Unlike preachers who emphasized the geographic outreach of that verse (Jerusalem, Judea, Samaria, and ends of the earth), Simpson saw the "Samaritans" as the outcasts of New York City, and the church's mission was to reach them: the poverty-stricken, recent immigrants, racial minorities, the addicted, prisoners, and prostitutes. These were the "neglected masses" longing to be free, but only the mighty Savior could reach them through His children's loving arms. Because of this focus, the eventual home of the Gospel Tabernacle, on 44th Street and 8th Avenue, found itself in the heart of "Hell's Kitchen," one of New York's neediest and most crime-infested areas. Soon after leaving 13th Street Presbyterian Church, Simpson wrote in the first issue of his magazine *The Word, The Work and The World,* concerning the power of Christ's love for reaching the neglected masses the world over: "A church that wants the poor, misses them, seeks them, will always find them, feed them and be filled with them."[5]

At this point in the story, the questions must be asked, "Where did this heart for the "neglected" come from? What had made this very successful and formerly proper Presbyterian clergyman become such an ardent lover of all people everywhere as well as a very effective evangelist? Roots often reveal how the tree grows.

Two hundred and forty years ago, Scotland and Prince Edward Island (PEI) resembled each other in many ways. Working the land was not particularly easy in either place and neither was life. Long, harsh winters, short summers, and the vagaries of weather made survival difficult. Religious oppression and lack of liberty in the 1700s had forced tens of thousands of Covenanters to make their way from their heather-hued hills of Scotland to the rich, red soil of a rugged island in the eastern maritime provinces of Canada, off New Brunswick and Nova Scotia, nestled in the Gulf of St. Lawrence. In their new homeland, the forests had to be cleared and cultivated before yielding a living. It became the British colony of St. John Island in 1769.[6] Some years after joining the Canadian Confederation on July 1, 1773, its name changed to Prince Edward Island (PEI).

Thus, the hardy Scotsmen left home and hearth by the shiploads for a chance at a better life in the New World. British North America needed people, and the Covenanters wanted freedom. They were farmers, fishermen, craftsmen, and storekeepers, and they labored long and hard in their adopted land to provide a better life for their growing families. James and Janet Simpson were part of that early wave of settlers who left their homes in the 1770s for the New World.[7] In PEI they found what they had longed for—peace and freedom, a place where they could live their life as they believed God so desired. Years later, this same lovely island became the setting for *Anne of Green Gables,* written by Lucy Maud Montgomery.

On a cold and blustery December 15, 1843, a baby boy, fourth of nine children, was born to James and Jane Simpson, third-generation Scottish immigrants. They named their tiny son Albert Benjamin. The Simpsons lived on the north shore of Prince Edward Island, near Cavendish, in the village of Bayview, overlooking Greenville Bay, which opens on to the Gulf of Saint Lawrence. Their house, situated on Simpson's Mill Road, was both home as well as headquarters for the growing Simpson family business. By the mid-1840s, this enterprising young shipbuilder, together with his brother, Alexander, who operated a grist mill and wool-carding business, had finally begun to enjoy the fruits of their labor. Together, they exported flour, oatmeal, and barley to markets in Great Britain via the Cunard Steamship Company[8] and imported farm and industrial implements from Manchester to sell in the busy general store. Queen Victoria had already been reigning for more than six years, and the sun never set on the Union Jack.

A PROPHETIC PRAYER

James and Jane had married in the nearby Cavendish Presbyterian Church a little more than six years before Albert's birth. They lost their first baby, James Albert, but had two other children: William Howard and Louisa; then baby "Bertie" arrived. Both parents were devoted Christians and committed members of Cavendish Presbyterian. They took their infant son to church to be baptized a few weeks after his birth. Jane Simpson had prayed that she might give her baby to God

> **Rev. Geddie asked God to make the "wee lad" a great man of God who would impact his world for Christ.**

as Hannah had with Samuel. She wanted her child to serve the Lord either as a clergyman or missionary. Providentially, the baby boy was baptized by Rev. John Geddie, the local pastor and strong voice for missions, who four years later became the first Canadian Presbyterian missionary sent to the New Hebrides. He eventually became known as "the father of Presbyterian Missions in the South Seas."[9] In his prayer, Geddie asked God to make the "wee lad" a great man of God who would impact his world for Christ.[10] Rarely has a more prophetic prayer been uttered.

Born of old Covenanter lineage, James and Jane, like their forebears, believed in "sound doctrine." It was founded on their love and loyalty to the Bible as God's Word and in Reformed theology. Colossians 1:18 expressed their core belief: "*. . . that in everything he (Christ) might have the supremacy* (NIV). Sunday attendance at the local Presbyterian

Church was followed by an afternoon reading Scripture and learning theology.

A few years later, despite living in relative isolation from the rest of the world, life came crashing down on peaceful Bayview community and the Simpson family. The "Panic of 1847,"[11] an economic crash caused by overheated speculation in British railroad stock, led to a series of bank failures, a steep increase in the Bank of England's interest rates, a sharp drop in the grain sales from Canada, and a serious currency crisis. Just a year later, Karl Marx and Friedrich Engels would publish *The Communist Manifesto* in England, which prophesied that capitalism as practiced in the Western World was doomed to failure, with a new a brighter day dawning for the common working man.

TO THE WILDS OF ONTARIO

James Simpson was one of those hard-working men who had built a business. But a perfect storm blew over the island. People stopped paying their bills at the store and demand for his boats dried up. Cunard stopped buying Simpson's produce, and his grain sales plummeted. The burgeoning Simpson business crashed. This local collapse was just a minor failure in the larger scheme of things, but it had major consequences for James and his family. Beautiful Bayview could no longer provide a living for James and his growing brood. He had to break the sad news to Jane that they would need to seek their fortune elsewhere, trusting in God's grace and guidance to find a new home. With such sentiments, the young father sold his business, settled his affairs as best he could, and prepared to move his family.

Simpson's older sister, Louisa, remembered the move, which took place in 1847. James chartered a local vessel, setting sail with seven families for Canada's "wild west." The trip was an adventure for his big sister Louisa, but Bertie, three and a half years old and never very robust as a child, was sick for most of the voyage. Arriving in Montreal, they boarded another boat for the Great Lakes and eventually ended up in Chatham, Ontario, midway between Toronto and Detroit. James found a house and moved in, and Jane began to settle into their new life in the fall of 1847.

TRAGEDY STRIKES AGAIN

James entered into partnership with a local shipbuilder and began to rebuild the family fortunes. Yet once again, it seemed that "Providence" was not smiling on the Simpson family. Not long after arriving in Chatham, a deadly outbreak of fever, one of the cholera epidemics which plagued many new towns, decimated the infant population of Chatham, likely part of the typhoid epidemic brought on by infected Irish immigrants a few years earlier which spread across the province. The deadly disease took Bertie's younger sister, Margaret Jane. His broken-hearted mother,

Simpson homestead in Chatham, Ontario

expecting another child and still struggling with the challenges of making a new home in this rugged frontier town, feared for her children. She insisted that James move the family out of Chatham immediately.

Thus, James found 100 acres of land about nine miles out of town and moved the family in 1850 to the undeveloped farm in the woods. Their new home was a rough log house. Skilled as a carpenter and committed to giving his family a decent home, James worked to convert the cabin into a comfortable house and furnished it with hickory furniture from the trees on the farm.

Chatham, seat of Kent County in southeastern Ontario, lies on the Thames River. Formerly a British naval docking yard, the town had become the northern terminus of the "Underground Railroad" for fugitive slaves fleeing the United States. The Simpson family would have been aware of this fact since pre-Civil War Chatham had as many as 25 percent of its population made up of fugitive slaves or their children.[12] As citizens of the British Empire, which had abolished slavery in 1833, the family must have been deeply impressed with the former slaves who were now working their own land in free Canada located at the Buxton community just outside of town.

James, though not a farmer, managed to wrest a livelihood from the soil. With hired laborers and his growing sons, he cleared the land, built a new house, and, ultimately, the farm became a relatively profitable venture. In due time, he became a prominent member of the community, an elder in the Chatham Presbyterian Church, and a member of the municipal council. Jane, refined and previously involved with local society in PEI, grieved the loss of her baby, Elizabeth Eleanor, born on the same day as Bertie's birthday. The heartbroken mother struggled at her life in the wilderness, with few neighbors other than some Gaelic-speaking farmers.

Eventually, life became more tolerable for James and Jane, who with her artistic gifts,[13] made their home attractive and comfortable. While living a fair piece out of town, the long Sunday wagon ride to church was an unbreakable commitment, unless the hard Ontario winters kept them home. As Bert grew older, his parents would occasionally leave the children at home and drive to church by themselves. Then, the future pulpiteer would transform the kitchen table into his "sacred desk," gather his "brethren" around, and preach to the captive congregation.[14] Likely as a "prophet without regard in his own country,"[15] young Bert had to put up with the occasional catcall or smart remark from his less-than-pious siblings.

DOCTRINE AND DISCIPLINE

Both parents were well-read according to the standards of the day. As such, they made the education of their children a high priority. Harold Simpson, son of one of Albert's cousins, wrote in his book, *Cavendish—Its History and People,* a description of James Simpson as "A strict disciplinarian, [who] set a high standard for his family and sternly enforced the rules. He believed in the efficacy of the rod, which was used on occasion."[16] The Simpson children attended public school and were expected to maintain high grades and also were required to read and memorize from the small, select library that Jane had put together. They regularly read English poets like Milton, Kirke, White, and Pollock. By age 10, Albert and his older brother, Howard, had read Gibbon's *Decline and Fall of the Roman Empire.*[17]

On Sunday afternoons, following morning church attendance and their mother's noontime meal, James would quiz the children on the

"Shorter Catechism" of the Westminster Confession, which didn't really seem very short to the Simpson brood. Young Bertie and his siblings took in daunting doses of dogma, which, while not always understood, hopefully found its way from head to heart.

To round out their education, they also studied theological tomes such as Baxter's *The Saints' Everlasting Rest,* Boston's *Fourfold State,* and Doddridge's *Rise and Progress of Religion in the Soul.*[18] Simpson later stated that he would almost break out into a cold sweat at the mere sight of the weighty volumes that stressed the utter sinfulness of mankind, the election of the predestined, and the irresistible grace that would save the totally depraved sinners, and keep them saved.[19] This kind of reading matter helped to form the mind of the sensitive and impressionable Bert. Louisa described him as "very timid and imaginative, and anything unusual left a deep impression on his memory. The thought of punishment would fill him with terror. I never saw him get a whipping; and if he ever got one, it was very tenderly administered."[20] As a result, his God-fearing parents sought to raise him in the way he should go, hoping and praying that their sovereign God would call Bertie as one of the elect. The only thing missing in his early spiritual development was a clear explanation of the simplicity of receiving that gospel of grace.

STONE OF REMEMBRANCE

At the age of nine, young Albert read the biography of John Williams, the missionary martyr of Erromanga, one of the recently reached South Pacific islands. It was as though God had placed another "stone of remembrance" in young Simpson's life. He was raised in an atmosphere of prayer, a deeply religious culture, and the study of heavy theological works. By his early teens, Simpson was becoming more and more conscious of spiritual things. The impressionable, often fearful lad,[21] who early on had sensed a desire to serve God, was becoming aware of his own sinful lostness. Thus, the twig bent— close to the breaking point.

Simpson late teens

"But the strain of all this terrific work upon a young and yet undeveloped brain and body was impossible to sustain long, and one night there came a fearful crash, in which it seemed to me the very heavens were falling."
—A. B. Simpson

CHAPTER 2
WHEN THE BOUGH BREAKS

"*T*HE FIRST RECOLLECTION OF MY CHILDHOOD is the picture of my mother, as I often heard her in the dark and lonely night, weeping and wailing in her room, in her loneliness and sorrow, and I still remember how I used to get up and kneel beside my little bed even before I knew God for myself and pray to Him to comfort her."[1] Those words from "His Own Story," an autobiographical sketch recorded in McKaig's *Simpson Scrapbook*, were penned at the request of friends and associates, to "put into permanent form the story of the things which the Lord has done for me."[2]

Doubtless, this early memory of young Bertie deeply impacted him, following the dramatic move from Prince Edward Island to the lonely farm outside of Chatham. The traumatic trip to Western Ontario and the subsequent "exile" to the lonely woodland homestead isolated his mother not only from longtime acquaintances and family on PEI but also from her new-found friends in Chatham. "Crushing her even more so was the recent memory of her little baby girl Elizabeth Eleanor," who had died just as they were settling in the town of Chatham. It was in this sad setting that "her little boy should find his first religious experience come to him in trying to grope his way to the heart of Him, who alone could help her."[3] Now she was taking up life in "one of the dreariest regions that could be imagined."[4]

A TINGE OF RELIGION
Simpson recalls his next reminiscence as having "a tinge of religion about it."[5] He had been playing with a friend's jack knife, a treasure for

any growing boy in those days. Unfortunately, Bertie lost the knife and the first thought that came to his mind was to pray. "I still remember an impulse came to me to kneel down and pray about it. Soon afterwards, I was delighted to find it. The incident made a profound impression upon my young heart and gave me a lifelong conviction, which has since borne fruit innumerable times, that it is our privilege to take everything to God in prayer."[6] Being raised in a pious home where prayer was a common part of life, the young boy already had experienced prayer. However, these two youthful occasions of going to God in prayer, while occurring many years before his conversion, made an imprint on his soul about taking "everything" to God, who hears and answers prayer.

Simpson was always grateful for his parents' consistent life and exemplary faith, yet he later commented, "The truth is, the influences around my childhood were not as favorable to early conversions as they are today in many Christian homes."[7] Since the Simpson family roots were found in the theological soil of the Scottish Covenanters, which did not expect "conversion experiences" but believed that infant baptism inducted the child into covenant. At some later point, it was expected that God would sovereignly bring that faith seed to full fruition and conviction of salvation. In the intervening years, Simpson's theological journey led him to the "new covenant" ushered in by Christ's sacrifice and entered into by grace and faith.

Simpson's comments about these childhood influences should be taken in context of an aging man dictating fragments of his memoir just a few years before his death in 1919. Possibly, he was contrasting the difference between a "well-ordered Puritan household" that emphasized God's utter holiness and righteous wrath rather than one less strict that focused more on God's love. He described his father as "a good Presbyterian of the old school and the belief in the Shorter Catechism and the doctrine of foreordination and all the conventional rules of a well-ordered Puritan household." His father rose daily before sunrise and lit a candle "sitting down in the cheerless room to read his Bible and tarry long at his morning devotions, and the picture filled my soul with a kind of sacred awe."[8]

PRETENDED PIETY

Yet young Albert soon demonstrated that while he was raised in such a devout setting, he still had to contend with his own "total depravity."

He later recalled one of the few whippings he ever received; such punishment always caused him great foreboding and loss of sleep anticipating the "wrath to come." It seems that he had been running around on a Sunday afternoon, judged a terrible desecration of the Sabbath by his father. Thus, it was decreed that he would receive a whipping early on Monday morning, since Sunday was too holy for a "hiding." Older brother, Howard, wiser in the ways of the world, suggested a way of escaping the impending punishment. "He told me with great secrecy to get up the next morning before daylight, about the time my father was accustomed to rise, to light the candle and go and sit down in a corner of the sitting room with the Bible before me and show proper spirit of penitence and seriousness, and he was quite sure my father would take the hint and let me off."[9] One can easily imagine Simpson with a wry smile on his face, as he shared this secret with his longtime secretary, Emma Beere, who recorded his reminiscences: "I am sorry to say that I was enough of a hypocrite to practice this trick, and sure enough, one morning when a whipping was coming to me, I stole out of my bed, and sitting down with a very demure and solemn face to practice my pretended devotions, I can still see in my imagination my quiet and silent father casting side glances at me from under his spectacles, as though to make sure that I was in earnest; and after finishing his devotions, he quietly slipped away to his work and nothing more was said about the chastisement."[10]

Simpson later recognized the value of those severe early years that "threw over my youthful spirit a natural horror for evil things, which often afterwards safeguarded me when thrown amid the temptations of the world."[11] As the third surviving child of nine children, young Bert was close to the "middle" and saw James and Jane's parenting style change to less law and more grace as the children came. "In our later family history," he noted, "these severe restraints were withdrawn from the younger members, as a more liberal age threw its influence over our home, but I cannot say that the change was a beneficial one."[12]

The growing boy was moving into adolescence, a critical period which deeply marked him. Young Albert had experienced sorrow early in life. His father's bankruptcy, the loss of their home in PEI, the long and sad trip to Chatham, as well as the epidemic and loss of his little sister all weighed heavily on him. While sharing his conversion story, Simpson recalled, in *The Fourfold Gospel*, "I remember when I was a child what a shock a funeral bell would give me. I could not bear to hear of someone's being dead."[13] Sorrow and death weighed heavily on his soul.

TEEN TRAUMA

Simpson had several scrapes with death during his teen years. One close call occurred when Bert and his buddies went for a dip at the local swimming hole. They spotted some wild grapes growing on the far river bank that only could be reached by swimming to them. Encouraged by his pals, Simpson struck out bravely. The problem was that he didn't know how to swim. Inevitably, gravity prevailed over folly, and he began to flail his arms and sink. In his own words: "In a few moments the water had got beyond my depth, and with a sense of agony, which I never shall forget, I found myself choking painfully under the surface.

> **The thought of death in such a hopeless state that ended in hell left him with sleepless nights and joyless days.**

In that moment, I still recollect, how the whole of my life came before me in a vision, and I can well understand the story told by drowning persons whose past histories seem photographed in an instant before their minds in the act of losing consciousness."[14] In his mind, he could see his obituary in the local paper. At the last moment, his pal's screaming caught the attention of some men fishing nearby, and they managed to reach him with their boat and haul him to the bank where he finally came to, much to everyone's relief.

On another occasion, he was thrown headlong over his horse when it stumbled. Fortunately, his mount fell under him. If he had fallen under the horse, he would have been crushed. Instead, he woke to find the horse gently bending over and nudging him, as though saying, "It's alright; I'm fine and you are too!" As Simpson dryly commented, "I am sure that [these] experience[s] greatly deepened my spiritual earnestness."[15]

About this same time occurred another close call. While visiting a house under construction, he climbed a scaffold, stepped on a loose board, and down he went. Instinctively, he reached out and grabbed a timber that held and frantically called for help. As his grip slipped, he fell into his father's arms. Simpson's terse sentence describes the seriousness of the situation: "The fall would have either maimed or killed me."¹⁶

The accumulation of these frightening experiences in such a short period of time troubled Bert, worrying him about his spiritual heart condition. He feared that he was not one of the elect and recognized his sinful inclinations. The deep sense of his depravity filled him with guilt and shame. The thought of death in such a hopeless state that ended in hell left him with sleepless nights and joyless days, crushed by a guilty conscience and sense of hopelessness.

FIRST RELIGIOUS CRISIS

As a teenager, Albert was tall and gangly. It was then that he entered what he termed, "my first definite religious crisis."¹⁷ For some time, he had desired to "study for the ministry." While not experiencing a dramatic "calling," there grew a certainty in his heart that he was to be a Presbyterian minister. However, a major obstacle blocked the way to his dream. His brother Howard, the eldest son and an excellent stu-

Presbyterian Church, Chatham, Ontario

dent, had priority and seniority. As firstborn, he had been dedicated to the ministry before birth, foreordained to the pulpit. And Albert was predestined to the farm. Part of Bert's spiritual struggle came from feeling overlooked in favor of Howard; this slight grated on his sense of fairness.

While this struggle was going on, Albert concluded that as a pastor, he would have to give up certain "worldly" activities. It just was not proper for a pastor to be involved in "worldly things, such as hunting and shooting game," as judged by his parents. Yet that is just what young Albert wanted to do.

So, the conflicted teenager took some of his hard-earned chore money and bought a shotgun, despite his mother's horror of firearms. She refused to permit them in her home after losing her brother from a shotgun accident years before. Nevertheless, young Albert "stole off to town and invested [the funds] in a shotgun." "For a few days, I had the time of my life," Simpson said. "I used to steal out to the woods with my forbidden idol and then, with my sister's [Louisa] help, would smuggle it back to the garret."[18] However, one fatal day, his mother discovered the forbidden firearm, and Albert was forced to return it to the shop, "losing not only my gun but my money too."[19] Shamed by his rebellion, the humbled huntsman decided that he would shun this world's pleasures and pursue his dream of becoming a minister, despite the odds against him. To change his destiny from farmer to preacher would require a family council.

One can imagine the hesitant son solemnly expressing his desire to study for the ministry. Recognizing Howard's right as first-born, Albert simply asked his parents' permission to go to college for pastoral training at no expense to the family. A farmer he was not, and he promised to earn his way to school. Since his father had expected Albert to work on the farm, giving his second son permission to go to college was, in fact, costly to his parents since they would lose valuable labor on the farm.

Nevertheless, the doubly honored parents blessed their son and consented to his going to college on his own. With that great hurdle cleared, young Albert had an idea how to earn and save money for college. He would accelerate his education by special study and tutoring to pass the rigorous entrance examination given by the local educational authorities. Successfully passing the exam would earn him a certificate to teach in the "common school" for younger children. Consequently, Bert, age 14, and Howard, 16, both began to study under the tutorship of a retired Presbyterian minister and, later, with their own pastor, Rev. William Walker.

They mastered Greek, Latin, higher mathematics, grammar, and English history. Their father gave each son a horse to ride the nine-mile trip from home to school and back again for their studies. Howard's poor health caused him to drop out while Albert continued alone. Soon, he moved into a boarding house in Chatham, entered high school at the age of 14, and dedicated himself to his studies. It was while living in town that the near-drowning incident happened.

PUNGENT PREACHING—DEEP CONVICTION
During late 1858, Bert attended evangelistic meetings in Chatham, led by H. Grattan Guinness, a 23-year-old fiery Irish evangelist—the Billy Graham of his day. Grattan Guinness, after successful evangelistic

Henry G. Guinness

tours in Wales, Scotland, and Ireland, had been "invited to help sustain the [Second] awakening that was sweeping North America..."[20] Arriving in Philadelphia in November 1858, he began an exhausting tour, preaching as many as 13 times a week. After Philadelphia, he went north to New York and other American and Canadian towns for six or seven months. This was young Bert's first encounter with a man whose mentoring relationship would eventually influence his eschatology, philosophy of Christian education, and his intense burden for the lost worldwide. [21]

Guinness was renowned for last-days messages that put the fear of God in his listeners. "Under his pungent preaching, Albert was deeply convicted ... Still under conviction he walked home for the weekend and got lost in the woods. He wandered upon some Indian graves that had been desecrated, and the gruesome sight greatly affected his sensitive spirit, not yet recovered from the effect of the drowning experience. His father found him and brought him home, but a long illness followed, during which he suffered intense spiritual darkness and often could sleep only with his father's arms about him. It was during this time that he was converted," wrote Simpson's sister, Louisa, many years after the event.[22]

Simpson later described what preceded his first physical and emotional breakdown: "But the strain of all this terrific work upon a young and yet undeveloped brain and body was impossible to sustain long, and one night there came a fearful crash, in which it seemed to me the very heavens were falling. After retiring to my bed, I suddenly seemed to see

> **He suffered intense spiritual darkness and often could sleep only with his father's arms about him.**

a strange light blazing before my eyes, and then my nerves gave way, and I sprang from my bed trembling and almost fainting, and immediately fell into a congestive chill of great violence that almost took my life. To add to the horror of that night there was a man in the house where I was boarding, suffering from delirium tremens, and his horrible agonies, shrieks, and curses seemed to add to my own distress the very horrors of hell itself. Next morning, I was forced to ask for a leave of absence and returned to my father's house a physical wreck."[23] Apparently, this boarding-house scene preceded Simpson's long and nerve-wracking trek home through the "First-Nation" cemetery, where his father encountered him in deep emotional distress.

THE TAUNTING CLOCK

Simpson picks up the story: "The physician told me I must not look at a book for a year, that my whole system had collapsed and that I was in the greatest danger. Then began a period of mental and physical agony, which no language can describe. I seemed possessed with the idea that at three o'clock on someday I was to die, and every day as the hour drew near, I became prostrated with a dreadful nervousness, watching in agonized suspense till it was passed, wondering that I was still alive."[24]

His anxiety as to whether he was predestined or not for salvation greatly contributed to his physical and mental collapse. For weeks, the sound of the clock's taunting ticking and the sight of the creeping hand moving toward the fatal hour caused him panic. Certain that he was about to die, he would cry out to God for mercy. "Fainting and terrified, I called my father to my bed side, telling him I was dying. Worst of all I had no hope and no Christ. Oh, how my father prayed for me that day, and I fondly cried in utter despair for God to spare me just long enough to be saved. After a sense of sinking into bottomless depth constantly, rest came, and the crisis was over for another day. I looked up at the clock and it was past three. But the day passed and still I was not saved."[25]

While readers of another age might question Simpson's mental stability and see him as an unbalanced religious fanatic, it should be remembered that people raised in a strict puritanical home, taught that God's election of those to be redeemed was sovereignly His to choose, took their religion very seriously. A person as sensitive to spiritual issues as young Albert Simpson understood the implications of Reformed theology. As a result, his recognition of his own sinfulness, without a full understanding of God's gracious gift of salvation to all, led to his collapse.

"THE FIRST GOOD WORK"

After months of dreading the crawling clock hand, the fixation slowly lost its grip, and Bert gradually began to regain health. While still convalescing, grace met the young seeker, now fifteen years old. "At length, one day I stumbled, in the library of my minister, upon an old [Scottish] book called Marshall's *Gospel Mystery of Sanctification,* and as I turned over the leaves, I came to a sentence which opened my eyes, and at the same time opened for me the gates of life eternal. In substance it was this, 'The first good work you will ever perform is to believe in the Lord

> "From this moment I am Thy child, forgiven and saved, simply because I take Thee at Thy word."

Jesus Christ. Until you do this, all your works, prayer, tears, and resolves are vain.'" He immediately threw himself to his knees and "looking up in the face of the Lord in spite of my doubts and fears I said, 'Lord Jesus, Thou has said, that him that cometh unto me I will in no wise cast out. Now I come the best I can, and I believe because Thou hast commanded me to believe that Thou dost receive me, that Thou dost save me, and from this moment I am Thy child, forgiven and saved, simply because I take Thee at Thy word, and I now dare to look up in the face of God and say, Abba, Father, Thou art mine.'"[26]

While unaware of what his future might hold, young A. B. Simpson came to know and experience not just a doctrine but the divine indwelling Person of Jesus Christ—His Savior.

Following his conversion, Bert returned to his rigorous "Entrance" preparation and at the age of 16, he secured his certificate as a "common school" teacher. For the next year, he had a class of about 40 students, one-quarter of whom were older than he. He wished and wished for a few whiskers or a hint of mustache to hide his youth. However, he discovered that he was able not only to control the class but also to aid them in their learning, clearly teaching them with a pleasant baritone voice that held them captive. This was the first indication of his unique verbal gifts and innate leadership skills, which he later developed and perfected.

Consequently, the first "fold" of the Fourfold Gospel synthesized by Simpson in the early 1880s became a living reality in his heart. As he later wrote in *The Word, The Work and The World:* "Christ is our complete Savior from guilt . . . from inbred sin, from sickness . . . for time and eternity."[27] This truth became the first "voice" of a growing four-part gospel chorus. This occasion in Bert's young life brought a singular peace to his heart and months of spiritual blessing. Sometime later before entering college, Simpson read Doddridge's *Rise and Progress of Religion in the Soul* and decided to write a "covenant" between himself and his Lord, committing himself to godly living in total surrender to God's will. This two-page document, handwritten in rather stilted King James English with much of the verbiage likely lifted from Doddridge's tome, became an anchor in his life. He later returned to it at least two other times to renew his vows to God, then signing and dating the text with a hearty "Amen!"[28]

Now forgiven of sins and sensing a new-found passion to preach the gospel, Bert buckled down and taught his students with all his skill and energy, saving his meager wages and preparing for the next step on his journey. Soon he was to face another examination, this time prepared by the Presbytery of London, Ontario, as an entrance exam. Passing it would permit him to matriculate at Knox College, the Presbyterian Seminary for Canada.

As young Simpson looked forward to this next step later that same year, across the Atlantic surfaced another "gospel" in the form of Darwin's *Origin of Species by Means of Natural Selection, or the Preservation of Favoured Races in the Struggle for Life,* published in Britain, November

1858. While this novel teaching on evolution took years to cross the Atlantic, this small cloud coming from "a man's hand" would eventually grow and deluge confusion and unbelief on the Christian Church worldwide.

A. B. Simpson, age 17

This selfish ambition became an increasing burden to his hungry heart that wanted more of God and less of himself.

CHAPTER 3
FOLLOWING THE CALL

*D*URING THE SCHOOL YEAR OF 1861, while teaching in the "common school" after his conversion, young Simpson's spiritual life grew exponentially. Many of the classic books written by Reformed saints of bygone days had become dear friends and guides rather than doctrinal drudgery. It was at this time that Bert read Doddridge's *Rise and Progress of Religion in the Soul*.

Later in the fall, while that most "uncivil war" raged in the United States to the south, Simpson set his sights on entering Knox College. The country boy was going to the big city of Toronto to study for the ministry. However, before young A. B. could put one foot in the hallowed halls of old Elmsley Villa, first home of Knox College, he had to prove that he was a ready and worthy candidate.

A PROPER EXAMINATION

For a young man aspiring to be a proper Presbyterian pastor at that time, the fences were high for entering seminary. The culture of the day held the pastoral ministry in high esteem. Consequently, to enter seminary, the first hurdle wasn't simply to send an "application" to a faraway school with an academic transcript and a few references. Albert and the other aspiring candidates had to appear before the London Ontario Presbytery to be properly examined. Tutored and sponsored by his pastor, Rev. William Walker, and being the son of James Simpson, a respected Presbyterian elder, these qualifications did not hurt Bert's candidacy. However, only after surviving a detailed cross examination by the pastoral board that lasted several hours were A.B. and his colleagues granted permission to begin their studies at Knox College.

As A. E. Thompson noted, "[Simpson] had studied so diligently under his ministerial tutors in high school and during the time he was teaching [grammar school] that, though he was only 17 years old, he was admitted to the third or senior year of Knox College's literary course."[1] The college required either the full arts course in the University of Toronto, with which it was the first seminary to affiliate, or three years of academic work in its own halls as a prerequisite to the three years course in Theology.

Because of his outstanding academic foundation, young Simpson became part of a select group of students admitted to the unique hybrid course, whereby he took the approved ministerial program at Knox College "literary course" as well as attending some lectures at the University of Toronto.[2] Bert's goal was the pastorate, and he concentrated on his theological and biblical studies at Knox while at the same time successfully completing the University advanced placement. Much of Simpson's love and command of the classics came from his studies at college.

STUDENT FINANCING

Although just 17, Bert proved to be a remarkably able student. Since he was financing his education, he took advantage of every opportunity to earn extra cash by competing for the "bursary prizes" or cash awards given for the best essays written on subjects chosen by the administration. In grammar school, he learned that he could write well and had won simpler prizes, such as books and diplomas. Now Bert was ready for bigger things.

Thus, ambitious Bert set out to win the writing competitions. In his freshman year, while matriculated in the third or final year in the Academic course, before entering the theological studies of the seminary, he won C$120.00 in a special competitive examination in the classics.[3] In his second year at Knox, his "Outline of Arguments in Favour of Infant Baptism" proved to be biblically and theologically correct. Due to the strength of his argument and literary excellence, he won the first prize of C$40.00, a substantial sum toward his first year's tuition. Ironically 20 years later, an older and more biblically-grounded Albert Simpson wrote regarding infant baptism: "But in later years I had to take back all the arguments and doctrinal opinions, which I so stoutly maintained in my youthful wisdom."[4] This later reversal of opinion would be part of a major sea-change in the life of A. B. Simpson.

The next year, 1863, motivated Bert much more after winning the Prince of Wales Prize, worth C$120. The subject was much grander: "The Preparation of the World for the Appearing of the Savior and the Setting up of His Kingdom." He worked long and hard on his rough drafts. But due to his propensity of waiting till the last hour to do the

> Because of his outstanding academic foundation, young Simpson became part of a select group of students at Knox College.

final version, he found himself facing an "all-nighter." The paper fell due the next morning by nine o'clock. With about eight hours left, A. B. was literally falling asleep at his desk. He sent out to the drug store for "something to keep me awake for six or seven hours at any cost, and as I sipped it through the night, my brain was held to its tremendous task."[5] And yes, despite hand cramping, which required A. B. to dictate the last part of the paper to his roommate, the composition was finished and given to the professor in time. After several agonizing weeks of prayer and waiting for the judges to grade the essays, the announcement was made. Simpson won the coveted prize and sufficient funds to cover his studies for the rest of that year. The following year, 1864, he won the top prize for proficiency in the classics and graduated with high honors from Knox College. Thus, his early study and diligence in the country school near Chatham, his short stay in high school, and the rigorous tutoring by his pastor prepared him for a future career as a writer as well as pastor and evangelist.

THE AMBITIOUS STUDENT

The *McKaig Scrapbook* is a fascinating anthology of "Simpsonalia" compiled by Dr. C. Donald McKaig, longtime professor at Nyack Missionary College (now Nyack College). In the section titled "My Own Story," is found the autobiographical sketch written by Simpson. In it, he admits to a marked personality trait: his ambition and drive to excel. He later learned that academic excellence is a worthy goal to seek, but never at the expense of one's spiritual experience. Three times in "My Own Story," Simpson speaks of his "motives [which] were intensely ambitious and worldly." This "selfish ambition which so controlled [his life]" became an increasing burden to his hungry heart that wanted more of God and less of himself. Because he was an outstanding student, he knew that he could succeed academically where others would fail. This self-awareness also resulted in his being conscious of a serious pride issue as he became increasingly mindful of his gifts and abilities.

Simpson reminisced about his days at Knox in "Student Days" in the December 1901 issue of *The Christian and Missionary Alliance* magazine: "The professor did not cram me full of instruction, but challenged me to rise to my best, do the work myself. He emptied me of my self-conceit, then roused the dormant forces of my mind and drew

> **This "selfish ambition which so controlled [his life]" became an increasing burden to his hungry heart that wanted more of God and less of himself.**

me out to think for myself. Drawing out, not pouring in, is true education."[6] Simpson's classmates were aware of young Bert's abilities. In the words of one of his fellow Knox students, Dr. J. W. Mitchell, "My earliest recollections of Dr. Simpson go back to the early [eighteen] sixties when he came up to Knox. Your photograph gives a fair representation of him as he then appeared, fresh from his father's farm and his country school teaching, giving little intimation of the mighty man of God that he would become in later years. . . . He had popular gifts of a high order, and I opine was eager to get into the field where he could exercise them, and was sure he would forge his way to the front."[7]

Another classmate describes him as "a most attractive young man—his body lithe, active, graceful; his countenance beaming with kindness, friendship, generosity; his voice rich, musical, well-controlled. Often, no doubt, flattery was showered upon him, and strong compliments were paid by admirers and relatives, all of which would tend to develop vanity and self-importance; but I never saw a trace of these traits, which are so common in brilliant young men, in young Mr. Simpson."[8] While his school pals didn't see pride in young Bert, he knew it was there, and it became a major issue in his later walk with Christ.

Simpson, age 21

Simpson recounts that when he first arrived at Knox College, he thought of himself as being proficient in a particular subject matter. However, his teacher aimed to show him his ignorance and unwise self-sufficiency. Simpson later was thankful for being shown how little he knew about so much. While undoubtedly an excellent student with good preparation, he had to learn what he didn't know before he could begin to share with others what he did know. While Knox College, as a training grounds for future Presbyterian pastors, was Reformed and Calvinist in theology, it was steadfastly orthodox and evangelical. While frosty rather than fervent might define the spiritual atmosphere, the students were not subjected to the faith-killing effects of "liberal or modernist" theology just beginning to be taught in major seminaries in Germany and Great Britain. In another generation or so, the effects of humanism and materialism would devastate the ranks of mainline denominations across North America by first infiltrating their seminaries, thus producing pastors who no longer believed in the faith of the fathers.

THE TEMPTATIONS OF CITY LIFE

In addition to the challenges at Knox College and the University of Toronto, A. B. had another area of life to explore. He had been raised in the strictest of Christian homes with heavy doses of Reformed theology and Puritan piety drilled into his head and heart from an early age. In Chatham, he had never personally experienced what he called the "temptations of city life." Now, far from the farm and thrown into college life, he had to learn to face these tests.

His first-year dormitory roommate was also in the special ministry course but was older and wiser in the ways of the world. Simpson described him as being "a very bright and attractive fellow [who] was a man of convivial tastes and habits."[9] He had excellent literary taste and was fond of quoting poetry. At the same time, alcoholic beverages found a prominent place on his side of the room. Weekly this bon vivant would host "oyster suppers" in their room, where his friends, mostly irreverent and irreligious medical school students with habits even worse than his roommate, came for free food, fun, and drinks. Bert had never witnessed such behavior before and felt uncomfortable and helpless. The coarse atmosphere and his roommate's cynical attitude toward spiritual things cooled the faith fervor of the naïve freshman. Simpson later expressed regret over the way those influences affected his prayer life and sense of closeness to God. In fact, an older and wiser Simpson later confessed: "I did not cease to pray, or to walk in some measure with God, but the sweetness and preciousness of my early piety was already withered. I am sorry to say that I did not recover my lost blessing until I had been the minister of the Gospel for more than ten years."[10]

As he began his second year at Knox, Bert was joined by his older brother, Howard, who had remained back in Chatham, teaching in a local school as his younger brother had done. They decided to room together. Both boys attended Cooke Presbyterian Church, and the pastor, Rev. John Jennings, took notice of them and their need for housing. Since many of the better-off church families boarded Knox College students, Rev. Jennings spoke about the promising students from Chatham to Mr. John Henry, a local businessman and founding member of Cooke Presbyterian. Thus Mr. Henry invited them to his home for an interview and apparently was positively impressed enough by the two Simpson brothers to open his home to them. Henry had two daughters; the oldest, Margaret, while two years older than "Bertie," as she called him, caught his eye. The same held true for Howard, who although older than Bert by more than three years, was a lowly first-year student. His tall "little brother" was already a notable second-year student who had won a literary prize and was gaining a reputation on and off campus as a "comer" with great potential.

THE "CHILD" PRODIGY PREACHER

Following the second year of study at Knox, ministerial students were deemed ready to do pulpit supply in local churches. For A. B., it was a way of earning valuable experience in the pulpit as well as an honorarium to help with his expenses. In more than one country church, the elders were surprised and concerned when the "child" sent out by the college showed up on Sunday to preach. With neither a wrinkle nor whisker, the trembling teen would mount the high pulpit and commence to astound the delighted parishioners with his resonant voice and hypnotic sway. A. W. Tozer described his preaching in *Wingspread:* "For orthodoxy it is blameless, for clarity and logic it is of the first order, and for beauty and effectiveness of delivery it beats anything these old sermon lovers have had for many a long day."[11]

Howard Simpson of *Cavendish* recalls telling the story of Bert's first test in the pulpit when he preached in Tilbury near his home. "We have referred to the important place of preaching in the Presbyterian

> **With neither a wrinkle nor whisker, the trembling teen would mount the high pulpit and commence to astound the delighted parishioners with his resonant voice and hypnotic sway.**

tradition. It was a severe test. His parents, his brothers and sister, his playmates and neighbors were in the congregation."[12] A. E. Thompson, his first biographer, wrote: "Yesterday he was Bert Simpson, their fellow, their rival in friendly contests of brain and brawn. Today he stands high above them in the pulpit . . . in the minister's place, in back of the open Bible where not even his godly father would appear to speak to them as a messenger of God . . . The boy, whose voice was to thrill five continents, did not fail."[13]

A BETTER PRIZE

While at college, young Bert wasn't just writing essays to get good grades and win cash prizes, he was also on the lookout for an even better prize, "a treasure," as Proverbs 18:22 affirms. Because he was a very ambitious young man who always reached for the best, the seminarian from Chatham had fallen in love with Margaret Henry, daughter of his landlord. He told University of Toronto students 50 years later "that he had left his heart at the door of a Toronto residence as it was opened by the fair daughter of the house."[14] The writer of Proverbs 30:19 talks of the "way of a man with a maid." Apparently, Bert's way with Margaret was the way of patience and persistence. In the little book, *Mrs. A. B. Simpson —The Wife or Love Stands,* written by Simpson's granddaughter, Katherine Alberta Brennen, we read the cryptically romantic description of their courtship:

> As I went walking down old St. George, the spirits of generations gone before seemed dancing around me on unseen feet. I felt as if I myself were living through the days, tales of which I used to hear by the hour, seated at Grannie's feet.
>
> Past Knox College . . . [where] Grandfather attended it, to study Theology and love.
>
> Margaret Henry, with her prim but precious ways—the eldest daughter of one of the founders of Cooke's Presbyterian Church.
>
> "Bertie Simpson! That tall, awkward, gawky country boy—Bah!" said Grannie Simpson, the size of a minute hand. But alas and alack!
>
> June—that delirious time—the air filled with the mating calls of bird and beasts, the very atmosphere pregnant with the plighted troths of youths and maids for generations.
>
> It was May—perhaps June itself. No one is really quite normal at that dizzy, uplifted time of year. Even theologians must have fresh air. Any man with the sheer audacity—to say nothing of will power—who could force one to walk in and out of a field of cows, still maintaining one's dignity and a firm tread!
>
> "My, my!" said Grannie Simpson. "As you will, Bertie, the hour is yours . . ."[15]

Thus, began a relationship between Albert B. Simpson and Margaret L. Henry. They "saw each other" during his years at Knox College, and a more unlikely couple would be hard to find. She, at just four feet, eleven inches, was tiny in stature but large in personality. Given the best education that money could buy at the Toronto Model School, followed by Miss Brown's private "finishing school," she proved to be high spirited, demanding, and opinionated. She had attended dance classes, frequented the theater, and was accustomed to the finer

Newlyweds Bert and Maggie Simpson

things in life. Young Bert, an artistic and ambitious farmer's son given to moods and melancholy, was conscious of his humble roots. James and Jane Simpson had come from a higher "social station" on Prince Edward Island, but the loss of the family business and exodus to Western Ontario resulted in a less secure financial position. However, they invested in their son's education as a way of reclaiming what they had lost. Young Bert determined to do his part and showed it by his desire to succeed and move up in life.

Together, Bertie and Margaret eventually forged a relationship often challenged by circumstances unique to each as well as their differences in opinion as to God's direction. Theirs was not an easy relationship, and it took decades before they were comfortable pulling together on the yoke that God had placed upon them.

A. E. Thompson's biography shares a little gem that shines a light on their relationship. Since the young seminarian, Albert Simpson, was in much demand for his pulpit skills, he showed his true feelings toward her when he took the "munificent sum of ten dollars as a fee for his Sunday services, [and] he at once proceeded to spend it for a present for his sweetheart."[16] Remembering that ten dollars in the 1860s would be worth ten times or more today, it is obvious that "Bertie" admired the tiny lady to the manor-born. While Margaret was older and more "high society" than her country beau, she gave her heart to the young man. In time, they would embark on a 54-year journey that would take them from comfortable respectability in the conventional church to living by faith on the cutting-edge of a full-gospel movement with worldwide implications. Such are the ways of God.

The Knox College senior graduated on April 15, 1865,[17] the same day as the death of Abraham Lincoln and about the same time as the cessation of hostilities in the United States Civil War, one of the bloodiest wars in U.S. history. Knox College graduated Albert Simpson with high honors.

During that same summer of 1865, a little-known incident occurred that proved embarrassing to the young graduate. Earlier, in his second summer's activities in 1863, Simpson had fulfilled his assignment by the Home Missions Committee to the Presbytery of Hamilton for the first three months (April-June). During this period, Simpson alternated preaching assignments at Welland, Crowland, and Port Colborne. Port Colborne was located east of Chatham on Lake Erie. He did well in all three churches and "his pulpit gifts were notable."[18]

Two years later, following Simpson's April graduation from Knox College, the minutes of the Toronto Presbytery, August 1, 1865, recorded that Simpson apparently had been engaged with a "Miss Carter" of Port Colborne, but the engagement had been dissolved in late June of the same summer. Before Simpson went before the Toronto Presbytery in August for his "trial discourses," leading to licensing as a Presbyterian clergyman, a letter sent to the Presbytery by Miss Carter's brother, dated June 25, stated that Simpson had improperly "resiled from [abandoned] that engagement," resulting in health consequences to his sister.[19]

This letter was followed by a second, sent to the Toronto Presbytery on July 25 by Miss Carter herself, declaring, "that during the period of Mr. Simpson's engagement with her, his conduct had been candid and honorable, and that they had parted kindly by mutual consent." The Presbytery dropped the matter, recognizing that Miss Carter's brother had maliciously timed his letter to damage the young man's career.[20]

Thus, on the next day, Bert and other Knox grads appeared before the Toronto Presbytery for their "public probationary trial." This was the last hurdle to clear before becoming officially recognized Presbyterian clergymen. With what had just happened and what was in front of him, one can only imagine the tension under which young Albert Simpson faced his board of examiners. And what a trial it was! They were carefully examined on their command of Biblical Hebrew and Greek, Bible, theology, church history and government. Additionally, their personal religious experience was given careful scrutiny. They also had to give an oral discourse from Scripture read before the learned doctors and submit written essays, with one in Latin. Simpson also had to preach a sermon on Romans 1:16, give a lecture on Matthew 4:1–11, and present an exposition on Romans 7.[21] All of this was done in a day! Successfully passing this trial by fire, Simpson was licensed as a minister of the Presbyterian Church of Canada.

A CRITICAL CHOICE

Following his appearance before the Presbytery for this final examination, A. B. had an important decision to make, which he described in his own words:

> *When I was a young minister of twenty-one, and just leaving my theological seminary, I had the choice of two fields of labor; one an extremely easy one, in a delightful town, with a refined, affectionate, and prosperous church, just large enough to be an ideal field for one who wished to spend a few years in quest of preparation for future usefulness; the other, a large, absorbing city church, with many hundreds of members and overwhelming and heavy burdens, which were sure to demand the utmost possible care, labor, and responsibility.*[22]

The first parish was found in Dundas, Ontario, described by Tozer as "a drowsy, delightful hamlet" not far from Hamilton. Because of its nearness to Lake Ontario, the Desjardins Canal was dug, connecting Dundas to the lake, and the Great Western Railroad ran through town. All of this made Dundas a prosperous small city and a promising place to minister. At the same time, the "absorbing city church" that Simpson mentioned was, in fact, located in the heart of nearby Hamilton. Knox Presbyterian Church was an affluent and important pastoral charge, then one of the most important churches in Canada. It had seen as former pastors some of the major Canadian Presbyterian pulpiteers. Only top-flight orators occupied Knox Presbyterian's "sacred desk." Yet young A. B. had received the call from the Knox presbytery when their former pastor retired.

The decision was difficult for such a young man, obviously gifted, but untried and unproven considering the responsibility. In Simpson's own words, "If I take the small church, it will demand little, and I will give little. Result, stagnation; I will get soft and cease to grow. If I take the large church, I will be compelled to rise to meet its heavier demands, and the very effort will develop the gifts of God which are in me. The small church may break me; the large church will certainly help to make me."[23] Conventional "humility" seemed to demand that he accept the call from Dundas, where he could grow and prove himself. On the other hand, his striving streak, always up for a challenge, told him not to accept the easy and predictable, but to accept the demanding call as from God and to learn and grow from it.

At the same time that he was deciding which church call to accept, the young graduate, just recently absolved of a serious charge, had to take a step that would "resolve" his problem of singleness. To pastor such a prestigious church unmarried was out of the question; thus, Albert rekindled the embers of the fire that previously had been kindled between him and the daughter of his landlord. Early in September 1865, Albert asked Margaret's father for her hand; he said "yes" and so did his daughter. In this rather hasty manner, they took the first step that bound them together for a lifetime of pursuing God's call on their lives.

The next mini-chapter in Katherine Brennen's book *Mrs. A. B. Simpson—The Wife or Love Stands* reads:

> "*On Tuesday, September 13, at Cooke's Presbyterian Church, Toronto, by the Rev. Dr. Jennings—Margaret Henry to Albert*

Simpson." *To all brides and grooms, it is an old, old story, yet ever new. 'I, Margaret, take thee, Albert . . . for better, for worse.'*"[24]

DOING THINGS IN A BIG WAY

Always one to do things in a big way, the young seminary graduate, Albert Simpson, preached his first sermon as the new pastor of Knox Church, Hamilton, Ontario, on Sunday, September 11, 1865. The next day, he met with the Knox Presbytery, where he was ordained and gained

> **Rev. Albert B. Simpson was in the pulpit of his first charge at the raw, young age of 21.**

the coveted "Rev." before his name. On the following day, September 13, he and Margaret were wed at Cooke Presbyterian Church in Toronto. The newlyweds took a honeymoon cruise on the St. Lawrence River. By Saturday, the 17th, they had returned to move into the pastoral residence on Main Street in Hamilton. The next day, Rev. Albert B. Simpson was in the pulpit of his first charge at the raw, young age of 21.

That same year across the Atlantic, William Booth founded the Salvation Army, to reach the down and outers of London, and Hudson Taylor founded the China Inland Mission that would reach the unreached peoples of China's interior. Both men and their ministries would model for the young pastor, just entering the pastorate in Hamilton, a vision and burden for the neglected masses at home and abroad.

The "regular" young pastor had gone "irregular" and wholeheartedly given himself to evangelize the neglected masses in the major cities of North America.

CHAPTER 4
THE REGULAR PASTOR

*W*HEN PHOTOGRAPHIC FILM IS PLACED in the chemical developer bath, the emerging image's shape gradually appears, becoming clearer over time. In a similar way, the growth and maturity of the newly ordained Rev. Albert B. Simpson slowly comes into view during his first pastorate in Hamilton, Ontario. From the first foggy form till the full-blown image, the process takes time and patience. God always has plenty of both.

One of the reasons why the young preacher received consideration to pastor such a prestigious church as Knox Presbyterian in Hamilton is because he had preached there as student pulpit supply for three months in the spring of 1861 before his graduation. The former pastor had moved on more than a year before. The church's "session," the local presbyters, wanted to find a quality preacher soon. They already had called two different well-known Presbyterian pastors who, at first, accepted and later declined. So, the "session was in session" until they had a new pastor.[1]

In those days, the premium was on good preaching, with good pastoring as a hoped-for add-on. It was not uncommon for Sunday sermons to be quoted in the Monday newspaper, sometimes in their entirety. The Hamilton *Spectator*, commenting on Simpson's speaking abilities remarked, "The reverend gentleman justified the high opinion that has already been formed of him and created a feeling of satisfaction that a man of so much promise has become permanently associated with one of our city's congregations."[2]

While Simpson's obvious youth, his six-foot bony frame, and serious demeanor made some parishioners a bit uncomfortable, the moment he stood behind the pulpit, opened the Bible, and began to speak, his youthful appearance was quickly forgotten. The saints reveled in his sermons. His granddaughter, Katherine Brennen, wrote that while still a student at Knox College, "standing on a soap box, Grandfather had the faculty of attracting great crowds who listened to his words."[3] His captivating voice, piercing eyes, rhythmic sway cadenced to his words, and meaty messages marked him as a young man of unusual gifts. Weekly, he spent hours studying and preparing his sermons, written in longhand and memorized. Fortunately, he had an excellent memory and spoke with freedom and conviction. But he was more than just a good preacher.

Because Knox Church had been without a pastor for some time, attendance had dropped, and the elders wanted the wandering sheep back home. And return they did, as Simpson's pulpit prowess quickly stirred the curiosity of the missing flock. One Sunday back to church was enough to keep them coming for more. Amazingly, the young pastor also carried on a remarkable visitation schedule, often visiting up to a dozen homes in a day. Within a year's time, attendance was back to pre-Simpson numbers. The sanctuary was full, and many new converts joined after coming to Christ. Interestingly, Simpson did not preach evangelistically. Altar invitations were not made following the sermon. Most converts came because of a pastoral visit or a personal inquiry by seekers.

THE REGULAR WORK OF THE MINISTRY

One of the leading Presbyterian pastors in Canada at that time, Rev. Thomas Wardrobe of Guelph, Ontario, preached evangelistically for decisions; few other of his colleagues followed his example. From the mid-1800s on, Finney and Moody made public evangelistic meetings popular in the United States, and Wardrobe strongly urged such meetings in Canada. He visited Simpson and invited him to take part in revival meetings in Guelph. However, young Rev. Simpson rather staidly replied: "I believe in the regular work of the ministry"[4] and turned him down. Many years later, Wardrobe was surprised and delighted to hear that his "regular" young minister friend had gone "irregular" and wholeheartedly had given himself to evangelize the neglected masses in the major cities of North America.

AN AWKWARD YOKE?

Though Simpson had received excellent preparation for the ministry at Knox College, his young bride, Margaret, had no such training. As Niklaus points out in *All for Jesus,* "Margaret, with no preparation for

Pastor Simpson of Knox Presbyterian Church

the pastorate but her conversion, Christian home, and high school education, stood at the entrance of an uncertain future. He would soar, and she would struggle. His vision of the heavenlies at times would obscure his earthly duties as father and husband, while her practical preoccupations would at times allow no honor for the prophet in his own home."[5] At the time she married Simpson, her faith was rather shallow and short-sighted.

Simpson affectionately called her "Maggie" or occasionally, "Peggy." Granddaughter Katherine Brennen described her "prim and precious ways..."[6] She was headstrong, emotional and sharp-tongued, pampered as a child, and accustomed to the best as the apple of her father's eye. She often found the life of a pastor's wife to be unbearable. Brennen described a day in their early marriage: "The days passed, filled with the thoughtful tenderness of a Christian husband—although but 21 years old. A strange terror of thunder possessed Grannie [Margaret]. No matter where he was, when skies darkened, home Grandfather would go to let her know that he was always near."[7]

> **All gold that is not tried in the fire is worthless in the tests of life.**

While Albert showed gentleness and grace, he also struggled with a slow-fused anger that, when ignited, sometimes exploded passionately. Inevitably, these scenes were followed by tears and pleas for forgiveness. Brennen describes a crisis moment in their marriage that had to do with his growing vision for the lost and Margaret's struggle to accept Bert's decisions that directly affected their family:

> *Still tortured and torn by conflicting emotions, Grannie's days were by no means filled with peace. Not daring to say "no" to the still small voice, Grandfather was in veritable agonies of prayer for the supernatural power to span the chasms and scale the heights. . . . Grannie tells of terrible moments when almost a glint of murder would come into his eyes. The devil always seeks to inflict the most terrible mental tortures upon them who are chosen to perform the most spectacular service for Him. The Lord always plays a gentleman's game with the Evil One. All gold that is not tried in the fire is worthless in the tests of life.*[8]

Even though Brennen's recollections of her grandparents' life together may be overdramatic, given that they were written more than 20 years after her grandmother's death, Bert and Maggie surely struggled with the age-old problem of balance between home and ministry. Such a scene as described above, involving a man venerated by generations of people the world over, is jarring. How does one reconcile such a picture with the great man of God whose vision for the lost and passion for Christ impacted millions worldwide? This young pastor and wife had to learn to follow Christ as any other couple, with their struggles, their sorrows, and their victories. Yet, A. B. Simpson eventually scaled those "great heights." The still developing "photo" was a long way from the finished portrait.

By all accounts, Albert and Margaret could not have been a less equally yoked couple. Yet despite years of marital strain from poor communication, lack of vision-sharing, and not understanding each other and the Lord's leading, God worked in both of them. More than 20 years into their marriage, they finally got on the same page. About that same time, Margaret began to realize that her husband truly was a visionary. Often when he turned to look for plodding Margaret and the family, he discovered that he was way out front, walking by himself.

SIMPSON AND CIGARS?

Brennen tells a humorous story about young Reverend Simpson and his ministerial colleagues. After becoming pastor of Knox Church, Simpson attended the meetings of the local Presbyterian ministerium, held in the pastors' homes. As described in *Mrs. A. B. Simpson—The Wife or Love Stands:*

> It was the custom of the ministers of the district to meet together to discuss all things in common. This little reunion, in its proper sequence, was held one day at the [Simpson] manse. An unaccountably strange odor of tobacco smoke began to steal upstairs. Suddenly the study door flew open and a towering figure of fury— all of four feet, one inch [four feet eleven inches] in its stocking feet—stood at the threshold. "SMOKING! Out of this house! Out of this house!" said Grannie Simpson, and as a body, the ministerial association moved on.[9]

Many years later at a "Friday Talk" given in the Gospel Tabernacle in New York in 1900, Simpson recalls those days:

> I remember long after I had given up that wretched habit of smoking, which was a real comfort to me in my early life, I did not miss it at all. I found that the Holy Spirit was a Substitute, but immensely better, a quiet, restful influence that put me to sleep. But years ago [1881], I had a tremendous breakdown and for months I was desperately miserable. I had not learned to know the Lord as my Healer. I remember those awful days of restlessness and

wretchedness, nights together that I never slept at all. I cast about for something and I remember it came back to me—"your old cigar. Why that will rest you, quiet you." And so, I tried it, but it did not give me any comfort, it just made me sick. I tried several times, but it made me sicker every time. I came to Marah and the waters were bitter. It just disgusted me, so I never learned the habit anymore; it was distasteful.[10]

Admittedly, it takes an effort to imagine A. B. Simpson puffing on a stogie; yet this account may be an encouragement for all who have struggled with the "wretched weed" or any other addiction. He was a young man raised in circles that had not yet concluded that tobacco's many forms and flavors carried with its comfort the added burden of addiction and serious health issues. Later holiness teaching that Simpson and others embraced recognized the body as the temple of the indwelling Holy Spirit. The "caretaker" who lives in that fleshly sanctuary must zealously maintain it for the indwelling Spirit of God. This was another lesson that young Pastor Simpson learned as he slowly developed as a man of God. Little by little, the one coming into view was taking on more of the appearance of the One who lived and ruled inside.

WILLING SPIRIT—WEAK FLESH

Thus, the young pastoral couple worked to make the needed adjustments while he honed his pastoral skills. By 1871, they had three sons, Albert Henry, Melville Jennings, and James Gordon, ages five, three, and less than a year old. Despite the church generously offering him two months of vacation two years previously, following the major remodeling of Knox Church, which Pastor Simpson supervised, he took only one month, which was too little too late. Because of his strict routine of Bible study, sermon preparation, and heavy visitation, Bert's frail constitution was cracking under the strain because of too much work and too little rest. His health eventually failed, and he crashed physically and emotionally.

In April 1871, he visited the family physician following an ultimatum by the church session and Margaret. The doctor ordered him to take an immediate leave of absence. By the end of May, Knox Church sent their cherished pastor on an extended tour of the British Isles and

Europe. The "tour" purposed to help Bert regain his health as well as gain some valuable "culture" as he traveled across Britain and the continent. During his European odyssey, Simpson wrote a series of letters to Maggie that revealed the heart of a loving husband and father and a maturing man of God.

"I have had some very sad and lonesome moments today, and had a long struggle with my despondent and unbelieving feelings . . . and I have been a long time in coming to see again that we have nothing to do but trust and love Christ."

—A. B. Simpson

CHAPTER 5
LETTERS TO MAGGIE

*I*N SEVEN YEARS OF MARRIAGE, this prescribed leave was Bert's first time away from Margaret and the family. He had traveled to church functions and been away from home for a few days at a time, but a three-and-a-half-month European tour was another story. His letters revealed a homesick husband after just a few weeks away from wife and family. Transatlantic mail depended on ship schedules, and he often waited two weeks or more to get mail from home. Several times their letters crossed on liners passing in the opposite direction. Delayed mail had to be forwarded from country to country, trying to catch the lonely traveler who was squeezing every ounce from his "culture" tour.

His letters invariably ended with loving remarks and numerous "KKKK" kisses for "Darling Maggie" and the boys. As the trip progressed, they disclosed a man regaining his physical and emotional health. The correspondence sheds much light on the young pastor, just 28 years old and six years into his first pastorate. The first letter of June 8, 1871, showed that Bert was on the mend.

> *I am now 155 pounds in weight while I find in looking back in my journal I was just 146 on the 15th of April, the day I was examined by Dr. Mullen. Nine pounds in six weeks is not bad. I hope it may go on, and it is comforting to hope that I have had the worst of it so far. The best thing I find is that my mind has resumed its old buoyancy and vigor. I can think and talk now and have got (sic)*

over the mental numbness which made me almost an imbecile the last two months I was home and which felt like a weight of lead upon my spirit. I am feeling a returning confidence in my powers under God, and I hope to go back better fitted than ever to do good in my own land.[1]

At six feet tall, Simpson was about half a foot taller than the average North American male at that time. So, weighing in at 146 pounds when his health failed, Bert Simpson likely looked like a tall beanpole.

"STUPID DULLNESS"

The European tour would give him a chance to recover from "the stupid dullness of the past months,"[2] as he described his condition before leaving in early May 1871. In his letters, he recounts the two-week trip from Montreal to Ireland on the rather dirty *SS Peruvian* of the Allen Line. Arriving in Scotland, he went by train to Edinburgh, where he attended a Presbyterian conference. Then he journeyed on to Ireland

SS Peruvian

and England. There, he spent several days in London, disappointed that Spurgeon was sick with smallpox. Thus, he canceled his visit to Spurgeon's famous Metropolitan Tabernacle. The rest of his itinerary took him from London to Brussels, then to Cologne and a cruise on the Rhine to Basel. He then traveled to Milan, Venice, Florence, Rome, Naples, and down and up the boot of Italy to Geneva, Switzerland. The last leg took him to Paris, London, Scotland, and finally home in late August. While physically taxing, the trip was "just what the doctor ordered" because it gave him opportunity not only to experience European culture but also to have a change of pace after the intense years of ministry in Hamilton.

The European tour letters disclose a man who loved and sorely missed his wife and children. They are full of humorous stories, like getting on the wrong train and being yelled at by a furious German conductor who spoke no English and threw the stupid Canadian who spoke no *Deutsch* off the train. "There is also the comical description, written from the Hotel de L'Universe in Brussels the evening of June 4, of crossing the English Channel." Halfway across the Channel, the wild waves were so bad that:

> *"Ere we were half an hour at sea, the deck and saloons were one mass of basins and prostrate human beings, men and women and children vomiting away at the most awful rate until soon in the abandon of their misery, they fairly lay down on benches and sofas, and thick as pigs, on the very floors."*[3]

Mercifully, the description will stop right there. Suffice it to say that the Reverend Simpson soon was in the scuttles with his own *mal de mer*, which left him in wet clothing for the rest of the channel crossing and the subsequent train ride to Ghent in Belgium.

EUROPEAN DECAY

Simpson's posts also reveal an observant eye, noting the heavy-drinking habits of Europeans, the gorgeous Alpine scenes witnessed while traveling by train and stage coach, and the many hotels where he stayed. He was saddened as he observed the famous "flower girls of Venice . . . young women nicely and modestly dressed, generally in white muslin . . . [who] come up to you with a bunch of bouquets and offer you one."[4] These poor young prostitutes worked the streets and plazas, where he was propositioned twice. Coming from Victorian-era Hamilton, Simpson was taken aback and saddened by the obvious moral decay of Europe.

Simpson was a forgetful traveler who lost and found his favorite umbrella, his Bible, his Bradshaw travel guide and train schedule, as well as other less-important items. His problems with money changing, train timetables, receiving cash remittances from Margaret, and many other mundane details fill the letters. Jokes and funny remarks to little Bert, Melville, and baby Gordon peppered the pages, as well as his constant words of love and concern for Margaret.

The letters are fascinating in that they reveal a Simpson not often seen. Most photos of Simpson show him as a serious, almost prophet-like man in his 60s and 70s. At the time of these letters he was 28, still growing into the man who would become a dynamic Spirit-filled pastor and leader, full of faith and vision. Simpson was 38 when he launched out onto the sea of faith to found the Gospel Tabernacle in 1881 and the "Alliances" just a few years later.

CHRIST IN ME

His mail discloses a man growing in commitment to Christ, and a deepening of his understanding of the "Christ-in-me/I-in-Christ" relationship that characterized his future preaching and writing. In a beautiful letter written the evening of June 11 from the *Hotel Suisse* in Basel, Switzerland, Simpson pours out his heart to his wife:

> *I have had some very sad and lonesome moments today, and had a long struggle with my despondent and unbelieving feelings, and I have been a long time in coming to see again what I have so often seen before but what I so often lose sight of utterly, that we have nothing to do but trust and love Christ; that we must not have any anxieties, for they all show that we love something else more than Him, and that we will have none if we only love him supremely.*[5]

This letter is likely the earliest written record of what became Simpson's hallmark "In Christ" message. He wrote: "I often wonder exactly what the apostle meant by 'Christ dwelling in our heart by faith.' But I have lately come to see that it just means Christ dwelling in our affection, i.e., our souls." He goes on to compare this to his relationship with Margaret.

> *Christ loved, and you know what it is to have any dear friend in your heart. Their form, their features, their character, their goodness, their acts of kindness, nobleness are all in your memory and*

affections and engraven most tenderly on your heart. Thus, I have you in my heart . . . Now it is by a kind of faith that this is so. Now let us just transfer all this to Jesus. In the same sense the apostle prays [Ephesians 4:13-20] that Christ may dwell in our hearts—not actually present but present to the mind and affections—loved, having a place in our tenderest feelings . . . O that we might realize this, to have Christ always in the heart . . . O that we might more earnestly and often send up this prayer for ourselves. Let us do so, my dearest wife; let us aim at being filled with the love of Christ and all the fullness of God.[6]

Here, a concerned husband strains to explain what he was beginning to understand about the uniqueness of "it is no longer I but Christ who lives in me." On the trip, he ministered to Margaret, read and meditated on the Word, and prayed these deeper truths into reality in his life. Because of his love for his wife, who was struggling in her walk with the Lord, he shared with her the "great secrets of a happy and holy life" that he had found.

NOT IN THE LETTERS

Like many husbands, Bert didn't tell Margaret all that he experienced in Europe. The trip had been ordered due to Bert's delicate health and need to get strong and fit. On one occasion, he excitedly wrote about traveling to the top of Mount Righi, 5,899 feet above sea level, on the little cog-rail steam engine. The next week while in Florence, Italy, he dared to climb the 414 steps to the top of the beautiful bell tower in the town Cathedral. Years later, Simpson described those experiences: "Well do I remember the day in Europe when I ventured to the top of the Righi in Switzerland by rail and again when I tried to climb the high Campanile stairs in Florence. As the paroxysm of imminent suffocation swept over me, I resolved that I should never venture into such peril again."[7] No, Maggie didn't hear about these frightening adventures. The tour definitely refreshed and energized Bert, but he was still far from full health.

His 1871 tour came on the heels of the hinge year, 1870, when Europe was rocked by riots, revolutions, and radical social change. Marx and Engels had published *The Communist Manifesto* a few years earlier, and the promise of a socialist "paradise without God" appealed to the ever-growing spirit of skepticism in universities all over Europe. Darwin's *Origin of Species* had been in print for a few years, and the idea of "origin without creation" was taking the intellectual centers by storm. Social unrest rocked Western Europe as people demanded liberty from oppressive governments, economic exploitation, and rapid urbanization. Nationalism raised its ugly head and brought peoples into conflict.

WARS AND RUMORS OF WAR

The Franco-Prussian War of 1870 saw France foolishly drawn into war with the German states led by the Prussian "Iron Chancellor," Bismarck. This short-lived conflict united the various kingdoms and duchies, making Germany the new European superpower, while weakening the corrupt French Second Republic. The conflict ended with the Siege of Paris and the brutal shelling of the City of Lights, causing the government to fall while losing the border provinces of Alsace-Lorraine to the Germans as part of the peace negotiations.

In Italy, forces for national unification and freedom of the Italian states from Papal rule resulted in the independence movement led by Garibaldi and Italy's Count Cavour. This brought about the eventual defeat of the Papal State and its army, and the Pontiff, Pius IX, became a virtual prisoner in the Vatican. These scenes of liberation and unification and the resulting loss of power over the Italian people by the Pope and Vatican were to later figure large in Simpson's eschatology, since he saw the institution of the papacy as the antichrist of the Book of Revelation.[8]

The heady airs of freedom blew at will across the Italian peninsula, and Simpson saw firsthand the results of battles fought in Italy and France. Bombed out neighborhoods, shelled buildings and bullet-pocked houses gave evidence of fierce fighting. He wrote from Geneva, Switzerland, on July 2:

> France is yet reeling from its late blood drunkenness and mad intoxication, but all Europe is agitated with the throes of some great coming revolution, and no man feels safe, and no country is safe or secure, and no man knows what a day may bring forth. I speak only what I have seen and heard in Scotland and England, and in

Ireland in Germany, in Italy and France and again I say, I turn from the dissolving social systems and the revolutionary atmosphere and the troubled conditions of this old and changing world to that great New Continent. I go back with a new love and a new hope for America, the hope for the world's future.[9]

HOPE FOR THE WORLD'S FUTURE

Simpson, always an avid student of history and a keen observer, learned much from his travels in 1871, which provided great material for sermons and popular lectures that he gave back in Hamilton. On the homeward leg of the tour, Simpson returned to England, where he visited Spurgeon's 7,000-seat Metropolitan Tabernacle, "finished with

> **Young Simpson, the preacher, was sufficiently experienced to evaluate Spurgeon's message respectfully and honestly.**

great simplicity and elegance, and well adapted for a large audience."[10] He heard the famous British Baptist preacher, stout and suffering from gout, deliver "a most excellent sermon," although less eloquent and powerful than he had expected. Young Simpson, the preacher, was sufficiently experienced to evaluate Spurgeon's message respectfully and honestly. The Metropolitan Tabernacle would lodge itself in Simpson's mind as a model for future reference.

In his letters, Simpson asks for his wife's dress size and gift ideas for the children and in-laws. While touring the continent and absorbing the beauty and history, his mind was very much connected with his return to Knox. He felt this tour required him to dutifully take in every possible historical site, scenic marvel, and cultural feature that the old world had to offer.

He even watched a few tennis matches at Wimbledon and saw the Canadian team play, although it did not fare well. The last letters reveal an anxious husband and father chomping at the bit to get back home. In the latter part of August 1871, Simpson returned to the open arms of wife and family and the appreciative audience that awaited him the next Sunday at Knox Church.

Knox Church of Hamilton, Ontario

With renewed energy and enthusiasm, Simpson took up his pastoral reins. Church membership eventually received 750 new members during the nine years he served there; all indebtedness was paid off. Numerous prayer groups, a Women's Aid Society and fervent giving to missions characterized the last years of his ministry there. Sadly, less than six months after he returned from his continental tour, tragedy suddenly struck the Simpson home.

DEATH'S STING

Margaret's elderly father, John Henry, fell seriously ill in Toronto. As his oldest daughter and closest support since losing his wife, Margaret traveled to be with him. Arriving just in time to spend a few hours before death called her father home, she received a telegram from Bert. Little Melville, just three and a half years old, was deathly sick with "membranous croup," i.e., diphtheria. The telegram read, "Melville very low." In agony, Margaret left her mourning siblings and rushed home to find her little boy dying. "As he was put into her arms, the baby's lips had only strength to whisper, 'Abide in me and I in you,' the verse that she had been teaching him. The little boy's head drooped—and he was still."[11] What followed was the long night of Margaret's soul. "There can be no God," her anguished heart cried. The grieving parents held onto each other as they bent under the heavy blow of death. Simpson later recalled that he had always felt helpless to counsel grieving loved ones, because he had not experienced the pain of burying one of his own. But holding his son's dead body in his arms after calling out to God and, seemingly, not receiving an answer, gave the brokenhearted father and pastor a new depth of compassion previously untouched.

In time, Margaret said that the little verse, John 15:4, which baby Melville murmured, "was the first message that ever sank deeply into

> **As he was put into her arms, the baby's lips had only strength to whisper, "Abide in me and I in you," the verse that she had been teaching him.**

[my] heart and that it prepared the way for the deeper experience in Christ into which [I] entered years afterward."[12] Abiding in Christ and He in her. In God's time, the truth that Simpson had written about from England was finally finding ready soil in her heart. Eventually the raw wound of loss gradually healed and little Mabel Jane, their first daughter, was born in late 1872. Their night of sorrow ended with joy in the morning.

AN UNEXPECTED MOVE

In October 1873, Simpson attended a convention of the Evangelical Alliance in New York City. This fellowship of evangelical Christians for closer unity and cooperation in ministry had been organized in London 30 years before and was now taking root in America. With widening horizons, the young pastor from Hamilton longed to be part of God's larger Kingdom movement. While in New York, he was invited by the Thirteenth Street Presbyterian Church in the city to be a guest speaker during the convention. Delegates to the convention from Louisville, Kentucky, attended the service at which Simpson preached. This amazing invitation given to a young pastor from a provincial Canadian city, whose reputation had preceded him, impressed the men from Louisville. Convinced by what they saw and heard from the young preacher, the Louisville delegation asked him to visit before returning to Hamilton. They then returned home to their church and spread the word. Simpson visited the thriving city and felt God's leading. Since the church was in full "pastoral search mode," his visit and preaching, plus the strong recommendation from the church's leaders, resulted in a call.

Arriving in Hamilton, Simpson found that he had to consider not one but three calls for his ministerial services. The Chalmers Church of Quebec had extended an invitation, as well as a "highly irregular" telegram from Knox Church of Ottawa, Ontario, announcing the arrival of a delegation to present their case for a call. Then there was the original request from the Chestnut Presbyterian Church of Louisville with its attractive salary package. Knox Church had no desire to see their pastor leave, but Simpson felt that this invitation from Kentucky was from God. The Knox session reluctantly agreed to release him, effective December 20, 1873. At his final sermon, preached on December 15, the night before his 30th birthday, his text was 2 Corinthians 6:1–2.[13]

"Now is the day of salvation," his sermon was quoted verbatim by *The Daily Spector,* Hamilton's newspaper the next morning. The article accompanying the sermon stated:

> *Last evening the Rev. A.B. Simpson preached his farewell sermon in Knox Church. The church was crowded long before the hour of service, and by the time the sermon began, a full 500 people came to the church door and found it impossible to gain admittance. The sermon was listened to with attention on the part of the congregation.*[14]

Simpson left Knox Church on a high note. In a matter of a few weeks, God had set Simpson and his young family on the next step in their faith journey. He had led Knox Church as far as he could and looked forward to the next step in ministry. He sensed a new challenge from God. Margaret, while comfortable in Hamilton, was glad to move south. The milder Kentucky weather meant fewer colds and sickness

> **He had led Knox Church as far as he could and looked forward to the next step in ministry. He sensed a new challenge from God.**

for her family and, likely, would have a positive effect on her husband's poor health. In addition, the church was offering a very generous salary of $5,000 a year, a welcome increase to the growing family's finances. The new pastor was relieved of all visitation duties, except for grave illness, and he was carrying in his baggage a healthy "sermon barrel," the result of nine years of study and preparation, which promised to ease his work load. To top it off, they were given two full months of vacation each summer. All in all, Louisville seemed to be an ideal situation for Simpson and his family.

Without a moment's delay, he took the train home and soon was in his office, determined to stay until he was baptized, sanctified, or crucified; whatever it was called, he wanted to be full of Jesus' Spirit.

CHAPTER 6
BLESSED ARE THE PEACEMAKERS

*F*ollowing eight years as pastor of Knox Presbyterian Church in Hamilton, Ontario, young but experienced Rev. Albert Simpson resigned after accepting the call from Chestnut Street Presbyterian Church of Louisville, Kentucky, the largest Presbyterian church in the city. Margaret was happy with the move, because it showed that her husband, now 31, was a rising star in the Presbyterian Church. The warmer weather appealed to Simpson, who was concerned about his less than robust health. Thus, the Simpsons packed their bags and boarded their children, Albert, Gordon, and baby Mabel, on the train for the long trip south to the Bluegrass State, arriving shortly before Christmas 1873 to "Kentucky cold" but milder than Hamilton. Simpson was installed as pastor of Chestnut Street Presbyterian Church on January 2, 1874.

"GOD'S PEOPLE FIGHT AND REMEMBER"

What they encountered upon arrival arrived was a microcosm of the church across the southern United States. The Civil War had ended eight years earlier. The Confederate Army had laid down arms; Robert E. Lee had offered his sword to Grant, and the Union was restored. Family feuds ended, and peace slowly returned to the nation—that is, except for the Church of Jesus Christ, Prince of Peace. The major Protestant denominations of the day, Methodists, Baptists, and Presbyterians, all had split over the issues of slavery and states' rights. These schisms resulted in the establishment of the "Southern and Northern" Baptists, Methodists, and Presbyterian denominations. Tozer remarked pungently: "The world fights and forgets; God's people fight and remember."[1]

To Louisville came Pastor Simpson and family from the Dominion of Canada, part of the British Empire, which had outlawed slavery in 1833. He had been raised in Chatham, Ontario, the end of the line for a branch of the "Underground Railroad." Likely young Bert had seen ex-slaves in Chatham who had fled the southern states to make their way north to freedom, where they started a new life on the Elgin Settlement begun by local Presbyterian clergy and black freedmen. Now years later, this Canadian couple arrived in a city that had been a major slave trade market. Located on the Ohio River, Louisville had benefited from being a commercial center near areas where cotton, tobacco, and other labor-intensive crops were raised.

Simpson immediately embarked upon this new ministry with determination. After a few months, more than 150 new names were put on the membership roll. Honed by his years in Hamilton, Simpson followed his practice of pastoral visitation, despite not being required to do so. Soon the young Presbyterian pastor was recognized as one of the most prominent church leaders in Louisville.

NOT SO WELL WITH HIS SOUL

About this same time, Simpson began to feel that all was not well with his soul. His outstanding preaching drew newcomers to the church to hear the gospel, but when it came time to talking with his parishioners of the deeper issues of the Christian life, his words sounded hollow to

> "Last night, I came here to hear Brother Moody speak, but before that happened, I saw Jesus, and He is all I need!"

him. Naturally pensive, Simpson saw things in his life that did not please him and knew that they could not please God either. From his early days as a school boy, he had always been ambitious, trying to be first and best. Perhaps this resulted from Bert's feeling overlooked as the second son and having to negotiate his father's approval to go to seminary at no family expense. He and Howard had vied for prizes in college, and even for Margaret's hand. Regardless of the reasons behind this trait, it deeply concerned the young pastor. Hearing of D. L. Moody's teaching about a deeper experience, a "baptism of the Holy Spirit" that gave victory over stubborn sinful tendencies as well as power for ministry, Simpson decided to give himself to prayer and "abiding" in the Lord for this new and more profound step in his Christian walk.

In mid-1874, he heard of a special meeting in Chicago led by Moody for seekers of this deeper walk with the Lord. He quickly caught the train heading to the Windy City and went to the big-top tent erected for the conference. Arriving early, he sat in on the testimony meeting and heard a plain-spoken brother get up and testify. "Last night, I came here to hear Brother Moody speak, but before that happened, I saw Jesus, and He is all I need!"[2] Simpson heard those words and felt God saying, "Go home and wait on me." Without a moment's delay, he took the train home and soon was in his office, determined to stay until he was baptized, sanctified, or crucified; whatever it was called, he wanted to be full of Jesus' Spirit.

JESUS GIVES US THE VICTORY

While waiting in prayer, Bert glanced at his library and saw a book given him, William Boardman's *The Higher Christian Life*. Like his experience as a teenager when seeking salvation, God spoke to him through a writer: "He who had justified us was waiting to sanctify us, to enter into our spirit and substitute His strength, His holiness, His joy, His love, His faith, His power, for all our worthlessness, helplessness, and nothingness, and make it an actual living fact."[3] He realized that the same One who came in to his sinful heart to cleanse and forgive did not then leave him to battle against sin on his own. This same Savior lived within to make him holy, useful for service and victorious over the swamp-sins that dragged him into the bog of despair.

In Thompson's biography, Simpson is quoted as he explains what this critical post-salvation moment that he called "Jesus Christ—Our Sanctifier" meant for him:

> We also believe, and this is the emphatic point in our testimony, that this experience of Christ our Sanctifier marks a definite and distinct crisis in the history of a soul. We do not grow into it, but we cross a definite line of demarcation as clear as when the hosts of Joshua crossed the Jordan and were over in the promised land and

*set up a great heap of stones so that they never could forget that crisis hour.*⁴

Simpson described what happened that made such a significant change in his life, as testified in his "Personal Testimony of Sanctification," given on September 12, 1915, at his first pastoral charge, Knox Church in Hamilton, Ontario, on the 50th anniversary of his ordination:

> *Throwing himself at the feet of that glorious Master, he claimed the mighty promise, "I will dwell in you and walk in you." Across the threshold of his spirit there passed a Being as real as the Christ who came to John on Patmos, and from that moment, a new secret has been the charm, and glory, and strength of his life and testimony. And he shall never forget how he longed to come back to the land of his birth and the friends of former years, and tell them that magic, marvelous secret, hid from ages and generations, but now made manifest in the saints, which is Christ in you, the Hope of glory. Henceforth it was not his struggles, his character, his ethical culture, his moral goodness, but his constant dependence upon the living One who has said, "Because I live, ye shall live also."*⁵

Simpson then enumerated the many blessings that came from that "death-to-self" moment that led to a deeper and richer life in Christ. From the spirit of victory over "his own intense nature, his strong self-will, his peculiar temptations, and his spiritual life that had been a constant humiliation,"⁶ came a mental efficiency from "the mind of Christ" and physical endurance found in His all-sufficient strength. A new dimension of answered prayer arose, where heaven's "checkbook" seemed to fall into his hand to fill out and sign in faith. It was following this deeper walk in Christ while at Louisville that "the glorious light of prophetic truth and millennial hope"⁷ became clear to his heart. Gradually moving from an optimistic postmillennial ushering in of Christ's reign to a Matthew 24:14-based "bring-back-the-King" theology, this critical point in Simpson's life was revisited many times over the rest of his life, as the Spirit revealed a new "foe for every day in the month, in the Christian's calendar,"⁸ as described in Simpson's fascinating booklet, "Thirty-One Kings."

All for Jesus describes the result of this turning point in Simpson's journey that began a new period of service marked by increased fruitfulness:

> *During the next forty-plus years of ministry, Simpson would repeatedly refer back to that moment of surrender to Christ as his Sanctifier, the One who alone could make him holy. It was the decisive turning point of his ministry in much the same way as the Apostle Paul looked back upon his conversion experience on the road to Damascus.*[9]

For the next several years, this "Christ-in-me" divine power for life and service empowered his ministry and broadened his spiritual bandwidth.

AN OLD MEDIEVAL MESSAGE

Not long after this watershed "deeper-life experience," another book had a profound effect on him. Given to him by a "kindred spirit" and member of his Louisville charge, Simpson called it "an old medieval" message. While it contained writings penned by men and women of the 15th and 16th centuries, the book, compiled by Quakers William Blackhouse and James Janson, was first published in 1839. Entitled *A Guide to True Peace*, it stressed "that God was waiting in the depths of my being to talk

> **Simpson struggled to calm his mind from the thousands of thoughts clamoring for his attention in order to hear God speak.**

to me if I would only get still enough to hear His voice."[10] As Simpson struggled to calm his mind from the thousands of thoughts clamoring for his attention in order to hear God speak, he eventually learned to catch the still, small voice in the depths of his being that began to speak with an inexpressible tenderness, power, and comfort. Thus began a learning process of hearing the whisper of "the Holy Spirit in my heart [that] was God's prayer in my secret soul . . . God's answer to all my questions, [it] was God's life and strength for soul and body."[11]

Refreshed and renewed in his inner man, Simpson, a true son of Issachar, understood the times and knew what to do. Coming from

Canada and never having been involved in slavery or the Civil War, the new pastor in town was a potential mediator between the warring church parties. Doubtless, Simpson arrived on the scene with strong feelings about slavery. Years later at the Missionary Training Institute, he recruited African-American students whose parents and grandparents had been slaves. Simpson's new Louisville parish, Chestnut Street Presbyterian Church, had been an exception to the rule. The Civil War had not split the congregation; yet, he recognized that he pastored "a wealthy, fashionable church without spiritual life," where there had been serious fault lines during the war. The former pastor had managed to hold the church together while other Presbyterian churches in Louisville suffered division. One historian has noted that the Chestnut Street Presbyterian church was "the only church in this city that remained undisturbed in its ecclesiastical relations during the war and at the unhappy period of the division in 1866."[12]

Because of Simpson's participation in the life of the Presbyterian Church while in Canada, he was quickly recruited by his Kentucky colleagues to do the same. Soon he was appointed as trustee at Center College, the denomination's liberal arts college, and appointed as a consultant to the Danville Theological Seminary. In addition, Simpson was one of the forces behind the organization of the Louisville chapter of the Evangelical Alliance. In all these activities, Simpson envisioned the church revived and recommitted to the task of reaching the lost.

THE WAR BETWEEN THE SAINTS

By the end of his first year, Simpson, troubled by the apparent divisive spirit among Louisville churches, believed that it would be eliminated only if the pastors met for prayer and reconciliation. Simpson sensed that God wanted to revive the church and save souls. Thus, he became a strong advocate for the Evangelical Alliance. Encouraged by him and other colleagues, the city's pastors met for a week of united prayer in early 1875 in various churches to consider holding united citywide evangelistic meetings, something they agreed on. Louisville had thousands of unchurched families devastated by alcoholism and the costly social ills of such a blight. Most of the pastors came willingly.

When the meeting was held at Chestnut Street Presbyterian, Simpson presented ideas for the joint evangelistic meetings. Tozer describes the first meeting:

Then knowing that if they were permitted to start talking they would talk their bristles up and the meeting down he suggested that they now get on their knees and call upon God for revival. It worked. As they prayed the fire grew so hot that everyone was melted except one old die-hard who ground his teeth shut, scooped up his hat, and stalked out for keeps.[13]

At the follow-up meeting, two pastors who had not talked since the beginning of the war in 1861 shook hands and restored fellowship. Because of Simpson's winsome way and gracious prodding, enmity was broken, and the pastors were ready to work together. At last, eight years after the cannons had silenced, the "unholy war" between the saints ceased and peace came to Louisville. Finally, they were ready to think about evangelistic meetings to reach Louisville's lost.

The 19th century had witnessed a new kind of mass evangelism arise, with gifted evangelists teaming up with popular gospel singers to reach the unchurched, often in neutral, non-church settings, such as

As they prayed the fire grew so hot that everyone was melted.

public halls, theaters, tents, or even open-air settings. Charles Finney, and later D. L. Moody, provided a model that others followed. Major Daniel Whittle, formerly an officer in the Union Army and colleague of Moody, partnered with P. P. Bliss, an outstanding singer and musician. God used this "dynamic duo" in many major cities with great success. Consequently, 24 Louisville pastors decided to invite the Whittle-Bliss team to hold meetings in their city.

Simpson became the go-to guy for inviting Whittle and Bliss and for the organization of the evangelistic campaign. Beginning in February 1875, Whittle and Bliss began a three-week evangelistic campaign in Louisville's Library Hall, which seated more than 2,000 people. Simpson saw firsthand the effectiveness of this kind of outreach to the unchurched masses. The daily noontime prayer meeting was followed by Bible readings at 3:30, with the main event at 7:30 p.m. Night after night, the hall was packed, attracted by Bliss's songs and the evangelist's preaching. Simpson noted the power of Whittle's straightforward messages based on Scripture centered around a single theme. While disarmingly simple, the format was effective, since hundreds of men, women, and children responded to the altar calls. The campaign ran from February 10 to March 12, 1875, deeply impacting the city for years to come. A strong desire grew in Simpson's heart to do more of the same.

During the campaign, Whittle suddenly returned home due to a family emergency, and Simpson took his place with Bliss's assistance. He preached from Luke 14:17 on the rich man's invitation to a feast—"Come, for all things are ready." He spoke of the feast prepared by Jesus Christ for all who would come to Him. As reported in the *Louisville-Courier* of March 1, 1875, the sermon "produced an effect which partook of the wonderful,"[14] with nearly 400 rising to their feet at the end of the message.

At the conclusion of the campaign, Simpson urged the pastors to continue holding evangelistic meetings, sharing the preaching, and using local musicians. The experience was another turning point in Simpson's life. For the rest of the year, Simpson preached evangelistically at church, as well as at Macauley Theater, despite being criticized for his "Sunday Theatricals." One hundred seventy-five members were added to his congregation.[15]

As a result of the climate of faith from the revival and his Spirit infilling, Simpson's interest in divine healing grew. He was asked to pray for a young man suffering paralysis. At the man's bedside, he prayed, and "suddenly the young man opened his eyes and began to talk to me." To Simpson's joy and astonishment, the man was miraculously healed. Consequently, Simpson began to pray for his own health, which improved. Later he shared this discovery with a devout Christian physician who declared such a doctrine as presumptuous. Simpson abandoned his belief and his poor health returned.[16]

"REGULAR PASTOR" NO MORE

One year later, Simpson, now an evangelistic preacher who had discarded his "regular pastor" mindset from Hamilton days, challenged his church to build a "tabernacle" to take the gospel to the unevangelized, thus beginning a two-year struggle. Simpson envisioned an unpretentious, yet attractive structure to be built and dedicated debt free.[17] In this contest between "economical" versus "sumptuous," the well-to-do leadership won the match. The church purchased a choice corner lot on Broadway and Fourth Avenue for $32,000. Simpson proposed a modern design—a semi-circular auditorium for excellent natural acoustics, with rising tiers of seats and gallery, with no one distant from the platform. With capacity for 2,500 people, the semi-octagonal structure formed a "family circle." The design was modeled on Rev. Dewitt Talmadge's famous Brooklyn Tabernacle, considered one of the finest public buildings in America for natural acoustics and comfort. Through the sale of the existing Chestnut Street property, plus a fundraising campaign, Simpson estimated that the $65,000 was feasible.

Thus, the cornerstone was laid on May 23, 1876, as a sign of God's blessing on the vision Simpson had for his church. In a metal box placed in the cornerstone, a few local newspapers were deposited, a manual of Chestnut Street Church, a small American flag, a gold ring, and a Scripture text, "Abide in me, and I in you," a last memorial of Albert and Margaret's little son, Melville. This motto represented a laying to rest of past pain, sorrow, and failures and looking forward to a better day. A few weeks later, Pastor Simpson and family left Louisville for a much-needed six-week vacation with family in Canada. Returning home at summer's end, Simpson discovered that construction had not gone forward.

"HE KEEPETH ALL OF HIS BONES"

Almost as soon as the Simpson family returned from their summer vacation, Pastor Simpson disappeared from view for several weeks. The October 1, 1876, issue of the *Courier-Journal* announced: "Rev. A. B. Simpson, having recovered from the slight gunshot wound which he received in the arm while out hunting a few weeks ago, will preach at Chestnut Street Presbyterian Church this morning."[18]

Simpson later remembered the incident in a 1915 issue of *The Alliance Weekly* where he relates what happened:

> I was reading last night an old Bible that had come down to me since the year '70 [1870]. It was pretty well torn . . . underlined and interlined with red, green, purple and black ink I saw the story of forty years inscribed in the margin There was a little verse, "He keepeth all his bones; not one of them is broken." I noticed in the margin, under a date of years ago, the words "God made this true." I remembered how as a rather headlong young minister I went on

my vacation and took my gun. It burst in my hands and I found myself fainting with blood pouring from my wrist. I thought the bones were shattered. I was away in the woods far from home. When I reached home, the first thing I did was to pick up that Bible, and God gave me that verse, "He keepeth all his bones; not one of them is broken." And though everyone said the bone was shattered, and the doctor watched against lockjaw and said the bones would come out in splinters, never a splinter has appeared. I have a scar to the day, and I haven't shot a bird since.[19]

The cryptic note in the old Bible revealed a young pastor who had not accepted the lesson learned years before when he bought and later lost the forbidden shotgun. He had vowed to not shoot again, and the consequence of breaking his vow resulted in a frightening experience and lesson learned. The issue was not guns or hunting but obedience to the "inside voice."

COMPETING VISIONS

During Simpson's vacation absence with the family, the building committee had tried to accommodate both Simpson's design and the desires of those wanting an imposing structure that "looked like a church," with stained glass windows and an elaborate, vaulted ceiling with ornamented ribs. Instead of the original $65,000 estimate, it had ballooned to $105,000, with $40,000 still needed to pay for the construction. Eventually, due to delays and cost overruns, the final tally jumped to $150,000.

For the next two years, Simpson and a group of the "stakeholders" locked horns over the design, financing, and, ultimately, whose philosophy of ministry would prevail. This ongoing struggle with Chestnut Street Presbyterian's leading movers and shakers resulted in serious strain in the Simpson home. Margaret did not want Bert fighting with the church, concerned that this could jeopardize his ministry and family's security. The strain was such that Simpson's health broke, physically and emotionally. The killing combination of overwork, constant pastoral and evangelistic work, plus the struggle over the Broadway Tabernacle, and stress on the home front, forced him to leave the pulpit for five months.

Exhausted, Simpson traveled to Clifton Springs Sanitarium, in central New York State, founded by Dr. Henry Foster, a godly physician of New England Methodist stock. He had felt called by God to open a sulfur water cure facility in 1850. As the first medical facility in the region, it quickly grew and prospered. One of Foster's principles

> The cryptic note in the old Bible revealed a young pastor who had not accepted the lesson learned years before.

upon establishing the sanitarium was his desire to minister to pastors, missionaries, and teachers who could not ordinarily afford such medical care. The biography of Foster's life by Samuel Adams, longtime chaplain at Clifton Springs, reveals a doctor with a definite call from God to establish a place for healing that recognized "Christ is the Healer." Adams relates how Foster had a definite experience of being filled by the Holy Spirit in 1849, before founding Clifton Springs. No doubt, Simpson and Foster must have had many conversations about this very subject, which became an important element in Simpson's Fourfold Gospel formulation.

Apparently, Simpson went there because of the institution's strong Christian principles. Likely, the fact that Clifton Springs operated on a charitable principle made it easier for Simpson to go there for an extended period. Foster pioneered in physical and mental health treatment, believing that the spirit was to be the first focus in treating people. Dr. Foster visited each patient daily, for years led the morning chapel services, and ministered to the soul while treating the body.

It is not known if Margaret and the children accompanied Simpson or if he remained there alone. His health leave began following a July 12 meeting of the session, when Simpson left the meeting early and turned the moderator's chair to another.

John Sawin records Simpson's remarks regarding his stay at Clifton Springs:

> *I used to get a good deal of help from electrical treatment. I remember the first time I went into the electric bath in Clifton Springs. I said this is exactly what I have felt a hundred times from the touch of the Holy Spirit, only it is very much weaker. Why, I said, I have something better than that, although I never turned it on my body. I have felt it a thousand times in my heart; now I see I can have it*

for my nerves and muscles, too. I never took another electrical bath, but I went to my room, and I may say very humbly that I asked the Lord to bathe me in the Holy Ghost, to submerge me, to make every nerve a tingling cord along which the divine current can flow.[20]

Today, reading "electric" and "bath" in the same sentence as a kind of medical treatment is a bit off-putting. However, the low voltage treatment allegedly provided benefits for the treatment of rheumatism, muscle and back pain, nervous system disorders, migraine headaches, arthritis, and neuromuscular issues. Thus, from mid-July to the latter part of January 1878, Simpson was absent from the Louisville church. By November, with their pastor still incommunicado, members began asking for action to be taken. In December, Simpson wrote the church, asking for the session's counsel "in regard to [my] future relations with the church."[21] The church had already written before Simpson's letter arrived, suggesting that he resign as pastor of Chestnut Street Presbyterian. Thus, the day after Christmas, the session met to consider the just-received letter of resignation sent by Simpson. His physician had consented to his returning to the church in January to serve until the effective date of his resignation, April 1, 1878, if the session should so decide. While it appeared that Simpson's stay in Louisville was about to close, God apparently had other ideas.

In two subsequent meetings, the session's efforts to receive Simpson's resignation was frustrated on both occasions, with a final vote cast on January 20, 1878. One hundred and thirty members voted for his permanence with thirty-seven cast for his resignation. Accordingly, Simpson returned to Louisville to take up his pastoral duties at a church divided and its leadership demoralized at their failure to oust the popular pastor. His first sermon delivered on January 27 from Philippians 3:13-14: "Brethren, I count not myself to have apprehended: but this one thing I do, forgetting those things which are behind, and reaching forth unto those things which are before, I press toward the mark for the prize of the high calling of God in Christ Jesus."

Simpson had returned as one, like Paul, making a new start in life, leaving past disappointment behind and pressing for the prize of the high calling of God in Christ Jesus. He returned to his normal heavy routine of pastoring his charge, as well as preaching regularly at Macaulay's Theater. For the next year and a half, Simpson ministered and watched the Broadway Tabernacle go up. He informed the session that he would not dedicate the church while it carried a $40,000 debt. The session overruled him and set a date for the "inauguration" of the new building on June 6, 1878, with the "dedication" scheduled for the next fall, believing that the debt would have been paid off by then.

At the inauguration, Simpson played a minor role as host pastor, with guest pastors preaching and leading the proceedings. Simpson spoke briefly, appealing to the congregation "to make one brave, final sacrifice" to retire the remaining debt that same day. In fact, it did not happen on June 6, 1878, but rather in mid-1881, when Simpson was already in New York. Ironically, the beautiful new building burned down two months after the balance of the debt was paid.

EVERY DAY IN EVERY WAY, BETTER?

In the summer of 1878, following the inauguration, Simpson attended a "Prophetic Believer's Conference" in Watkins Glen, New York, while vacationing, coming under the influence of noted Bible teachers whose premillennial stance regarding the return of Christ contrasted with Simpson's Reformed postmillennial roots. The prophetic conference's emphasis influenced Simpson's migration from postmillennial to premillennial teaching.

Following his European "cure tour" in 1871, Simpson had increasingly become skeptical of the optimistic postmillennial perspective that taught Christ's return at the end of a thousand-year period caused by the Christianization of the world. Instead of seeing things as "every day in every way, getting better and better," he was seeing that the increased knowledge and power of the "civilized" Western world was simply making sinful man more efficient in violence, crime, and war. Thus, the cry at the conference was for men and women to consecrate themselves to the task of worldwide evangelization, fulfilling the Great Commission, and preparing the way for Christ's return.

After the conference, Simpson traveled to Chicago, deeply impacted by what he had heard. While there, he had a very disturbing dream. He saw himself in an auditorium, seated with thousands of Christians. On the platform was a multitude of Asian men, women, and children, who appeared to be Chinese. Most troubling, they said nothing. No sound came from their lips, but they stood wringing their hands and imploring with their faces, as though appealing to the audience. Like a mimed

Macedonian vision, their wordless cry seemed to say, "Come over and help us." Simpson woke from the dream in a sweat, deeply convicted by the utter despair of those faces. He felt that God was calling him to leave all and become a missionary to China.

"GO, BERTIE, GO!"
He wrote to his wife and shared the strange vision. When he returned home, he brought it up with Margaret. She pushed it aside and said that he was free to go to China, alone, while she and the children would stay home. In Katherine Brennen's colorful account of her Grannie's recollection of the "China vision," she told him, "Go Bertie, go! And heaven be praised if I can rid myself and the children of a lunatic!"[22] Despite Maggie's wanting no part of it, Bert contacted the Presbyterian Mission

> **"Go Bertie, go! And heaven be praised if I can rid myself and the children of a lunatic!"**

Board and presented himself as a missionary candidate. The eventual reply from the mission indicated that Simpson had a serious case of the "terrible toos"—too old, too unhealthy, too many kids, and too late.

While the vision didn't take him to China, it stirred in him a passion for the lost worldwide, recalling missionary John Geddie's prophetic prayer over him as an infant 35 years before. Apparently Geddie, years later, recognized there was something special about that baptismal moment in the Cavendish Presbyterian Church on Prince Edward Island in early 1844, since he purposely sought out young Pastor Simpson in Hamilton, Ontario, more than 20 years later, on one of his rare furlough returns to Canada, to remind the young pastor about his foretelling prayer of dedication.

In addition to his burden to reach the unreached of Louisville and other great cities of North America, Simpson's eyes now were focusing on a wider field—the world. Looking back on this moment, Simpson later recognized it as being another step in his life that soon would send him in a new direction.

DADDY'S GIRL
In April 1878, the Simpsons welcomed the birth of their second baby daughter, Margaret May Simpson. The lovely baby, "Daddy's girl," grew

up to become an accomplished pianist and musician, able to take her father's hastily-written poems and tunes and transcribe them for use at the Gospel Tabernacle.

That same month, Simpson revisited his "Solemn Covenant," first written and signed as a young Christian in January 1861. This third recommitment to his early vows was part of the move of God in Bert's life because of all that had happened in Louisville. The quest for the filling of the Holy Spirit in purity and power had soon been followed by the newfound desire to reach the lost. His struggles with the church regarding vision or vanity brought him to the recognition that he was not free to do in Louisville what God was putting in his heart. His refusal to dedicate the new Broadway Temple and the sense that his time in Louisville was coming to an end resulted in increased pressure and unrest in the Simpson home. Margaret was not in agreement with Albert's differences with the church leaders about the Broadway Tabernacle. Heated discussion resulted in words and wounds as Bert, now 36 and Margaret, 38, would soon enter their middle-age. Unfortunately, what he was hearing from God was not yet audible to his struggling wife. What he saw as God's clear leading away from Louisville to a new larger challenge terrified Margaret.

A CHURCH OPEN TO ALL CLASSES

While the "China vision" did not make him a missionary, it put in motion an inevitable process. The charming southern town was too provincial, too set in its way, too satisfied with the status quo for what God had put in Simpson's heart. The hinge moments of the Louisville years were pushing him toward the major North American metropolis, where most missionary boards and societies had their headquarters—New York City. There, he envisioned pastoring a "people's church" committed to reaching the neglected masses. He dreamed of a church open to all, free of pew rent and monthly dues, committed to investing its freely given resources to reach the unreached across the whole spectrum of world need. For him, Jerusalem, Judea, Samaria, and earth's ends were attainable for all who would trust God and obey His commands.

When a call came from the fashionable 13th Street Presbyterian Church in New York in November 1879, Simpson took time responding. He traveled there and spent three weeks to meet with the session, preaching three straight Sundays and seeking to determine God's will regarding the decision. Margaret was aghast and adamant in her opposition. Hadn't her husband declared some years before that New York City was "corrupt sin-committing, Sabbath-breaking, mammon-loving, God-defying Gotham," and did he not disguise his disdain for the city? Now, he wanted to take their four young children to be raised there?[23] Her frustrated fury at his determination to go where she refused to follow led her to destroy Simpson's diary entries from his time in New York,[24] where she apparently read and saw his thoughts about her soul state and the challenge before him. Deeply hurt and confused by her anger, he began a new diary soon after where he registered his emotions, prayers, and plans:

> *November 10th, 1879, Monday night*
> *To the Lord Jesus Christ I commit these pages. May He guide every word and make it a holy, happy record. M. took out the pages I had written for the past two weeks here; God so permitted her foolish and sinful hand. Poor child. I have prayed and prayed for her until of late I cannot pray without intense distress. I leave her with Him, trusting that He will lead her to repentance and salvation. She has suffered much of late. She is possessed of an intense bitterness, and I am full of pain and fear. I was much exercised as to whether I should ask my brethren of the Session to speak to her and beseech her to be reconciled, but after conferring with one of them, I found it would be vain, and I wait in silence upon God. I trust my own heart may be kept righteous and merciful in everything.*[25]

This is another jarring moment for all who have honored and revered the memory of this couple so mightily used of God. Here one peers into the secrets of a family committed to God but divided by fear and anger. The visionary husband does not understand the mother's heart, which begs to not have her growing family raised in the devil's playground. Ripped pages and harsh words strained a marriage already stressed by the last few years in Louisville. Faith, dread, and confusion reigned in the Simpson home.

On Sunday, November 9, Simpson presented his resignation to the Louisville church. It was not accepted by the session for consideration. In fact, the leadership spoke against it and wrote a memorial praising the pastor's gifts and burden for the lost. Simpson writes: "They also passed on a motion of Mr. Jones, my most persistent adversary in my plans of work, a series of resolutions of which I am quite unworthy, most remarkable in their warmth and strength of commendation."[26] Despite the previous struggles between the session and their strong-willed pastor, they did not want to let him go. Yet Simpson, while gratified by the generous gesture, was convinced as to God's will. Therefore, he firmly re-submitted his resignation the next evening, and it was reluctantly accepted.

A STATE OF HARDNESS AND REBELLION

For the next several days, Simpson visited his parishioners, who were still in shock over his resignation. Margaret continued to "be in a state of hardness and rebellion" which did not ease as the date of their departure for "godless Gotham" approached. The day arrived, and the Simpson family boarded the train in Louisville. To add insult to injury, Margaret and the four children took their seats in one car while Daddy moved to another coach where he spent most of the trip in thought and prayer, preparing for the new challenge. Arriving at New York on Saturday, November 22, Simpson preached the next day. His laconic journal entry simply reads: "My first Sabbath in New York. Preached A.M., Acts 1:7, 8. Much aided." A more appropriate inaugural message would be hard to choose for one whom God used to reach across the global continuum of need with the gospel within the next few years. He would need all of the power and enabling of the Holy Spirit to do what God had in store for him.

One can imagine their horror when the shabbily dressed immigrants trooped noisily into the beautiful sanctuary with their snotty-nosed children in tow. Simpson's fond dream became the church's worst nightmare.

CHAPTER 7
SEALED ORDERS

*O*N THE NIGHT OF HIS ARRIVAL IN NEW YORK, Simpson wrote in his journal: "I asked today for a verse for New York and received a blank. God made me willing to leave all to Him and go with sealed orders."¹ It is clear from reading the next entries that there were many questions in Bert's mind still waiting for an answer. He began a house search, seemingly fruitless, but decided to entrust it to God. Beginning his new ministry, he was "flying blind," faith walking in the dark.

Since the 13th Street Church's session was anxious to set the date for his installation, Simpson prayed in his diary for clarity:

> *Peculiar burden tonight in Session meeting. My installation proposed and requested at an early day. Does the Master clearly bid this? Or does He hold me back at present and keep me free for wider work—as I have desired—as an Evangelist? Or does He bid me receive this special charge at present and let Him open the way in future for whatever else He may have? I will surely by His grace do whatever He shows. I want and must have His way and full blessing or I shall be unable to live. Lord let me not err."²*

Over the next several days, while Margaret was still angry and distant, Simpson pressed on, prayed hard, and prepared to go to work. He felt led to "write the vision" as God told Habakkuk and trust Him for its fulfillment. Finding a home at last and able to obtain needed furniture, the Simpson family moved into their New York parsonage on December 5, 1879. Despite his wife's continued resentment about the move, she slowly began to show signs of acceptance. For months, she alternated between harsh words and sorrow for her anger. Often, he would return home to find his children crying and his wife distraught. "My wife is under an influence of excitement and morbid resistance. And I cannot be free with her without distress and self-condemnation. My children were in tears when I returned tonight and in strife," he wrote.[3] Simpson prayed for grace and guidance for his family affairs.

FREE CHURCH

Originally begun as a "free church" that did not charge pew rent, the 13th Street Presbyterian Church started as an evangelistic outreach to the poor of lower Manhattan as the Third Free Church—Presbyterian. A simple sanctuary was built, and several pastors served there till 1839, when Rev. Samuel D. Burchard became pastor. Born in New York, Burchard moved to Kentucky as a youth for health reasons; he received his education at Center College and Danville Theological Seminary, where Simpson had served as trustee while in Louisville.

After Burchard arrived, the church's original evangelistic emphasis focusing on the poor, regardless of color, and earning a reputation as an "abolition church" changed its strategy. The humble hall was sold, and the congregation moved north to "the fields" on 13th Street in 1847, and a more traditional format followed with the introduction of pew rent. This resulted in a split, but the affluent in the new neighborhood were reached. After 40 years as pastor, Burchard's charge had become wealthy and the seventh largest Presbyterian church in New York City. However, all was not well; the social forces that had driven the church north 30 years before again threatened to overrun it. Once again, the neighborhood had changed. Affluent members moved farther north or over to Brooklyn, "leaving as driftwood Jews and Catholics," as reported in a commemorative discourse by Pastor Burchard.[4]

In 1877, despite these pressures, the church's finances seemed secure, but two years later, with Pastor Burchard's resigning under the shadow of alleged financial impropriety, the session decided to permit Burchard to retire on his 40th anniversary as pastor, with a substantial financial settlement easing his departure. The church took out a $15,000 mortgage and presented the full amount to the departing pastor in August 1879. This decision left the church with a considerable debt assumed despite the New York's Presbytery's explicit position that congregations were not to mortgage property without properly notifying the Presbytery. Thus, Simpson was called to the 13th Street Church under these circumstances.

Simpson's strong evangelistic preaching and visitation to all of the parish families within the first three weeks of his arrival led to an increase in congregants, following Pastor Burchard's resignation.[5] Simpson's energy and passion for souls confirmed the wisdom of inviting him to pastor the church. Nominal members became converted followers of Christ. Within

13th Street Presbyterian Church

just a few weeks after his arrival, almost every public service saw people coming to the "inquiry room" to pray for salvation. Eventually, he began holding street meetings in Little Italy, a poor neighborhood south of his parish. Soon, at least 100 newly arrived immigrants who had no spiritual hope were reached by the still-young pastor and friends from his church. The evangelistic team took the simple gospel of Christ to America's newcomers, and they embraced the message and the messenger.

One of Simpson's first challenges at 13th Street Presbyterian was the long-debated practice of pew rent. This method of church funding was widespread and trans-denominational. Most North American Protestant urban churches served middle- and upper-class white families. New arrivals to America came from predominantly Catholic or Orthodox countries, while Jews fled pogroms in Eastern Europe. Ireland, Italy, Poland, Russia, and other European nations sent their "huddled masses yearning to be free" by the shiploads. They tended to be poor, with little or no education, and gravitated to the large Catholic or Orthodox churches representing their national origins. These churches welcomed the immigrants and served as cultural and social centers that catered to the indigent who could not afford to pay to pray. However, the churches did little to eliminate the spiritual poverty of the needy newcomers. The wandering Jews settled wherever they could find housing and employment and were generally despised by other immigrants as well as native-born Americans.

A PEOPLE'S CHURCH

While not universally popular, Protestant churches found pew rent to be an efficient revenue stream. Whether or not a family attended services, their pew rent secured their seat; it was reserved. Either way, their monthly fee kept the church coffers filled. Simpson and others opposed this practice and longed to see it eliminated. A. B. Simpson's long-dreamed vision was for a "people's church" that was open to all, rent free, welcoming the rich, middle-class and poor; old American stock and European new arrivals as well as former slaves and freedmen, Asians and Jews would find safe haven in the Body of Christ. He longed to lead a congregation where color, class, caste, and social status meant nothing. While seemingly idealistic, even naïve, he felt that such

Little Italy—1890s

a place would clear the path for the unreached and unchurched to find their way to salvation.

When Simpson invited his Italian friends to attend the fashionable 13th Street Church, the saints were shaken, and the session was shocked. Such a thing just would not do. When Simpson requested that the new believers be baptized and received into membership, the church leadership gently but firmly suggested that Simpson find them a church where they would feel "more at home."[6] This attitude grieved his heart, as when he struggled with the Chestnut Street session leaders in Louisville to embrace his vision for all lost—rich and poor.

Before accepting the pastoral call to 13th Street Presbyterian, Simpson had clearly shared his vision with leadership regarding the neglected and unchurched in New York and his goal of making the church an evangelistic center where all were welcome. As long as this idea was a distant dream, the session leaders enthusiastically agreed. One can imagine their horror when the shabbily dressed immigrants trooped noisily into the beautiful sanctuary with their snotty-nosed children in tow. Simpson's fond dream became the church's worst nightmare. As always, the issue at hand was whether the church was to serve itself or seek the lost. While these well-meaning people loved their pastor's passion, they did not share his commitment to reach all classes and bring into the congregation those whose status showed that they "did not belong."

SETTLING IN

Despite the disappointments and setbacks encountered in the new pastorate, life at the Simpson home gradually regained some sense of normalcy and calm. Pastor Albert enjoyed working with his hands and built a bookcase for his office. This brought him satisfaction and much-needed shelf-space for his growing library, as well as saving money. Many times through the years, the family would find him occupied with home projects, which provided a much-needed break from his heavy routine of preaching, visitation, writing, and editing.

THE GOSPEL IN ALL LANDS

One of the motivations that led Simpson to New York was the idea of an illustrated "missionary magazine." The "China vision" and Simpson's growing conviction of the relationship between the fulfillment of the

Great Commission and the Second Coming of Christ had drawn him to this center for world missions. On his first days in New York, he visited dozens of church families while working late at night on the inaugural issue of *The Gospel in All Lands (GAL)*. Intended as a resource for Christians and churches, the monthly magazine would carry articles submitted by mission leaders and missionaries, country profiles, and unreached regions and peoples still awaiting a gospel witness. He saw its potential as a contribution for missions mobilization in North America, going far beyond denominational periodicals and missionary prayer letters. What he proposed would require a monumental investment of time, energy, and personal finances.

He chose Africa as the first issue's focus as the European powers were preparing for the "great scramble for Africa."[7] Like most missions-minded people then, Simpson approved of this move by the Europeans to establish or reinforce their colonial claims. What seemed to be an altruistic answer to David Livingstone's call for "Christianity, Commerce, and Civilization" for Africa was, in reality, a mad rush to raid the "dark continent" and rob the treasure chest. Trustingly, the Protestant missions community saw this as a long-last answer to the problem of the closed continent. Time would soon reveal the true motives behind this development.

Over the next year, Simpson's diary reported decisions for Christ every Sunday. He struggled physically due to the move to his new church and multiple preaching engagements. In addition, pastoral visitation and his duties as writer and editor of *GAL* were taking their toll. His meager energy reserves required time to recover from Sunday duties, and the lack of church staff meant more work for the pastor. In a little over a month, following his arrival in New York, Simpson single-handedly wrote and edited his first 52-page edition of the missionary magazine, featuring Africa.[8] His diary recorded almost daily his delight at the progress on the magazine, asking God for strength and energy to complete the publication while maintaining his normal heavy church workload.

The Africa edition, published in February, was followed by an equally large China issue in March. He wrote and edited most of the articles, including contributions from other writers. The magazine's first run was 5,000 copies, which he mailed to individuals, churches, colleges, seminaries, and mission organizations. Within two months of the first edition, rave reviews came in praising the mix of well-written articles and lavish use of maps and engravings. In March, the Japan edition came out, and April featured Brazil. Eventually, other editions highlighted India, the Middle East, and other areas of the world.

For the next year and a half until the summer of 1881, Simpson managed to juggle his pastoral duties with the magazine's demands. The congregation continued to grow by conversion growth. Margaret was more at peace about living in New York and slowly "catching up" with her visionary husband. Simpson's children, the oldest entering the teen years, were learning their way around town. First-born Albert and brother, James Gordon, soon discovered lifestyle choices that ultimately would adversely affect them. Little Margaret, now three years old, was "Daddy's little girl."

At the same time, gray clouds of exhaustion, depression, and poor health hung over Simpson. By mid-1880, overworked and under-rested, fatigue forced him to stop all activity for more than a month to restore his strength and ability to work. At that time, he turned over the role of publishing and financial management of *GAL* to publisher Eugene R. Smith, a Methodist layman from Baltimore. For the next 16 months, Simpson would continue to write editorials and contributions to *GAL* until he turned the project over to Smith.

Until late 1881, Simpson managed to keep all of the "balls in the air:" multiple weekly sermons, visitations, evangelism, and writing for the magazine. The church's finances improved drastically so that within a year, most of the $15,000 mortgage had been paid, with the balance pledged to be liquidated by year's end. Simultaneously, Simpson's interest in missions increased; but as he became more aware of the lack of commitment to missions by most of the Protestant Church, his prior sanguine outlook about the fulfillment of the Great Commission and Christ's return grew more realistic. He did not cease to believe in the close connection between the two. Rather, he felt that 13th Street Presbyterian Church exemplified the less-than-passionate burden that their pastor felt. He wrote about the staggering amount of money spent on construction, decorations, and furnishings for churches in America. At the same time, missions giving was literally pennies on the dollar. He marveled at the huge sum of money spent on pet food as compared with the meager investment made for world evangelization.

Simpson's reading of a book written by Rev. H. Grattan Guinness, the hell-fire evangelist of Chatham days, entitled *The Approaching End of the Age: Viewed in the Light of History, Prophecy, and Science,* greatly influenced his eschatology. Guinness linked the Papacy with the Antichrist of Revelation and his rise before Christ's return. This reading led to the last step in Simpson's migration from postmillennial to premillennial teaching. Accordingly, he became increasingly convinced that the return of Christ was very near. He was convinced that most of the Old and New Testament prophecies had been fulfilled. He wrote in the February 1881 issue of *The Gospel in All Lands* that "we must be living very near the world's great crisis."[9]

Simpson's views on the missions enterprise consequently changed. He no longer believed that the denominational agencies were preparing the right kind of missionary to reach the lost around the world. He envisioned a new breed of missionaries, "God's irregulars," equipped with one or two years of biblical, theological, and practical training in missionary training schools rather than theological seminaries. His personal experience and observation, having served on boards at Knox College and Danville Presbyterian Seminary in Kentucky, convinced him that they were preparing the few willing to go who were often educated beyond the needs of the people to be reached. His idea of a training school was modeled after Guinness's East London Training Institute, as well as a few similar schools in Germany and Sweden. He wrote in the *GAL*, February 1881: "There is a great and growing missionary work for godly women. They are doing nobly at home in raising means. But God wants more of them abroad . . . Is there no woman who reads these lines in whose heart the half-suppressed whisper is *go*?"[10]

It seems clear that Simpson, either consciously or not, was reaching a point of no return. Despite the apparent success of his pastorate, the struggle that he experienced in Louisville regarding the Broadway Tabernacle was similar in degree to what he was facing at 13th Street Presbyterian. Perhaps the first major blow to his dreams for the transformation of his charge from a wealthy upper-class church to a "people's church" open to all occurred when the session refused to receive the Italian immigrants. Despite the leadership's assurance that they were in full agreement with Simpson's vision of a church sharply focused to reach out to the least and lost of New York, it became patently apparent that they were not willing to go where their pastor wanted to lead them.

In late spring 1881, Simpson's health was failing.[11] He had never really recovered from the previous year's exhaustion and month-long absence. He struggled to keep up with his full docket of church ministry. Church members were making excuses for his reduced routine of visitation because he was "not strong." Following his Sunday morning and evening sermons, he needed until Wednesday to recover. Thus, not having true conviction that God could and would heal him, he consulted with a prominent New York physician who "insisted on speaking to me on the subject of my health and told me that I had not constitution strength enough left to last more than a few months. He required my taking immediate measures for the preservation of my life and usefulness."[12]

NO MAN CAN WORK LIKE HIM

Because of his doctor's stern words, amazingly similar to what had been told him by another physician 10 years earlier while pastoring in Hamilton, Ontario, Simpson took a leave of absence and traveled to Saratoga Springs in upstate New York to "take the waters" of that health spa center. Simpson describes his state of mind and heart upon arriving there:

> *With broken health and its accompanying gloom and conflict, one afternoon we stood on that [Indian] camp ground and heard the Jubilee chorus sing these words: "My Jesus is the Lord of Lords, no man can work like Him." The words rang in our heart like a heavenly message and the sinking spirit took a new hold of Him. A few weeks later we found the dear Lord as a Healer and wonder-working God and from that time began all the blessed work of which our present visit was a part.* [13]

Simpson later described that scene and the effect of the words sung by the Jubilee Singers:

> *... [The words] fell upon me like a spell. It fascinated me. It seemed like a voice from heaven. It possessed my whole being. I took Him to be my Lord of lords, and to work for me. I knew not how much it all meant; but I took him in the dark, and went forth from that rude, old-fashioned service, remembering nothing else, but strangely lifted up forevermore.* [14]

The "Jubilee chorus" that Simpson described was a choral ensemble of African-American college students, sons and daughters of freed slaves. Following the Civil War, Northern Baptist missionaries opened a college in Nashville, Tennessee, in 1866, Fisk University, for newly emancipated slaves. The Jubilee Singers made yearly summer tours to raise funds for the school as well as recruiting new students. Like many spirituals of that era, there exist various sets of lyrics. The spiritual, "Ride on King Jesus," which Simpson heard, has a lyric which sings:

Ride on, King Jesus! No man can hinder me. Ride on, King Jesus, ride on, no man can hinder me. (repeat)

He is King of kings, He is Lord of lords, Jesus Christ, the first and last, no man works like Him.

King Jesus rides on a milk white horse, no man works like Him. The river of Jordan he did cross, no man works like Him.[15]

Simpson was deeply impressed by the refrain, "No man works like Him," and later used them in the gospel song that he wrote in 1897, "No Man Can Work Like Him," which became one of the Alliance's favorite songs and put into word and melody that truth that his Lord worked like no man.[16]

A few weeks later, in early August 1881, Simpson and family went to Old Orchard Camp in Maine. This beachside summer camp later became the setting for many important Alliance conventions. While there, Simpson attended few meetings. Most of his time was spent in rest, prayer, meditation, and waiting to see what his Lord of lords was going to do. Dr. Charles Cullis, an Episcopal doctor and layman, was one of the speakers. He had gained notoriety for the practice of praying for his patients as part of his treating them, with many being miraculously healed. He became the pioneer in teaching on the Bible basis for believing in healing as part of Christ's atoning work in North America.[17]

Simpson still remembered the Louisville incident when he had prayed for a deathly sick young man who was almost instantly healed. He recalled enjoying improved health until the Christian doctor told him that such faith was presumptuous. As a result, doubt had crept in and delicate health, heart palpitations, and lack of energy and stamina returned. He had lost what prayer had found. Now his lapsed faith was given new reason to believe.

What impressed Simpson most were the testimonies of sensible, honest men and women who simply told about the amazing healings in their lives. Sensing that the hopeful refrain of the Jubilee Singers was more than just wishful thinking, Simpson decided that he would be Berean, and go to "the Scriptures to see if these things are so." In Simpson's own words, he describes this watershed moment in his Christian life:

> *One summer I heard a great number of people testify that they had been healed by simply trusting the Word of Christ, just as they would for their salvation. It drove me to my Bible. I determined*

Old Orchard Campgrounds

> *that I must settle this matter one way or the other. I am so glad I did not go to man. At His feet alone, with my Bible open and with no one to help or guide me, I became convinced that this was part of Christ's glorious gospel for a sinful and suffering world and the purchase of His Blessed Cross for all who would believe and receive His word. That was enough. I could not believe this and then refuse to take it for myself, for I felt that I dare not hold any truth in God's Word as a mere theory or teach others to do what I had not personally proved. And so, one Friday afternoon [probably Aug 5, 1881] at the hour of three o'clock, I went out into the silent pine woods [at*

Old Orchard Camp]. I remember the very spot, and there I raised my right hand to heaven and in view of the Judgment Day, I made to God, as if I had seen Him there before me face to face, these three solemn vows:

> *1. As I shall meet Thee in that day, I solemnly accept this truth as part of Thy Word and of the gospel of Christ and, God helping me, I shall never question it until I meet Thee there.*
>
> *2. As I shall meet Thee in that day, I take the Lord Jesus as my physical life for all the needs of my body until all my life work is done; and God helping me, I shall never doubt that He does so become my life and strength from this moment, and will keep me under all circumstances until His blessed coming and until all His will for me is perfectly fulfilled.*
>
> *3. As I shall meet Thee in that day, I solemnly agree to use this blessing for the glory of God and the good of others and to speak of it or minister in connection with it in any way which God may call me or others may need me in the future.*[18]

As Simpson later expressed it in his seminal book, *The Fourfold Gospel*, he believed that healing for the physical body was in the Atonement of Christ, part of the redemptive work of the Lord Jesus on the cross. As Romans 8:11 expressed it, the same Holy Spirit that resurrected him from the dead quickens or brings life and health to our mortal bodies. The Old Testament promise of Isaiah 53:4–5 found its New Testament fulfillment in Matthew 8:16–17 and 1 Peter 2:24: *By His wounds we are healed* (NIV).

In the same way that Jesus Christ is Sanctifier, living in the believer through the Holy Spirit, giving victory over sin and Satan and providing power for holy living and acceptable service, this same Spirit of Christ lives within the believer to heal and give divine health. The concept of "The Lord for the body and the body for the Lord,"[19] as well as the Lord for our soul and spirit, both derive from the "Christ in me" theology that had grown up in Simpson. That theme became the major motif of his ministry from this time forward.

By faith in the Lord for his body, Simpson returned to his cottage. While he could not testify to Margaret that he felt better physically, he declared that he had received by faith healing from the Lord and had decided to live that way. The next day, Saturday, they left for New Hampshire and checked into a hotel near Mount Kearsage. Hearing that Simpson was in town, the local pastor asked him to preach the next day at the Congregational Church. Accepting the invitation, he sensed God telling him to testify about his newfound belief in healing. Then the battle began. Since he still felt no better, he hesitated to preach what he had just accepted but did not yet feel in his body. So, he preached a sermon from his "barrel." He later said that he could hardly get the words out, so convicted was he by his lack of faith and disobedience. He quickly left the church, went outside and lay down in a nearby field and begged for forgiveness, promising to be true to what he believed.

That same afternoon, he was asked to speak in the evening to a small group in his hotel. In obedience, he humbly told them what he had discovered just two days before, that healing was in the Atonement, that Christ died for our sins and the effects of sin, including sickness. It was his first of countless times to preach on the same subject. Finishing, he was at peace but still felt no different.[20]

Mount Kearsarge, New Hampshire

The next morning, some young people at the hotel asked Pastor Simpson to climb neighboring Mount Kearsarge with them. Instantly A. B. Simpson remembered the terrifying experience aboard the little cog railway in Switzerland back in 1871, when he thought he was choking to death at the nearly 6,000-foot peak of Mount Rigi in the Swiss Alps. He recalled the same strangled sensation while trying to climb the hundreds of steps of the cathedral bell tower in Florence, Italy, only a few weeks later. Walking up a flight of stairs had been a trial for his weak heart.

THE WOLF AND THE SHEPHERD

Now, every cell of his brain said, "Don't go," while his soul was urging him to trust God and try or die. He sensed the Lord telling him, "If you fear or refuse to go, it is because you do not believe that God has healed you. If you have taken Him for your strength, need you fear to do anything to which He calls you?" So, Simpson set off with the youth and soon felt his heart racing, his breath short, and his strength failing. Again, in his words:

> *At first it seemed as if it would almost take my last breath. I felt all the old weakness and physical dread; I found I had in myself no more strength than ever. But over against my weakness and suffering I became conscious that there was another Presence. There was a Divine strength reaching out to me if I would have it, take it, claim it, hold it, and persevere in it. On one side there seemed to press upon me a weight of Death, on the other an Infinite Life. And I became overwhelmed with the one, or uplifted with the other, just as I shrank or pressed forward, just as I feared or trusted; I seemed to walk between them and the one that I touched possessed me. The wolf and the Shepherd walked on either side, but the Blessed Shepherd did not let me turn away. I pressed closer, closer, closer, to His bosom, and every step seemed stronger until, when I reached that mountain top, I seemed to be at the gate of heaven, and the world of weakness and fear was lying at my feet.*[21]

The wolf and the Shepherd, death on one side and Infinite Life on the other. From that time until about a year before his death in 1919,

Simpson walked ever closer to the Good Shepherd and accomplished the work of three or four "normal" men. Literally, the climb up Mount Kearsage was the capstone of this decisive moment in his life that changed the direction of his ministry from that time forward.

FAITH TRIED BY FIRE

In just a few weeks, Bert and Margaret returned to their New York home with new energy and determination. While still a painfully slender six-footer, Simpson was enjoying health as never before. He preached about the indwelling Christ who makes people holy and healthy. Though it was a new message to his parishioners, the sermons were well received. Following his extended absence and subsequent healing, Simpson was quickly challenged in his renewed faith in the Lord for the body. His three-year-old daughter, Margaret, came down with a serious case of diphtheria. Mother Margaret had already lost her three-year-old Melville Jennings to the same disease years earlier. She demanded that Bert call the doctor, but he refused. Instead, he anointed his daughter's fevered brow and claimed God's promises for her recovery. He spent a lonely night with her while his wife feared for the worst. The next morning, her throat was clear, and the little girl awoke ready to get up and play.[22]

Eventually, some began to wonder if their pastor was becoming a bit fanatical. At this same time, Simpson was about to do something so drastic that it would affect his standing as a Presbyterian minister. Over time because of his study and preaching about Moses and the passage of the children of Israel through the Red Sea, Simpson became convinced that the proper method of baptism was by immersion. Despite winning a cash prize while in seminary for his essay on infant baptism, he was now convinced that baptism demonstrated the public witness of the inward act of trusting Christ for salvation and death to the former self life.

On a chilly autumn afternoon in 1881, a simple Italian Baptist Mission located in the "poorest district of New York" was the scene of another watershed moment in Simpson's life. Feeling isolated and condemned by his friends for his "eccentric fanaticism," he humbly asked the Italian Baptist pastor (believed to have been Antonio Arrighi, who, at the time, was the only known Italian Protestant clergyman in North America) to baptize him, right there in the "humble little frame schoolhouse" that served as a church for a congregation too poor to own a building. [23] Mrs. Simpson was not there to witness this last nail in the coffin lid of her husband's Presbyterian career. It is likely that Simpson sent the 100 Italian converts that he had won to the Lord to this Italian Mission after 13th Presbyterian's session refused membership to them. Thus, Simpson probably chose this modest venue for his baptism because of the previous relationship. Following the simple immersion service, the Baptist pastor and wife left for another engagement. Alone in a cold changing room, Simpson fell to his knees and rejoiced as he felt the warmth of the Lord for his willingness to enter a deeper level of obedience and death to all that he once held dear. While not sure of where this step would lead, he left the humble chapel confident in the Lord's leading.

Always desirous of being honest with his church, he immediately informed the New York Presbytery on November 7 of his baptism by immersion and his inability to perform infant baptism. He then informed 13th Street's session of his intention of resigning from the New York City Presbytery to become an independent pastor. Once again, these momentous events caught Margaret by surprise and again, caused her to struggle. With five children ranging from teenage Albert to one-year-old Howard Home, no salary, and living in a rented home, the long-suffering wife once again found herself questioning Bertie's decisions. She had finally begun to feel at home and at peace with New York. Then, suddenly in August, her sickly husband was miraculously healed, and she now lived with a real-life Lazarus whose burial wrappings had been cut off by God's healing power.

The morning of that same day [when Simpson presented his resignation to the New York Presbytery] the elders called on Mrs. Simpson at home to express their profound sympathy. Her husband said, "They remarked as they condoled with her that they felt they were attending his funeral."[24] Thus, while apprehensive but with no harsh reaction as had occurred when he resigned from his Louisville charge, Margaret tried to stay within shouting distance of her visionary husband.

The Lord had torn open Bert's sealed orders and now he felt, at age 38, a new man, free and ready to obey his Commander's orders. Years later, daughter Margaret would remember: "He once told me that he had not grown up until he was 38, and we know that most of his outstanding work was done after that."[25] For 38 years, Simpson struggled with debilitating health issues and a growing vision of God's will for him. He more than made up for the first half of his life with the amazing burst of energy and lasting ministry in the second half.

"He shall not make you think much of yourself, nor so much of Himself, but He [the Spirit] will make you think a great deal of Jesus."

—A. B. Simpson

CHAPTER 8
THE WANDERING GOSPEL TABERNACLE: 1881 TO 1887

*I*N BLIND FAITH, A. B. SIMPSON RESIGNED from 13th Street Presbyterian Church on November 7, 1881,[1] in obedience to the Lord's leading. Simpson believed that God had called him to reach the neglected masses of New York City, something he believed not possible at 13th Presbyterian due to the conflicting visions of ministry.

On the following Sunday, Simpson held a meeting at the Caledonian Club, in the third-floor cold, "cheerless dance hall," as he described it. The first meeting was well attended, since his resignation from 13th Street Presbyterian had been breaking news in New York; many friends and journalists were present. Local church news was newsworthy and press attention was beneficial. At that first meeting, Simpson stated his goal for his new evangelistic venture and announced a follow-up meeting for prayer and conference the following Sunday.

At the subsequent Sunday meeting, five women and two men attended what Simpson considered the founding service of the Gospel Tabernacle. Twenty years later, Simpson mentioned that the first official service had a "less encouraging attendance;" yet two of the original attendees were still part of the Tabernacle. The original Caledonian Hall no longer stands, having long since been torn down. Located at 8 and 10 Horatio Street, it stood just two blocks down from 13th Street Presbyterian Church and the nearby Simpson parsonage on 123 West 13th.[2]

Following that unpromising beginning, the band of believers continued to meet at Caledonian Hall on Sundays. The little flock also met at the Simpson home for a mid-week teaching and training service, Simpson later admitted in *Living Truths*, (March 1907 edition), that initially, he had no intention of starting a church. His goal was to establish "an evangelistic work, leaving the converts free to join various churches."[3]

Upon further thought and conversation with Dr. Judson, a fellow pastor and friend, Simpson was encouraged to care for his own sheep.

New York Caledonian Club, 8 and 10 Horatio Street

"The mother is always the best nurse of her own children," said Judson.[4] Simpson saw the wisdom in those words, since some of the new converts were already asking for baptism and the Lord's Supper. None of the "children" wanted to be sent away.

Accordingly, the small congregation of 35 members met in Simpson's home, where they officially organized as the "Gospel Tabernacle of New York in February 1882."[5] Simpson noted that since there were not enough "men to go around and fill the various offices, . . . some of our first trustees had to be 'elect ladies.'"[6] This new experience of recognizing giftedness and ability for ministry by women characterized the early Alliance and Simpson's growing view of the role of women in ministry, vividly noted in *Anointed Women*.[7]

Simpson desired to reach the unchurched of New York, especially the middle class, which he felt had been neglected in most major U.S. cities. He had seen the same need in Louisville. Thus in New York, he targeted the great class of those considered neither rich nor poor. Many ministries flowed from Simpson's leadership and encouragement to open rescue missions, homes for "fallen women," orphanages, training schools, and healing homes. At the same time, Simpson kept his focus on the unreached. His goal for new believers following conversion was to provide a strong, self-supporting base upon which he could establish a significant evangelistic outreach at home and abroad. Simpson modeled the Gospel Tabernacle on Spurgeon's Metropolitan Tabernacle in London, attended by thousands of men and women, with poor, middle, and upper classes all seated together.

FOLLOWING THE CLOUD

Due to conversion growth, the Gospel Tabernacle moved to the Academy of Music in January 1882, where it remained for a month. Then the "cloud moved" and the Tabernacle relocated to Steinway Hall at 71–73 East 14th Street. Simpson was aided there by Mr. and Mrs. George Stebbins, well-known gospel singers,[8] as well as British pastor, Rev. E. W. Oakes, one of two men from the original group that met at Caledonian Hall in November of the previous year.

During those first months, the rent was paid out of pocket by Simpson, who did not wish to burden the early adherents of the new ministry. This soon changed as the congregation "asked the privilege of taking hold with liberal hands and self-sacrificing love," and public offerings began.[9] This development relieved the financial burden from Simpson and his long-suffering wife, still straining under the challenge of feeding and housing her five children and no pastor's salary to support them. As a result, they were living in a small four-room apartment on their meager savings, occasional love gifts from friends and Margaret's inheritance from her father's estate.

Need for another hall arose due to previous engagements at Steinway Hall, thus the wandering Tabernacle band moved to Abbey Park Theatre on Broadway, near 22nd Street. They began meeting there on

March 19.[10] Simpson's Tabernacle followers grew by conversion growth, joined by a few mature Christians, inspired by the goal of reaching those overlooked in America's largest city.

By May 1882, the Tabernacle leased the Grand Opera Hall on 8th Avenue and 23rd Street at $2,000 a year, a considerable sum for the fledgling flock.[11] In this more permanent venue, meetings were held

Grand Opera Hall House

nightly as well as Sunday morning and evening. The hall held the auditorium, Sunday school rooms, pastor's office, and printing house.

That same summer of 1882, L. B. Heller of Newark, New Jersey, another well-to-do Simpson admirer, donated a big top "gospel tent," erected on 23rd Street between 7th and 8th Avenue. Despite its being the only vacant lot in that part of Manhattan, the owner, William Noble, did not charge for its use. The neighborhood was home to brothels, the turf of the infamous McGloin gang,[12] and sprinkled with sleazy saloons and gambling dens. Services began at this outdoor venue on Friday, June 14, and went on for more than four months. Simpson and his followers held nightly evangelistic meetings and gave out tens of thousands of gospel tracts. Over the next several months, more than 300 New Yorkers were converted, becoming part of the growing Tabernacle family. With the arrival of cold weather, the Gospel Tabernacle band moved back to the Grand Opera Hall.

The following year, a journalist reporting on the 1883 summer meetings stated that the tent was nearly full to its capacity of 2,000 people, and those attending were orderly and intelligent. Conversions and healings were a nightly occurrence. The writer described "Brother Simpson" as a man in the prime of life, slight of build, fair complexion that contrasted with his black hair and beard. His preaching was described as direct and simple, and he was an "earnest exhorter."[13] Nightly at the end of the message, he would invite forward those who were seeking God's grace.

THE FAMOUS "FAITH HEALER"

After more than a year as an independent pastor and evangelist, Simpson was no longer a respectable clergyman. Rather, he had become a popular figure, famous for the almost non-stop ministry of the Gospel Tabernacle, and the numerous reports of miraculous healings under his ministry. He was highly criticized by former pastoral colleagues, who did not believe in the new-fangled doctrine of "divine healing." Reporters who openly questioned Simpson, calling him a "faith healer," were among the steady stream of visitors to his office in the dingy Grand Opera Hall. He did not seek publicity and simply saw himself as a pastor and evangelist.

Such a doctrine had at that time the scornful designation of "Faith Cure." And it was cordially disdained on all sides by the shepherds of God's flock.

Reporters that asked for verification of healings were given the names of members of the Tabernacle and others who had been healed. One skeptical reporter visited five of those named. After confirming their stories, he published their testimonies. Simpson emphasized that the healing ministry was not the major thrust of his work, but merely one phase of the total work of Christ for those who would believe. However, the sensation caused by the publicity drew newcomers.

A few years later, Simpson wrote in the Yearbook of *The Christian Alliance:*

> "In the spring of 1883 . . . a [healing] Home was opened at 331 West 34th Street and was the scene of many blessed manifestations of the Divine Presence and power during the ensuing year."[14]

Regarding the Berachah Home healing ministry, the article continues:

Soon after the organization of this work, several persons connected with it were divinely healed through faith in the name of Jesus. Many persons from a distance soon began to come for inquiry and instruction. The principle involved in these healings is intelligent and Scriptural faith in God on the part of the person concerned, springing from thorough conviction and not through any personal power in the pastor or other workers. All cases have been carefully instructed, and the need was soon felt for a Home where they could be received for rest, teaching, and spiritual quickening.[15]

Berachah was actually the second healing home, since Simpson had previously opened his own home on West 13th Street to receive the sick. Obviously, Margaret was not overjoyed at having her home transformed into an "institution," inadequate due to the lack of space and proper facilities as well as the presence of small children who needed a home of their own. Due to Margaret's plea and Simpson's prayer, a wealthy follower donated a house that became the Berachah Home.

Many of Simpson's closest early associates first met him at the tent and tabernacle meetings where they themselves received physical healing, restoration from discouragement, a deeper walk in the Holy Spirit, and a sense of renewed calling. Those involved included Dr. George Pardington, Rev. Kenneth Mackenzie, Rev. E. D. Whiteside—who later became the "Apostle to Pittsburgh,"—and Rev. Walter Turnbull—eventual head of the Nyack Missionary Training Institute. All met the visionary pastor, whose burden for the lost and willingness to obey had led him on this faith journey. As a result, they felt compelled to join Simpson.

After his own healing, Mackenzie, who had witnessed the attacks on Simpson, described his pastor's miraculous transformation:

In appearance, he was almost cadaverous, pale and emaciated. His large frame gave emphasis to his physical frailty . . . But I should note here that Dr. Simpson eventually grew robust in appearance and exhibited in glorious measure the vindication of His faith in the sustaining power of the Lord Jesus. I envied him his capacity to drink copiously of milk, which soon had the effect of filling out his shrunken tissue until he became a really heavy man.[16]

The tent meetings continued until late October when cold weather forced them to rent P. T. Barnum's Roman Hippodrome, later renamed the Madison Square Garden. Beginning on Sunday, November 4, 1883, Simpson took the Tabernacle members to the huge arena, barely prepared for the upcoming church service. Despite having no heat in the arena, the day dawned bright and the Tabernacle crowd was "full of hope and earnestness and the services much blessed."[17] This first Sunday worship celebrated two years of independent gospel ministry in New York City. Simpson preached the passage, "Cast thy bread upon the waters and thou shalt find it after many days," and it was clear that God had thrown open an ever-wider door in the big city.

The Garden was an open-air arena with a canvas roof. It regularly featured P. T. Barnum's Circus, as well as flower shows, equestrian events, beauty contests, and Women's Christian Temperance Union meetings. D. L. Moody had held evangelistic meetings there seven years before, where thousands were converted. The Tabernacle met in the chilly arena all winter until January 1884. Despite prayers raised and pleas to the Garden owners, the much-promised, long-awaited furnace was never lit, thus forcing the shivering saints to abandon the Garden, returning to the warmth of the Grand Opera Hall until April 1884.

After a half dozen venues in three years, Simpson felt that the Tabernacle needed a permanent home. He envisioned a plant building, an "extremely cheap edifice of corrugated iron, from $1,000 to $2,000, and holding a large audience on one floor."[18]

The Tabernacle congregation took up the challenge and raised funds to purchase four lots on 32nd Street, part of the area now occupied by Penn Station. A sizable down payment of $13,000 was made, but the lawyer handling the negotiations made off with the money and the deal fell through. Despite this frustrating setback, a much better location and opportunity fell into Simpson's hands, one that would resolve the problem of Simpson's wandering tribe for the next three years. And therein lies a strange story.

"SEE IF HE DOES NOT GIVE IT TO US"

At the time of the Tabernacle's travels around lower Manhattan, the show biz district ran along West 23rd Street, between 6th and 7th Avenue, populated by dance halls and theaters. Some were imposing, like the white marble Grand Opera House at 8th Avenue and 23rd Street,

Madison Square Garden, 1880s

where Simpson's church had met. In need of a more permanent home, Simpson began negotiating with the owner of the old Armory on 23rd Street, near 6th Avenue, a run-down building once used as a stable and later a church.

Long before Mel Gibson thought of it, British-born producer, Salmi Morse, born Salomon Moses, planned on playing his "Passion of Christ" in New York, and he saw the old Armory as just the right site.[19] In 1879, he had previously run the play in San Francisco, openly opposed by all Christian clergy, resulting in a loss of money. After eight performances, the play was shut down by the police, the actors booked and fined, and Morse had to leave town. New York was to be no different. He faced opposition from Protestant and Roman Catholic churches.

Just as Simpson was about to close the deal on the Armory for a reasonable yearly rental, Morse made an offer the owner could not refuse. He proposed to lease the building for 15 years, with an annual payment three times more than Simpson's, promising to invest up to $100,000 to transform the run-down building into a proper theater. The owner gladly accepted; and over the next several months, major remodeling and decoration worth more than $70,000 transformed the old barn. During this time, he sought a license for his "Temple Theater."

Simpson was deeply disappointed by the loss of this great opportunity. In contrast, one of the Tabernacle women asked, if he had "heard the good news." Simpson did not see anything good in what had happened, but she explained that the Lord had sent Morse and his production to "fix up the old ruined armory for us, as we [are] poor and without means, and that just as soon as it is all ready, see if He does not give it to us."[20] Simpson had encountered a sister with more faith than even he had!

The mayor, William Russell Grace, turned down Morse's theater license application because he "thought the play sacrilegious."[21] Although it was described as a simple reenactment of the life of Christ, like the Oberammergau "Passion Play" in Germany,[22] Morse got nowhere with city hall. Grace's term ran out and the new mayor, Franklin Edison, also refused to issue a license to Morse.

The producer pressed on, continuing rehearsals up through February 1883 in his Temple Theatre. When police arrived to make sure he was not operating without a license, an offended Morse replied, "My object is too dignified for me to try to bring out the Passion surreptitiously or to evade the law."[23]

Then, Morse tried another tactic. He planned a "private dress rehearsal" in another theater and issued invitations to hundreds of prominent citizens. The scandalized public's reaction regarding the "dress rehearsal" worked to Morse's advantage. According to newspapers, at least 2,000 people crowded into the theatre. "The Passion" became the hottest ticket in town. This ruse soon ended when the authorities showed up at another "rehearsal." The New York Times reported:

> Gentlemen whose clothes and air were clerical mingled in the throng; the Hebraic element was noticeable, and there were many actors and actresses whose successes, such as they were, were made years and years ago. Sealskins and diamonds were as plentiful as at a Wallack or Union-Square matinee, and everybody seemed to expect an evening of uninterrupted pleasure. An uninterrupted evening was not to be. Suddenly the producer's attorney stepped in front of the footlights. He emphatically expressed his regret that in the midst of a beautiful concert of sacred music, Mr. Morse had been arrested by the police. A storm of hisses filled the house, and cries of "Shame! Shame!" were heard in the balcony and orchestra.[24]

But the show did not go on. Simpson and his followers watched to see what would happen next. Morse received his theater license within a few months—public outcry no doubt having much to do with the

Salmi Morse

decision. However, due to continued legal action against it by various Protestant churches, the play was doomed, and after investigating possible production of the play in Cincinnati or Louisville, Salmi Morse gave up. Tragically, Salmi Morse soon passed off the scene under suspicious circumstance in early 1884. There are two versions regarding his demise: one is that he drowned in a bathtub and the other that he was found floating in the North River.[25]

As a result, the owner auctioned off the Temple Theater. The new owner found that he had bought a theater that didn't look like one. Morse's Temple Theater had been decorated in what Simpson called, "ecclesiastical style for a religious play, with seven golden candlesticks for lamps and decorations to match."[26] The production company gave up the lease and offered the improvements for $5,000. Simpson recalled: "We prayed over it, and God stopped us from going too fast. The building was finally put [on] the market, and sold at auction, and the gentleman bought whom we prayed would buy it. The result is that we have been enabled to come in here without paying a penny for improvements."[27] The new owner rented the theater, which became the 23rd Street Tabernacle, for the original asking price before Salmi Morse showed up. God kept Simpson from "going too fast" by holding up the needed funds. For more than a year Simpson had been watching and praying for this building, and the "Lord who provides" did just that.

THE LITTLE GEM ON 23RD STREET

Clearly the faith-filled woman from the Gospel Tabernacle got it right. The "little gem," as Simpson called the theater, became the new home of the Gospel Tabernacle and reopened on Sunday, March 23, 1884 as the Twenty-third-Street Tabernacle.[28] While now a house of worship, it was necessary for the Tabernacle to honor a previous commitment. Thus, a

> God kept Simpson from "going too fast" by holding up the needed funds.

version of Shakespeare's *Othello* held a rehearsal there on April 10. *The New York Times* reviewed it, approving of the use of black performers on stage rather than white actors with theater makeup for black face.[29] While the thespians rehearsed the Bard's timeless lines, Simpson led the congregation in rousing song while seated in the front of the theater, separated by the thick playhouse curtain, oblivious to the rehearsal underway on the stage nearby.

The newly opened Twenty-third-Street Tabernacle soon hummed with activity. There were nightly evangelistic meetings, Sunday morning and evening services, Friday afternoon healing meetings, and young people studying at the Missionary Training Institute, held on the stage. "Simpson was strongly influenced by Grattan Guinness, and the Nyack [Missionary Training] Institute [later moved from New York City to Nyack in 1897] was 'conceived in eschatological consciousness.'"[30] The building also housed Simpson's budding printing concern for the first edition of *The Fourfold Gospel* as well as housing the editorial office of *The Word, The Work and The World*.

By this time, the Tabernacle's "Missionary Union for World Evangelization" had several volunteer candidates from the institute in preparation for work overseas and fund-raising had begun to send the "Congo Band"[31] to Cabinda (part of the former Portuguese Congo), in Central Africa on the north coast above the Congo River. Later in 1884, the Tabernacle hosted the first "Fall Bible and Missionary Convention," where the deeper life, healing, and missions were taught morning, afternoon, and evening.

One of the featured speakers at the convention was Rev. H. Grattan Guinness, founder of the East London Training Institute as well as the

Livingstone Inland Mission (LIM), which had already established several mission stations on the lower Congo River. The Gospel Tabernacle's Congo Band would be sent to an area just north of the LIM's area of ministry. In 1888, Guinness opened the Congo Balolo Mission on the upper reaches of the Congo River that was renamed the Regions Beyond Gospel Union, later renamed Regions Beyond Missionary Union (RBMU), so named after the Apostle Paul's desire "to preach the gospel in the regions beyond you" (2 Corinthians 10:16).

Simpson's iconic missionary hymn title, "to the Regions Beyond," took its cue from the RBMU's name, as well as its publication, *The Regions Beyond* magazine.[32] Doubtless, Guinness's visit to the Gospel Tabernacle gave Simpson ample time to gain valuable insight and experience from Guinness, who had already walked down the road that Simpson was just beginning.

The Bible and Missionary Convention, a several-day event, became an annual feature of the Tabernacle and eventually introduced Simpson, his ministry, and the Fourfold Gospel to a wider audience in the United States and Canada. It combined the best elements of the camp meetings, revival services, prophetic conferences, and missionary meetings. Rousing song, powerful preaching, prayer for the healing of body and soul, and fervent testimonies of God's great power were all part of the convention.

THE CONGO BAND

In November 1884, the five-member "Congo Band" led by John Condit, embarked on Simpson's ill-fated pioneer attempt at missions. Condit, along with Frank Gerrish, Jeans Jensen, William Quayle, and William Pearson had recently graduated as part of the first class of the Missionary Training Institute in July of that same year. As described in *So Being Sent . . . They Went: A History of the CMA Mission in Cabinda: 1885 to 1957,* Condit and his four colleagues sailed for Great Britain in late November 1884.[33] After spending Christmas and the New Year in London, they continued their journey down the coast of West Africa, arriving in Cabinda, a newly-declared Portuguese Protectorate. The ill-prepared missionary team remained in the coastal town for one week, trying to get established. Unable to purchase property for a self-supporting mission station, they had to trek down the barren coast of the Congo River to the north-bank town of Banana, where they met British Baptist missionaries from Mukimvika, their station on the south bank of the massive river. The Congo Band sailed across to the Baptist mission station, where they found refuge with their new British friends.

While two of the team went up river to purchase property for their mission base, Condit fell sick to the "fever," most likely malaria. Being a fervent believer in divine healing, he refused to take quinine offered by the more experienced British veterans. Steadfastly, he maintained his decision to trust the Lord until near death, when taking the medicine

> Despite the setback, the indomitable pastor pressed on to reach those who had never heard the good news of Christ.

was too late. Thus, Condit died, and his demise resulted in the collapse of the missionary effort. Within another month, three of the team members sold their outfits, purchased tickets, and returned home. One of the five, Frank Gerrish, stayed on and worked successfully with the Baptists until June 1888. While there, he was seconded to the Baptists and the Gospel Tabernacle supported him. He returned to the Tabernacle in mid-1888 to a hero's welcome, only to die from his weakened condition from constant fevers. This initial effort that ended in failure came as a serious blow to Simpson and the growing Tabernacle ministry. Despite the setback, the indomitable pastor pressed on to reach those who had never heard the good news of Christ.

THE BETHSHAN CONFERENCE

Just a few months later in that same year, 1885, Simpson, Margaret, and their oldest son, Albert Henry, traveled to Britain where they attended "The Conference on Divine Healing and True Holiness." Often called "The Bethshan Conference," it was convened by the leaders of the Bethshan Healing Home, W. E. Boardman and Mrs. Elizabeth Baxter. Boardman, who chaired the conference, was the same man who had authored the book on the "higher life" that led Simpson to a deeper experience of being filled by the Holy Spirit while in Louisville, an experience that revolutionized his ministry.

This was Simpson's first visit to Europe since his 1871 culture and health leave. As one of the 23 representatives from North America, he quickly stood out among his peers and was invited to speak on several different occasions. It was a kind of "coming-out party" for the relatively unknown Simpson. Many of the bigger names from America, such as Dr. Charles Cullis, Rev. A. J. Gordon, and Dr. Asa Mahan did not attend. Arriving the end of May, the 42-year-old Simpson radiated vigor and vision, despite the still-raw memory of the Cabinda fiasco. The Bethshan Conference introduced Simpson to the broader community of holiness and healing proponents in North America, as well as those from England and Europe.

As Nienkirchen points out in his book, *A. B. Simpson and the Pentecostal Movement*, "The internationalization of Simpson as a spokesperson for the faith-healing movement was the consequence of his involvement in an International Convention on Holiness and Divine Healing held at Bethshan, London, in 1885. . . ."[34] In reality,

> **Oh, I don't want conventions without that warm, loving heart and that present Christ!**

except for the first meeting held at the Bethshan Home, all the other meetings were held at the much larger Agricultural Hall nearby. They had opened at Bethshan, but the hall was jam-packed, with hundreds left outside. The participants met morning, afternoon, and evening for five days, generally to a full house.

Simpson went to London keenly interested in the various positions regarding sanctification. There were the "erradicationists" from the Wesleyan wing and "supressionists"[35] from the Keswick camp. Since his profound experience of Spirit-infilling in Louisville 13 years prior, Simpson had discerned an ever-growing understanding of the role of the Spirit of Christ as the One who takes residence in the believer's life. His was a position best labeled "habitation," and it emerged at the London Conference.

At the beginning of the second day, on the morning of June 2, Simpson was invited to give the opening Bible reading from the Gospel of John. He proceeded to give a dove's-eye view of the Holy Spirit's work in that gospel, reading and briefly commenting on the Spirit's person and ministry. Simpson called it "that beautiful chain of divine teachings about the Holy Spirit in the Gospel of John, the most heavenly of all the

New Testament writings, coming quite fresh from the heart of the dear Master." From John 1 to 20, he pointed out the Spirit's role in salvation and regeneration as well as being the coming Advocate and Comforter, the very same Spirit of Christ in the life of the believer. At one point in this impromptu talk, he said:

> *The people who want to see the Holy Ghost, never can receive Him; the people who want a sign and evidence, never can get this blessing. But you know Him—you don't see Him . . . He shall not make you think much of yourself, nor so much of Himself, but He [the Spirit] will make you think a great deal of Jesus.*

At the end of the address when commenting on John 20:21, Simpson described how Christ pronounced peace on the disciples and then breathed on them:

> *When He said this, He breathed. He just gave the living touch Himself. It was His own life, not something else; it was the very Spirit that was in Him—The Holy Ghost that had been in the Incarnate Jesus. "He breathed on them, and saith . . . receive ye the Holy Ghost." And so, He hovers here Himself—Himself, the marvelous, the mighty—breathing His warm living breath. Oh, I don't want conventions without that warm, loving heart and that present Christ!*[36]

After listening to the addresses and testimonies given on the first day of the Conference, Boardman had invited Simpson to do the Bible reading. Thus, was his opportunity to share his maturing view of sanctification, central to his "Christ-in-me" theology.

As succinctly summarized in Van De Walle's *The Heart of the Gospel*, "Simpson [preferred] his view of habitation to either eradication or suppression."[37] This unrehearsed sermon became known as "Himself," made famous with the words of the first verse of the hymn he later wrote:

> "Once it was the blessing, now it is the Lord. Once it was the feeling, now it is His Word. Once the gift I wanted; now the giver own. Once I longed for healing, now Himself alone."[38]

He saw this deeper work of the Spirit in the believer's life as resting in Him, abiding, obeying, and dying daily in order to live victoriously.

Following that first time before the conference, Simpson spoke on three more occasions, as well as giving final words from the North American delegation on the last day of the conference. Simpson's notoriety was enhanced by the unsolicited testimonies of two women

> **During these early years, it is apparent that God had touched the once weak and weary man—body, soul, and spirit.**

giving witness to their healing through the ministry of Simpson and the Berachah Home in New York City. In terms of historical perspective, the "Conference on Divine Healing and True Holiness" became a major moment in Simpson's life, giving him wider exposure and higher profile in the growing worldwide holiness and healing movement, precursor to the amazing move of the Spirit early in the 20th century.

One interesting historical note occurred at the Bethshan Conference. In the evening meeting on the same day when Simpson gave his "Himself" address, a Mr. J. W. Wood of Adelaide, South Australia, testified to the work of God "Down Under":

> *I have left many dear ones there who are united with Christ by a living faith: who have been saved, and cleansed, and healed. I do praise God that I have a threefold Gospel to preach and not a one-sided one; not a Gospel for the soul only, leaving the other two parts of man entirely out of it—for that partial kind of gospel is what we have generally been having, the salvation of the soul only.*[39]

Upon his return to New York with his family later in the summer of 1885, Simpson continued to minister at the Twenty-third Street Tabernacle. Evangelism, healing and deeper life teaching, the missionary magazine, the growing educational work of the Missionary Training Institute (MTI), the healing homes, social concerns, and the popular Bible and Missionary Conventions occupied Simpson's days and nights.

In addition, he had to deal with the fallout from the failure of the Congo Band. For the faithful followers of the Tabernacle, this was one of the few initiatives of their beloved pastor that had not gone well.

Simpson and his growing leadership team analyzed the reasons for the failure of the Congo venture and went back to the drawing board. They expanded the program from one to three years in 1885. Classes included literature, philosophy, natural science, history, theology, Bible books, Greek, missions, and music. Students gained valuable practical experience at the summer evangelistic tent meetings and the various rescue missions in New York. Over the years from its foundation till the MTI found a permanent home, it operated at eight different sites.

All of this was taxing on body and soul, yet Simpson soldiered on without a break. During these early years, it is apparent that God had touched the once weak and weary man—body, soul, and spirit—and made him a new creation in Christ. Happily, by this time, Margaret finally was on the "same page," and she was staunch in support of her Bertie. Their journey to this point in their marriage had been difficult.

"DIVORCE HIM, MARGARET!"

Just a few years earlier, after Simpson left the Presbyterian Church, living by faith and ministering to the "neglected masses," his older brother, Howard, also a Presbyterian clergyman in Indiana, came to New York for a visit and spoke openly against his younger brother. Though there had been sibling rivalry from the day that Bert received permission to go to college and prepare for the ministry on his own, while Howard was sent as the firstborn, he apparently resented his "brat brother" as recalled by Katherine Brennen.[40] Bertie had beaten him to college by a year. Bertie had won the hand of fair Margaret. Bertie took all the

> "He is my husband—with great gifts and powers given him by God." Margaret stood strong by her man.

prizes in college. Bertie was called to one of Canada's most prestigious Presbyterian churches in Hamilton as his first pastoral charge. Bertie, Bertie, Bertie, "never knew His place; always bobbing up, can't keep him down," Howard declared to Margaret. "These meetings are not of God, but of the devil. Divorce him, Margaret. Bertie always seemed a little queer." However, honor was afforded to the prophet. She responded: "He is my husband—with great gifts and powers given him by God."[41] Margaret stood strong by her man.

AN "ALLIANCE OF CHRISTIANS"

After attending the October 1885 Deeper Life and Missions Convention at the Twenty-third Street Tabernacle, the leaders of the Old Orchard Camp Meeting Association in Maine invited Simpson to take that same conference format to Old Orchard in 1886. Thus, the next year in August, Simpson led the first Old Orchard Convention, the place of his miraculous healing five years before in 1881. There the seed was planted for the establishment of an "alliance of Christians" who believed the message of the Fourfold Gospel and had a passion to reach the lost across the whole continuum of world need: from Jerusalem to the farthest reaches of the globe.

Chicago businessman, W. E. Blackstone, gave a passionate address: "The Need of the World and the Work of the Church." It was there and then that the immense spiritual poverty of the "heathen" and the

> **For Simpson, the key to understanding Christ's return and establishment of His millennial reign is found in Matthew 24:14.**

miserly response of the church became apparent. He stated that more was spent by North Americans on dog food than foreign missions. He convinced the listeners of the truth that the return of Christ was contingent on the evangelization of the lost worldwide. His strongly prophetic premillennial message and the hearty agreement by those at the convention prompted Simpson to declare that the last two days of next year's Old Orchard Convention would be dedicated to considering the establishment of a missionary society. In June 1887, a draft constitution of the proposed society was printed in *The Word, The Work and The World*.[42]

Some years earlier, Simpson had been hopeful about the various efforts of denominational missions when he first published *The Gospel in All Lands* in 1880. However, this optimism diminished as he observed how little was committed to the work of reaching the lost compared to the total income of the major denominations. During those same years, his postmillennial teaching from earliest youth and seminary days was in transition. In the last few years of his ministry in Louisville and while at 13th Street Presbyterian, he was influenced by three major premillennial voices in North America: D. L Moody, A. J. Gordon, and A. T. Pierson, all of whom became close friends to Simpson, often speaking at Alliance conventions in New York and other cities. The other major influence came from Great Britain, the writings of H. G. Guinness. His book, *Approaching End of the Age: Viewed in the Light of History, Prophecy, and Science*, profoundly influenced Simpson's views.[43]

As Simpson transitioned from one school of eschatology to another, his own understanding of the end times matured. As a "premiller," he was and is hard to categorize. In some of his writings on the subject, one can see dispensational and pre-tribulation tendencies, even what some might consider a bit amillennial. "There is a millennium for the soul as well as for the church. There is a kingdom of peace and righteousness and glory into which, in a limited sense, we can enter with Him here."[44] At the same time, he clearly maintained his historical interpretation of the "last-days" passages found in Ezekiel, Daniel, and Revelation. Years before while on his first visit to Europe, he had seen firsthand the overthrow of the Papal states and the virtual imprisonment of Pope Pious XI in the Vatican in 1871. He saw this as fulfillment of prophecy regarding the defeat of Antichrist in Revelation 17.

However, Simpson's unique position on Christ's return was a melding of eschatology and missiology. Dr. Ralph Winter, a leading 20th century missiologist, claimed that Simpson was the first Christian missions thinker to weave those two doctrinal threads into one. For Simpson, the

The Simpson's at Old Orchard Camp—circa 1885

key to understanding Christ's return and establishment of His millennial reign is found in Matthew 24:14:

> *And this gospel of the kingdom shall be preached in all the world as a testimony to all nations, and then the end will come* (NIV).

He also believed that the sanctification of the church and the return of the Jews to Israel were key to understanding "immanency," as meaning "very soon," yet contingent on the Church doing its part, not only waiting for but hastening the coming of the day of the Lord.

Interestingly at the 1886 Old Orchard Convention, a large part of the program was dedicated to preaching on healing and prayer for the sick. The message of Christ the Healer captivated the people of God, and many were made whole. The September 1 issue of *The Word, The Work and The World*, carried several pages of testimonies of healing, either at Old Orchard or at other Simpson-led meetings. One of them was given by Mrs. A. B. Simpson, who testified to her belief in healing and gave witness to the healing of her "little child [Margaret] having been healed of croup, another [Mabel] of diphtheria, and later a son [Gordon] of scarlet fever. She also bore testimony to God's tender care in supplying their temporal wants."[45]

THE GOSPEL FOLDED FOUR WAYS

As a result, when the Old Orchard "Christian Convention" met, July 31 to August 9, 1887, "for the promotion of Christian Truth, Life, and the Word,"[46] the grounds were packed with people excitedly anticipating something special. On the Saturday preceding the convention, hundreds gathered to pray for the upcoming event, with a strong sense of the presence of God. At that convention, which saw The Christian Alliance and The Evangelical Missionary Alliance come into being, Simpson's inaugural sermon bore the title "The Fourfold Gospel." When he returned to New York, he preached four successive sermons at the Gospel Tabernacle on each of the "folds." Possibly the mention of the "Threefold Gospel" by the brother from Australia at the Bethshan Conference in 1885 planted the seed in Simpson's mind for a "Fourfold Gospel," since he already had more than "three folds" in 1885. The gradual migration from postmillennial to a premillennial position gave him a fourth: Jesus Christ—Coming King. None of the "folds" were unique to Simpson, but

Simpson, seated in middle of Gospel Carriage

his succinct, Christ-centered theology codified what a growing body of the evangelical church had come to believe by the end of the 19th century.

Two thousand were present at the Old Orchard opening meeting and 4,500 at the closing service. During one of the meetings, Ina Moses, a young woman who had been on crutches for three years, demonstrated God's healing power when she dramatically threw away her crutches and walked without aid. The whole assembly burst forth in spontaneous praise and sang the doxology. Messages on the deeper life, missions, and the return of Christ, as well as prayer for the sick, drew people from up and down the East Coast of the United States and Canada.[47]

As promised, the last two days were spent in special sessions dedicated to establishing a missionary society to reach the lost worldwide. God oversaw the direction of the conference, which led to the formation of the "alliance" that Simpson envisioned. As the convention closed on a high and joyful note, Simpson returned to New York as the recognized leader of a newly birthed movement that would impact the world for God's Kingdom—The Christian Alliance and The Evangelical Missionary Alliance.

He went from being the "sickly pastor with delicate health" to the robust, energetic dynamo whose abilities and production in ministry were nothing less than amazing.

CHAPTER 9
TWO ARE BETTER THAN ONE: 1887 TO 1897

*T*HE YEAR 1887 USHERED IN MAJOR EVENTS that affected people around the globe. The British Empire celebrated the golden jubilee of Queen Victoria, while the United States commemorated the centennial year of its Constitution. Late in the year, one of the worst natural disasters in human history was recorded—the massive flooding of the Yellow River in China, with fatalities estimated between 900,000 and 2 million. This horrendous disaster emphasized the cold, hard fact that men and women were dying by the tens of thousands daily, the majority with little or no witness of the gospel of Christ.

And what happened the last two days at the Old Orchard convention demonstrated Simpson's conviction of this awful truth and his determination to do something about it. Since leaving the confines of the Presbyterian denomination in late 1881, after more than 17 years of "respectability," he had morphed into a well-known evangelist and pastor of the booming Gospel Tabernacle, a "faith healer," and something of a missions fanatic. In founding not one, but "two Alliances," Simpson declared from the first steps of this new movement that he was not starting a "denomination." He had left that world with its bylaws and barriers. His were the wide-open spaces of a world not overly crowded with preachers trying to impact the lives of the unevangelized at home and abroad.

Simpson carefully chose the word, "alliance" since it had little religious connotation, other than "The Evangelical Alliance," the cross

Margaret and A. B. (right foreground) at Old Orchard Camp

denominational body founded in Great Britain that later came to America in the 1870s. Simpson had attended its first conference in New York and soon became an ardent promoter of the movement. The term, "alliance," derived from "ally," referred to the coming together of a family through marriage or a union of peoples or nations. The term was used frequently in European diplomacy to describe the alignments between countries "allied" on a common front for a specific reason, without abandoning their national sovereignty and identity. The "alliances" that Simpson proposed would welcome anyone from all evangelical denominations that agreed on and supported the message of the Fourfold Gospel and were committed to the mission of reaching the lost in "the regions beyond," as expressed in his famous missionary hymn.

Accordingly, at Old Orchard, two distinct but related Alliance organizations were founded. One, the "Christian Alliance," was established for like-minded believers who would meet for the promotion of the Fourfold Gospel, as well as for prayer and support for the recently formed missionary society called the "Evangelical Missionary Alliance (EMA)." The first group regularly met for preaching, teaching, prayer, recruitment of workers, and fund-raising. The second "society," the Evangelical Missionary Alliance, was the mission agency purposed to train, prepare, maintain, and manage the missionaries sent abroad. The board membership of the two Alliances was almost identical.

One Alliance would hold its meeting, finish its business, and close the books; then another recording journal would be opened and practically the same group would proceed to "take hours to make minutes." After 10 years of this rather awkward arrangement, the two "Alliances" were merged in 1897 as "The Christian and Missionary Alliance." This entity was often referred to as "The Society," since Simpson wanted to avoid the appearance of denominational inclination.

BRANCHES AND DUCKS

Since Simpson feared that critics would accuse him of starting a new church and trying to steal sheep, he insisted throughout his lifetime that The Alliance was a missionary society. What happened is simple: Alliance groups sprang up all over North America because of Simpson's writings and the large conventions that were held across major North American cities. The local body of believers, called "branches," welcomed believers from all kinds of denominations who became part of this "alliance" of Christians—Methodist, Baptist, Presbyterian, Episcopal, Brethren, Mennonite, Congregational, and many more. The branches normally met on Saturday or Sunday afternoon for their meetings. The members were told to remain in their home churches and support them. The "society" was not a church but a two-armed body of believers who desired to preach and practice the full gospel and fulfill the Great Commission to bring back the King.

As the saying goes: "If it swims like a duck, and quacks like a duck, it's probably a duck." And the duckling grew up to be a Body of believers that Christ would have called "a church." In the branches, the message of Christ as Savior, Sanctifier, Healer, and Coming King was taught. Many unchurched people visited the branches because of the testimonies of healing, the demonized being delivered, and lives being transformed. Many of these curiosity seekers were saved, and many new converts who were not comfortable in denominational churches attended the branches. Eventually, yielding to their requests, the local "superintendents," later called "pastors," began serving the Lord's Supper. The new believers asked to be baptized and were. As a result, little by little, the duckling grew, swam faster and farther, and the rest, as they say, is history. It was only in the 1970s that the Alliance "society" was finally declared a "denomination." For some of the early veterans still alive at that time, that word sounded more like "abomination." Since that time, the struggle for the C&MA has been to retain the essence of the early movement while not petrifying into a monument to the past or becoming just another nice evangelical denomination.

After three fruitful years in the cramped facilities of the 23rd Street Tabernacle, a larger home was needed for the burgeoning work and "headquarters" of the two Alliances. After prayer and searching, the castle-like Hepworth Tabernacle on Madison Avenue and 45th Street was purchased for $126,000, equivalent to a multi-million-dollar sum today.

Hepworth Tabernacle

This move uptown afforded Simpson opportunity to reach a more affluent area. By the same token, the move also saw many of the downtown Tabernacle members lost due to the distance from their homes.

Ironically, this monument to a former pastor's vanity recalls an interesting note that Simpson published in the November 1, 1882, issue of *The Word, The Work and The World*. Entitled, "Men's Foolish Words," the editorial commented that Rev. Hepworth, pastor of the aforementioned tabernacle, had declared that belief in divine healing was foolish, presumptuous, and an affront to God's sovereignty. He asserted that today's world needs facts, not religious fancy. Within just a few years, this once rich and powerful congregation led by a critic of Simpson's healing ministry, had to put its multi-domed temple up for sale at half of its real value. Thus the "foolish of this world" purchased the physical remains of a once influential congregation.

While the massive iron-roofed sanctuary seated more than 2,000 people, it lacked the necessary accommodations for the Tabernacle's many ministries. So, after two years, this building was sold for an excellent profit, making it possible to purchase a key parcel of land at 8th Avenue and 44th Street. Thus, the cornerstone for what became the Alliance headquarters and permanent home of the Gospel Tabernacle was laid in January 1889. By the end of the year, the building was already in use, and was dedicated in May of the next year, with a membership numbering about 1,000 and attendance much higher. The Tabernacle had three pastors, housed the administrative offices of The Alliance as well as the Missionary Training Institute (MTI), dormitories, and the Beracah Home.

Missionary Frank Gerrish, of the ill-fated Congo Band, returned to New York and the admiring members of the Gospel Tabernacle in mid-1888. More experienced and wiser by years, Simpson saw Gerrish as the potential leader of a new Congo team to be sent out shortly. The Congo veteran consulted with Simpson, providing valuable information and insight. However, weakened by his service in the Congo, he died by year's end. Thus, the final page of the first chapter of Simpson's missionary vision sadly ended.

UNFRIENDLY FIRE AND CAUSTIC CRITICISM

A few years later, biting criticism came against Simpson from Mrs. Fanny Guinness, wife of Henry Guinness of the East London Missionary Training Institute. Henry Guinness was the "fire and brimstone" preacher whose sermons convicted teenage Bert Simpson in Chatham

> **Mrs. Guinness accused Simpson of sending people to their death because of his teaching on divine healing.**

years before. Simpson had modeled the New York Missionary Training Institute on the Guinness Institute model in London. Yet despite their friendship, Mrs. Guinness, in the January 1891 Regions Beyond missions periodical, accused Simpson of sending people to their death because of his teaching divine healing and telling the new missionaries to trust God for their health.[1] Such unfriendly fire from such an unexpected source had to be painful.

Fanny Guinness

Even more caustic criticism came unexpectedly from a November 1889 *Boston Journal* article written by Navy Lieutenant Emory Taunt, who had surveyed the Congo River basin for the U. S. Navy in 1885. While on his expedition, he met Frank Gerrish and learned of the Congo Band fiasco. The *Journal* obtained Taunt's report to the Secretary of the Navy, regarding Simpson:

> "It is useless to send missionaries to the Congo unless they are supplied with ample means for establishment and for permanent support; should [religious societies] neglect this provision, they are sending their people to certain death."[2]

The *Boston Journal* article continued:

> Taunt's sermon [in his report to the Navy Secretary] was prompted by the fate of six (sic) men from Twenty-Third Street in New York City, who left their mother church for Africa with only $500 between them. One promptly died; four others had their passages home charitably paid by the Baptists; the sixth joined another mission.[3]

This "taunting" attack was riddled with factual errors. The Congo Band was made up of five, not six, men. The tickets of the three, not four,

Lt. Emory Taunt

men who returned to the homeland were paid by the sale of their outfits, not through Baptist charity. Every member of the Congo Band took out an outfit worth several hundred dollars as well as $500 cash. However, despite the detail errors in his overwrought report, the fact remained that the Gospel Tabernacle's Missionary Union for the Evangelization of the World[4] had sent out a team woefully underprepared for such a daunting mission.

Obviously, Simpson had to respond to these attacks coming from all sides and did so in *The Word, The Work and The World* and later in New York newspapers. The earliest years of what became the Alliance missionary effort were times of painful learning for Simpson and those sent out by the mission.

When the flurry of adverse comments regarding the Cabinda debacle had finally calmed down, another situation arose that caused Simpson and the Tabernacle members more chagrin. In early 1890, without advance notice, seven volunteer missionaries appeared at the Gospel Tabernacle, announcing that they were on their way from Kansas to the Sudan, today encompassing Guinea, Burkina Faso, Mali, and Cote d'Ivoire. What they lacked in funds and training was equaled by their fervor and faith. While not formally becoming Alliance missionary candidates, the Tabernacle congregation adopted them wholeheartedly. Simpson put the five men and two young women up in the Berachah

Home for several weeks until they were able to raise their passage for Africa. They sailed on May 15, 1890. By year's end, four of the seven had died of "fever." Mrs. Guinness caustically mentioned the deaths of these volunteers, again attributing their demise to Simpson's teaching on divine healing.

THE REGIONS BEYOND

However, all was not lost, since Simpson and the MTI faculty diligently worked to better prepare those who were to be sent out. Those of the Kansas volunteers who survived eventually joined The Alliance and became effective missionaries in French West Africa. Thus, Simpson continued to preach and promote missions and teach divine healing, and the MTI was filled with men and women ready and willing to go. By 1888, several candidates were prepared. The commemorative history, *After Twenty-Five Years,* celebrating the first quarter century

> **Despite the initial Cabinda misfortune and criticism from all sides, the vision continued strong.**

of Alliance ministry, states: "Our chosen fields are the 'regions beyond,' the unoccupied portions of the heathen world, and so our missionaries have been led into the most difficult and remote regions . . . such as Kwang-Si in South China, the province of Hunan in Central China, the borders of Tibet [and most recently the country of Annam], the tribes of Mongolia, the unoccupied region of the Congo and the Niger of Africa, and some of the neglected republics of South America."[5] This was an unreached people group (UPG) mission that blazed trails long before the term UPG came into vogue decades later.

Despite the initial Cabinda misfortune and criticism from all sides, the vision continued strong, the volunteers came forward, and support through prayer and funding confirmed that God was in the movement. In fact, one of Simpson's most amazing and sarcastically criticized abilities was that as a fund-raiser. The annual conventions held in New York and around the country became venues for receiving offerings in cash and jewelry, faith pledges, stocks, and even real estate. It was not unusual for great outpourings to come in totaling $100,000 or more in just one convention. These offerings occurred at the New York convention, Old Orchard, and all over the country. For many years until after Simpson's death, almost all funds for missions were raised during the "missionary conventions," whether those held in major cities or in the local Alliance branches, where missionaries on home assignment presented their fields. The "pledges" were raised and received by the branch leaders and pastors. The missionaries did not raise money; they raised vision and the members responded.

During that first decade through 1897, the Alliance began sending out a small number of missionaries to India, China, Japan, the Congo, French Sudan, and the Holy Lands (Palestine). There were 13 missionaries serving by 1890. Sensing that the International Missionary Alliance (new name for the Evangelical Missionary Alliance after Canada joined), was not accompanying the growth of the homeland Christian Alliance branches, Simpson issued a challenge to the growing constituency to make a "pledge to the Prayer Alliance" for world missions.

> **The Alliance began sending out a small number of missionaries to India, China, Japan, the Congo, French Sudan, and the Holy Lands (Palestine).**

Simpson noted at the 1890 Old Orchard convention, after preaching on prayer and challenging those present to be part of the Prayer Alliance, that he later sat by the open window till late that night hearing from a nearby cottage "the voice of prayer goes forth all night long . . . that the mighty God would work with all His power and glory."[6] And God did answer prayer, soon.

At the first Round Lake convention in western New York State, a dramatic surge in interest occurred. At the early Tuesday morning Bible study session, the speaker, after reading from Christ's last words in Mark 16:15, said, "How simple and practicable it would be to send the Gospel to every creature in the next ten years."[7] This offhand, unassuming remark sparked a move of the Holy Spirit. Suddenly, "The Spirit of God swept over the people, and they were moved to tears and roused to holy enthusiasm and almost every person present rose to their feet, and pledged themselves to unite in prayer and work, with a view to the evangelization of the whole world within the present century."[8] Several offered themselves as candidates; one minister even put his little daughter on the altar.

WOMEN IN MINISTRY

The image of the pastor placing his little daughter, Isaac-like, on the altar as one destined to be part of world evangelization was a prophetic picture of Simpson's position on the issue of women in ministry. As pointed out in another of Paul King's excellent treatments of A. B. Simpson and the early Alliance, he wrote in *Anointed Women: The Rich Heritage of Women in Ministry in The Christian and Missionary Alliance:*

> While the egalitarian vs. complementarian debate persists on in the 21st century, A. B. Simpson and The Christian and Missionary Alliance of the earlier 20th century were far ahead of the times, pioneering a forgotten ingenious unifying middle path that was both intrinsically complementarian (affirming male headship) and at the same time granting virtually full freedom for women in ministry, including pastoral ministry and performance of all pastoral functions, providing latitude for both personal conscience and unity. This position evolved more than a century ago through a decade or so of prayer, study of Scripture, and dialogue.[9]

King's research documented nearly 400 women who served as pastors in The Alliance over a period of approximately 75 years, as well as hundreds more who served as evangelists, Bible teachers, and conference speakers. On the first Board of Managers, women were part of the early governance of the fledgling movement.

Convention song leader, Miss Louise Shepherd, converted after hearing a salvation message, was one of the many early examples. At the seminal Round Lake conference of 1891, she stood and admitted that following her conversion, she had never been overly stirred by missions. However, at that service, "she had been really aroused to foreign missionary work" and offered personal jewelry worth $250, adding an equal amount in cash sufficient to support one missionary for a year. At that time, Simpson estimated the average cost of a year's missionary's support was $500. Spontaneously, others came forward and laid "pins, rings, watches, chains, and other precious heirlooms," which had a total value of more than $1,000. Through the rest of the day, additional funds and gifts poured in and two more young men offered themselves for missionary service.[10]

A MISSIONARY EXPLOSION

Simpson called for 100 new candidates, and they came forward. He encouraged sacrificial giving, and Round Lake became the first of dozens of conventions where tens of thousands of dollars poured in. From that time forward, continual overseas expansion grew. Alliance leaders looked back on Round Lake as the trigger event for a "missionary explosion." By 1893, there were 180 Alliance missionaries working on 12 fields with sufficient financial support for them and more. And in another two years, the number had soared up to almost 300![11] Simpson embarked on a seven-month trip in 1893 to visit the fields of the Middle

> By 1893, there were 180 Alliance missionaries working on 12 fields with sufficient financial support for them.

East, India, and the Far East, where he saw more than 100 missionaries. This tour helped him understand the challenges faced by these new overseas workers, which reflected his pastoral concern for them and the changes in their preparation at the MTI.

By 1897, realizing that maintaining two parallel organizations did not optimize their effectiveness, the Christian Alliance, and the International Missionary Alliance became one, making The Christian and Missionary Alliance simpler and more efficient. Simpson was elected president and chaired the Board of Managers. The objectives continued to be the same, to evangelize the neglected classes at home, promote the teaching of the "Alliance distinctives," and to go to the "regions beyond where the story has never been told."[12]

TO THE JEW FIRST

The special "Easter Convention," April 14 to 18, 1897, calling for the "Ratification of the Union of The Christian and Missionary Alliance" (C&MA) was held at the new Missionary Training Institute on the Nyack Campus, 20 miles up the Hudson River. The training school had to move because it had outgrown the still-new facilities at 44th Street and 8th Avenue. The last senior class of the New York MTI was graduated that weekend and a special offering went toward the cost of construction of the new MTI building, to later become known as Simpson Hall.

The Friday April 16 evening meeting ran from 7:30 to 9:30, and on the program were printed the words: "Our Work for Israel and the Heathen World, The Jew First." Simpson believed Romans 1:16, *For I am not ashamed of the Gospel of Christ, for it is the power of God to salvation to everyone that believe, to the Jew first and also to the Gentile* (NIV). As the new C&MA was being ratified, that inaugural meeting clearly imprinted the spiritual DNA of The Alliance. For decades, the Annual Report of The Christian and Missionary Alliance given yearly to Council delegates included the year's reports for the Foreign Department. The order of the reports began with Romans 1:16, and the Jewish and Holy Land work as the first reports.

Throughout his lifetime, Simpson was a strong supporter for the evangelization of the Jews. In *The Coming One,* a volume presenting Simpson's position regarding the end times, he clearly stated his views. "Jewish mission work is not the principal work of the church, but it is one of its commissions: *'To the Jew first, and also to the Greek'* (Romans 1:16). We must not let this work monopolize us. If we do, we will be disappointed. We must remember that the spiritual Israel is a remnant. This is not Israel's day, but God is saving some even today, and we ought to be doing all we can to give them the gospel."[13]

In the same book, he tells an anecdote about two rabbis who looked on the ruins of Jerusalem. One rabbi wept while the other smiled. "Brother, why dost thou weep?" asked the smiling one. "I weep because I see foxes running over the walls of the city of my fathers. Why dost thou smile?" "I smile because this is what God said should come to pass, and the word of promise is as true as the word of judgment, for He has also said, 'Jerusalem shall yet be the joy of the whole earth.'"[14] This simple little story of an optimism based on the faithfulness of God's Word is akin to Simpson's belief that God had not abandoned His people. One day, they will run to the arms of their Savior and Lord Messiah, Jesus.

Simpson's burden for the Jews resulted in the early deployment of missionaries to what was then called "the Holy Land" field. In 1890, the first two Alliance missionaries, single women, Misses Elza Robertson and Lucy Dunn, both members of the Gospel Tabernacle, were sent out to Jerusalem. These courageous pioneers established the mission in Jerusalem and developed a strong ministry among women and children. However, due to the "macho" culture found in Palestine, The Alliance sent two men to reach the men. In 1904, a year after Missionary A. E.

Thompson arrived on the field, he erected a "Tin Tabernacle," a wood-framed building sheathed in corrugated iron on property bought in the Old City. By 1913, Thompson had built an imposing stone chapel, with walls one meter thick at 55 Street of the Prophets, in the Jewish Quarter. It was and remains, the only Protestant church in the walled city of Jerusalem.[15] Today it is home to a multi-cultural Alliance congregation.

This merger of the two Alliances into The Christian and Missionary Alliance was not without criticism. Many former friends felt that Simpson had morphed the movement into a denomination, despite his

> **By 1913, Thompson had built an imposing stone chapel, with walls one meter thick, at 55 Street of the Prophets, in the Jewish Quarter.**

protests to the contrary. Some pastors and churches that previously had enthusiastically participated in Alliance conventions and supported missionaries began to oppose passively or actively the growing Alliance ministry.

Simpson struggled to keep a clear sense of mission before the constituency to not threaten other evangelical churches and missions. He kept the organization lean and frugal, used the conventions and publications to present the Alliance message and mission, and thus fund the new volunteers with no onus on denominational mission agencies. The MTI continued to grow and prepare needed workers for the Alliance work abroad and at home.

The first decade of the two Alliances that merged was a "God thing," a movement of people committed to a unique message and a singular mission, led by an exceptional leader. One reporter from the *Baltimore Sun* described Simpson at the Old Orchard convention:

> *In all, fully 20,000 people were in the grove. At least 10,000 of these remained for hours and hung breathlessly on every word Dr. Simpson uttered. His hold on the vast audience was remarkable. He could sway them at will. If he said, 'sing very softly and tenderly,' the mass would just breathe the melody of some hymn. Then at a word, they would fairly shake the ground. So, during his sermon,*

*they would drink in every word. His discourse was more like a talk than a sermon, not nearly as much of a rhetorical or oratorical effort as in former years.*¹⁶

His text was Luke 10:2 ". . . Pray ye therefore the Lord of the harvest, that he would send forth labourers into his harvest," but the theme constantly repeated was, ". . . Simon, son of Jonah, lovest thou me more than these?" (John 21:15) "The *Sun* reporter is able to say from absolute proof that The Alliance received today, what could be taken to any bank and sold for $70,000."¹⁷

When considering all that Simpson accomplished as pastor of the Gospel Tabernacle, president of two "Alliances" until 1897, leadership

> **Not long after the turn of the century, hundreds of branches spread across the U.S. and Canada, seeking out the "neglected masses" with the full gospel of Christ.**

of the mission, directing and teaching at the MTI, holding conventions across the country, often physically wearing out those who accompanied him, publishing books and tracts, writing hymns, and editing the official Alliance weekly publication, one can only wonder at the remarkable transformation. He went from being the "sickly pastor with delicate health" to the robust, energetic dynamo whose abilities and production in ministry were nothing less than amazing. His calm but captivating personality gave great leadership to a movement that had begun in a cold New York dance hall. In just a bit more than 15 years, that unassuming beginning had expanded into a compelling cause that already fielded hundreds of workers in more than a dozen countries, reaching the unreached.

Not long after the turn of the century, hundreds of branches spread across the U.S. and Canada, seeking out the "neglected masses" with the full gospel of Christ.¹⁸

A. B. Simpson, circa 1890

"My father had a great heart, but an exceedingly lonely one. He was naturally sensitive . . . I never saw him angry either, though tears often came to his eyes."

—Margaret (Simpson) Buckman

CHAPTER 10
GROWING PAINS: 1897 TO 1912

*A.*B. Simpson understood the day in which he lived and knew what to do. After founding the two Alliances just 10 years before, he had seen the International Missionary Alliance grow by leaps and bounds. Missionaries went out to Africa, the Middle East, India, China, Japan, South America, and other lands. One of the major heartbreaks that faced this outward movement was the high number of deaths recorded in Africa, Asia, and South America. Malaria, thought to be the result of "bad air," had already killed dozens of Alliance workers overseas. Though scientists had earlier discovered the parasite that caused the disease, in 1897, it was British physician and scientist, Sir Ronald Ross, who determined that the maddening mosquito was the disease carrier. As a result, the word went out and missionaries adopted the humble mosquito net, and the number of fatalities fell.

Early in 1898, the U.S.S. Maine exploded in Havana's harbor. Whether by Cuban rebels or enraged Spanish forces, the event led to the Spanish-American War, a short-lived affair that lasted about three months. Spain was soundly defeated, losing Cuba, Puerto Rico, and Guam. In addition, the United States annexed The Philippine Islands and paid $20 million indemnity to Spain. Simpson, as well as other mission leaders, strongly supported the war against Spain due to its cruel colonial practices, their devastating effects on the occupied lands, and its policy of hindering access by Protestant missions to these lands. By the end of the year, The Alliance looked forward to sending workers to these newly freed colonies.

During those first 10 years, the movement had become known as "The Alliance" and continued to grow alongside the Gospel Tabernacle, an independent church pastored by Simpson. The weekly missions magazine, after several title changes, finally became *The Alliance Weekly*—a venerable name used for decades before eventually becoming today's *Alliance Life*. With the growth of the numerous ministries that flowed from Simpson's fertile leadership, many capable men and women came to work with him. Whether at the MTI, the magazine, the Alliance Mission, or the Tabernacle, these collaborators from many denominational backgrounds joined forces with Simpson and The Alliance because they identified with the message and mission. Simpson did not ask them to abandon their denominational roots but to link arms with him in advancing this "alliance" of believers. They were Simpson's "allies" for the cause of Christ, which they subscribed to wholeheartedly.

A certain ambivalence, whether conscious or not on Simpson's part, can be sensed regarding the question of what The Alliance was to become. While forcefully declaring from the start his opposition to establishing another denomination, Simpson did encourage the branch leaders to receive members, issue membership cards, maintain financial

This charitable but candid evaluation pointed out some serious flaws in the C&MA's administration.

and business records, and hold weekly meetings. At the same time, he advised the branch superintendents to hold their meetings on days and hours to avoid conflicting with existing church programs.

After more than 16 years as a Presbyterian clergyman, Simpson understood the structure of a denomination. Highly regulated, often inward-looking and self-serving, the struggle for freedom to follow God's leading could be handicapped by the burden of boards and bylaws. For this reason, the Alliance organization was made as simple as possible, with decision-making agile and rarely far from Simpson's watchful eye. Overhead was kept at a minimum, and missionaries were expected to live faith-filled, frugal lifestyles. Under Simpson's leadership, most of the financial support for the overseas workers did not come from an established budget but from pledges and offerings taken annually at missionary conventions across the United States and Canada. The importance of these annual events for the ongoing funding of the missionary endeavor required long and exhausting tours by Simpson, other invited speakers, and furloughing missionaries.

The "missionary explosion" that followed the Round Lake convention in 1891 brought blessing as well as headaches. By 1895, the Alliance missionary force had grown to almost 300, making it already the fifth largest agency among American missions in less than 10 years.[1] Eventually with the rapid expansion of the overseas work and the unpredictable financial base, missionary "allowances" suffered cuts due to lack of funds. Without the sacrificial attitudes of the field workers, these shortfalls would have devastated their morale. In some cases, the unprecedented growth led to painful problems that strained the Society and reflected personally on Simpson's administration of The Alliance.

THE WOUNDS OF A FRIEND ARE FAITHFUL

Wise counsel came from an unexpected quarter, *The Missionary Review of the World*, July 1899 to December 1900 edition.[2] This periodical was edited by Dr. A. T. Pierson, friend and longtime supporter of Simpson

Dr A. T. Pierson

and the C&MA. It contained a five-page report from the Editorial Department and was written by Pierson himself. This charitable but candid evaluation, given by a close comrade and astute observer of the burgeoning missions movement in North America, pointed out some serious flaws in the C&MA's administration.

He began by mentioning the obvious fact that The Alliance had undergone very rapid growth that had outpaced the organizational management and competence of the mission, coupled with the constant strain of providing for the financial support of the missionaries. He called into question the over-centralization of the leadership role by Simpson and his wife. He as president and Board chair and she as the missionary treasurer for many years, essentially administered the mission. The editorial went on:

> *And the time has fully come when Mr. Simpson and his wife should hand over the Alliance work to a large, competent, counsel and trustworthy body of men and women, retaining no control whatever over either funds, workers, or methods, save as wisdom and piety enable them to counsel and direct. We are fully persuaded, after close study of the Alliance and its mode of business, that too much power is wielded by one man, and that this is bad for both the man and all concerned.*[3]

Such a statement coming from a close friend and associate of many years, doubtless deeply wounded Simpson, while possibly incensing Margaret, less sensitive than her husband.

The *Missionary Review's* editorial continued with some wise suggestions: the need for financial transparency for the abundant giving toward missions and the accountable management of the funds were obvious measures to be taken. Pierson mentioned the multiple $100,000 offerings received at major Alliance conventions. He suggested that this over-dependency on mega-offerings opened the C&MA to constant criticism and questioning. The practice also resulted in the lack of a predictable working budget.[4]

One last suggestion from Pierson addressed a glaring error in the early Alliance:

> *It seems to us also that missionary workers have been too easily accepted, too superficially prepared, and too hastily sent forth, in not a few cases—all these being the necessary risks of a work that has with such unusual celerity sprung to maturity.*[5]

The accuracy of this observation can be confirmed many times over by the overly optimistic deployment of missionaries with minimal training and less confirmation of their character, call, and competence in those early years.

The truth of Pierson's observation was borne out early in Simpson's first mission venture with the "Congo Band" led by John Condit, which resulted in Condit's death, the abandonment by three of the other four team mates three months after arriving on the field, and the failure of that initiative. While this initial attempt's lack of success did not seriously hurt Simpson's reputation, it did shine a light on this shortcoming.

This overly optimistic tendency was also pointed out in Pierson's editorial, which brought up the dismissal of Emilio Olsson, a Swedish missionary and Bible Society colporteur who visited Simpson in late 1896. He presented a wildly speculative plan for the evangelization of South America in four years with one hundred men. "I believe that South America can be evangelized in four years. One good missionary can reach 10,000 people a month, 100,000 per year, and 400,000 in four years. One hundred missionaries could reach 40,000,000 people in four years."[6]

He presented his proposal in the January 22, 1897, issue of the Alliance publication. Simpson, ever enthusiastic, quickly agreed with the strategy. Olsson, a converted sailor of 38 years, had worked with the British Bible Society and had trekked thousands of miles all over the South American continent, distributing more than 20,000 Bibles. That same year, he was ordained by The Alliance, made superintendent of the C&MA mission of South America, and was sent on a four-month trip to Great Britain and Sweden before leading a team of six young missionaries to be deployed in several South American fields, thus initiating his aggressive four-year plan. The full account of the short-lived association of The Alliance with Olsson is told in *Roots and Branches: The History of The Christian and Missionary Alliance in Brazil*. Olsson's working relationship with the C&MA lasted about two years and left the South American work in shambles.[7]

No doubt Olsson was a courageous worker and had adventure in his veins. However, after the missionaries in Buenos Aires revolted under his leadership and petitioned the New York board to investigate, he was called back to New York to meet with the mission leadership. When his decisions and financial management were questioned, he bristled and refused to subject himself to interrogation. As a result, he was dismissed from the mission. The following laconic note appeared in the C&MA

publication on July 1, 1899: "Rev. Emilio Olsson has been dismissed from The Christian and Missionary Alliance, and any of our readers who wish to know the facts in his case may write to the Foreign Secretary, 690 Eighth Avenue, New York City."

The next issue of The Christian and Missionary Alliance magazine included a three-page statement regarding the reasons for the decision. Olsson had gone to the newspapers and a missions magazine accusing Simpson and The Alliance of breaking the working agreement and withholding funds due for his support. Olsson even published a 52-page

> "We cannot lengthen the cords without proportionately strengthening the stakes."

booklet with the polemical title, "THE Rev. A. B. Simpson's Misstatements REFUTED BY Emilio Olsson." Pierson's *Missionary Review* picked up the story and questioned the C&MA's dealings with Olsson as part of the Editorial Department's observations regarding Simpson's administration.[8] This imbroglio revealed Simpson's tendency to sometimes "lay hands" on the untrained, unprepared, unruly and occasionally, unscrupulous, with unintended consequences. The predictable result of this article by Pierson doubtless caused Simpson embarrassment and misunderstanding before the public.

STAKES VS CORDS

At the same time, the number of Alliance branches in North America was quite small as compared to the large contingent of missionaries serving overseas. Simpson depended on the big-city conventions and the *Alliance Weekly* as the major vehicle for promoting missions and propagating Alliance distinctives and raising support for the missionaries. While Pennsylvania, New York, Ohio, and Eastern Canada quickly became hotbeds of Alliance activity, large swathes of the mid- and far-west went virtually untouched for years. Simpson depended on capable and sacrificial leadership from the district superintendents, often made responsible for more than one state. Men like E. D. Whiteside and H. M. Shuman in Pennsylvania and J. D. Williams in Minnesota recruited and deployed new workers and opened numerous branches in their regions. For years, weak or nonexistent leadership hurt the cause on the

West Coast. Under able direction, The Alliance in Canada gradually grew, although not always welcomed by the major denominations in the Dominion. The strong emphasis on sanctification and healing put off many who felt that the C&MA was becoming isolated and detached from the larger Body of believers who were less committed to these key doctrinal positions held by Simpson and his followers.

One major headache for Simpson was the balancing act between the needs overseas and those at home. A perennial challenge, the thorny issue of "broadening the base," strained the Society. In 1906, 25 states still had no branches and 100 major cities were without even one Alliance worker. By 1906, *The Alliance Weekly* sent forth a "louder call" from every region for more local leaders, calling it a "very short-sighted policy" that would send "all our means" and "the best and brightest of men and women" to the mission field without an equal investment in local branch leaders.[9] The issue clearly presented the problem: the overseas work depended on the homeland base, and "we cannot lengthen the cords without proportionately strengthening the stakes" in North America.[10] This "stakes vs. cords" tug of war burdened Simpson and the evolving Foreign Department responsible for the care and administration of the far-flung missionary force. Simpson spent many sleepless hours in thought and prayer over these thorny issues.

Because of the growth of The Alliance and the number of candidates coming to New York to study, the Missionary Training Institute's recently dedicated facilities on 8th Avenue soon proved to be woefully inadequate by 1896. With 50 students in the school's dormitory, there were another 150 spread throughout Manhattan in boarding houses and private homes. Potential student's applications were rejected for lack of space, a development which grieved Simpson's heart. A larger campus needed to be built, but to do so in the city would cost hundreds of thousands of dollars, while an equivalent educational plant could be built in a suburban area for less than $100,000.

NYACK ON THE HUDSON
An early supporter of the Gospel Tabernacle, Stephen Merritt, an undertaker by trade and pastor by vocation, lived in Nyack, a town on the west side of the Hudson River about 20 miles upriver from Manhattan. There, affordable real estate was available overlooking the river, running up the hills above the Tappan Zee. In short time, suitable property was

A. B. Simpson, upper center, officiates Missionary Training Institute cornerstone ceremony

purchased on "the hillside" and the cornerstone for the institute building was laid on April 17, 1897. A veritable "frog-strangler" storm drenched the work site the day before, leaving it a field of mud, and Simpson called for an impromptu prayer meeting. Two chartered trainloads of people were coming up from the city, and they would hardly be impressed with the swampy bog before them. "Before the prayer meeting was over, the sky cleared, and the clouds rolled away, and the sun shone in all its glory, and a stiff drying wind blew briskly over the land. By three o'clock, when the services began at Nyack, one would scarcely have suspected that there had been a shower."[11]

The move of the Missionary Training Institute proved to be an excellent decision. Since he personally believed that Christ would return soon, Simpson decided against building more expensive buildings of brick and mortar. Perhaps he thought, *There is no need to go to such expense because the Lord might return before the buildings wear out.* His enthusiasm and economy exceeded his eschatological estimates. Needing a tabernacle to hold Alliance conventions and camps in Nyack, Simpson's third son, James Gordon, took on the job of foreman, and with his crew of young men, a beautiful wooden tabernacle, now site of Pardington Hall, was built in just 20 days for about $25,000.

Without doubt, those buildings erected under Simpson's leadership at Nyack are a testimony to the quality of workmanship and the excellent virgin timber used.

With the Missionary Training Institute moving to Nyack, Simpson became a land developer. He and some colleagues bought a large plot of land on the "hillside" and parceled it into lots for homes. They invited people to purchase land and build homes in the Nyack Heights "Christian community," free from the noise and coarse influences of city life. By that time, Simpson recognized the danger of raising children in "the devil's playground." Thus he, with a few colleagues and well-off friends, began The Nyack Heights Improvement Company[12] in early

> **The business venture eventually failed, criticism followed, and the company faced serious financial loss.**

1897. Over the next few years, lots were offered, and opportunity was given to invest in the company. Sale of preferred stock furnished capital for the company for clearing the land, laying out streets, and installing gas and water lines and other improvements. Unfortunately, just a few lots were purchased, including one by Simpson where he built a home for Margaret and the family. The business venture eventually failed, criticism followed, and the company faced serious financial loss. Consequently, Simpson took total responsibility for the failure by buying out his partners, assuming the financial loss.[13] Earlier, Simpson had successfully sold property in New York at a significant profit. However, the Nyack Heights undertaking showed that Simpson, seen as a "prophet" by many, was definitely "non-profit" on that occasion. The criticism directed toward this real-estate venture added to a growing list of personal attacks.

FAITH OR FAKE HEALERS?

Over the many years of Simpson's ministry, another jab that he and The Alliance felt came from the teaching on Christ the Healer. He was criticized from all sides regarding that doctrine. Renowned Presbyterian theologian Benjamin B. Warfield, in *Counterfeit Miracles* (1918), derided the many so-called "faith healers" and their less-than-consistent testimonies before the church and the world. Interestingly, in the same chapter where Warfield attacks Simpson's teaching of healing in the Atonement, Warfield points out the many charlatans and imposters found in the healing movement. Yet at the same time, he mentions Simpson in glowing terms: "Perhaps Doctor A. B. Simpson of New York, who has been since 1887 the president of The Christian and Missionary Alliance, founded in that year at Old Orchard, Maine, has been blameless in the public eye as a healer of the sick through faith for as long a period as any of our recent American healers. The fame of others has been, if more splendid, at the same time less pure and less lasting."[14] While being lumped in with some unsavory characters, Simpson at least received a backhanded compliment from Warfield. He was never accused of profiting from his prayer ministry with the sick, in contrast to some of the others who did well by doing good.

Two personal friends and fellow ministers of Simpson, Kelso Carter and Rowland Bingham, had early on been strong advocates of divine healing. They later retracted their support of the position. Since Carter had been one of Simpson's close colleagues and collaborators during the initial years of the Gospel Tabernacle, his departure from the teaching and his book, *Faith Healing Reviewed After Twenty Years*, deeply disappointed Simpson. The same for Dr. Bingham, who as a young man had been a close associate of Rev. John Salmon, the pioneer Alliance leader in Canada, who mentored Bingham. Salmon had been healed of a life-threatening kidney disease when Simpson was holding a healing convention in Buffalo, New York. Salmon had already come to accept that healing was in the Atonement, and he wanted to be anointed and prayer for, but "found no clergymen in Toronto who believed in the practice."[15]

Trusting God for the needed fare and hotel costs, Salmon prepared to travel to Buffalo, despite his weakened condition. He prayed and asked his Heavenly Father for the needed funds and a letter came in the next mail with $14.00. Arriving in Buffalo, Salmon attended the meeting and was anointed with many others at the close. He was instantly healed and immediately joined the team in prayer for others. Then he gave his testimony and became the new leader of The Alliance. As a result, Salmon taught and practiced prayer for the sick based on Christ's atoning work as he learned from Simpson. Many years later, when the Bosworth brothers were holding evangelistic services in Toronto,

Bingham, the then head of the Sudan Interior Mission minimized the healing ministry of the Bosworths, pointing out those not healed as a result of prayer rather than recognizing the many who were restored in health. His disavowal of divine healing was another disappointment.

Simpson never permitted divine healing to become the tail that wagged the Alliance dog. However, from his earliest healing experience at Old Orchard Camp in August 1881, Simpson never soft-pedaled the teaching, although his understanding of healing and divine health matured over the years. A major reason he felt compelled to preach on healing and prayer for the sick came after the death of President James A. Garfield, who was shot in July and died on September 19, 1881. Simpson, at that time still rejoicing in his newfound health, longed

> **He was never accused of profiting from his prayer ministry.**

for someone to go pray for the dying president hospitalized in nearby New Jersey. God seemed to lay it on Simpson's heart to go and pray for Garfield. "Will you go?"[16] Simpson hesitated and did not go, and the president died from wounds made by the assassin's bullet. He felt that he had broken his vow made to God at Old Orchard to clearly teach what he had learned. Convicted by his inaction, from that time forward, Simpson obeyed God and shared the message and ministry of divine healing to the larger Body of Christ.

SIMPSON'S FOUR-WHEELED CHARIOT

Not all of Simpson's critics regarding divine healing came from the "opposing theological camp." On occasion, he also came under intense "friendly fire." One of his worst detractors was John Alexander Dowie, a colorful Scotsman raised in Australia who came to America in 1888, first settling in San Francisco. After a few years on the West Coast in the "healing business," he moved to Chicago and eventually established Zion City and the Christian Catholic Apostolic Church.[17] Dowie heard about Simpson and the amazing healing ministry at the Gospel Tabernacle. Sensing an opportunity, he proposed to Simpson that they barnstorm the country together, praying for the unwell and doing well by it. As A. W. Tozer describes in *Wingspread*, Simpson simply responded: "No, Brother Dowie, I have four wheels on my chariot. I cannot agree to neglect the other three while I devote all my time to the one."[18]

Simpson's refusal infuriated Dowie, who set out to discredit the "Fourfold" founder of the Gospel Tabernacle. He planned a series of lectures in major cities where he intended to "tear Simpson to shreds and then tramp on the shreds!"[19] At the first city on the tour, Pittsburgh, Pennsylvania, Dowie was dining before going to the lecture hall. His fish dish proved to be a problem since a tiny bone lodged cross-wise in

John Alexander Dowie

his throat. He got neither the bone nor a word out. After a long delay, the crowd awaiting the "Simpson shredder" tired and left. Dowie canceled the rest of the tour and went back to Zion. When Simpson was told what had happened, he simply replied: "Oh, Dowie, yes, I committed that man to the Lord long ago."[20]

Much more serious long-term effects on The Alliance came from the historic, sovereign move of the Holy Spirit right after the turn of the 20th century. It began first in the Midwest, spreading to Los Angeles in 1906, with the Azusa Street revival that ushered in the Pentecostal movement. However, as is persuasively presented in Paul

King's research-rich book, *Genuine Gold: The Cautiously Charismatic Story of the Early Christian and Missionary Alliance*, supernatural manifestations of the Holy Spirit occurred soon after Simpson opened the Gospel Tabernacle, long before the turn of the century. King recounts that people came to the Tabernacle and were miraculously healed with no one praying for them, while others fell to the floor unconscious and bathed in the presence of God. Thus, "manifestations and practices often associated with the Pentecostal and charismatic movements such as trembling, shaking, shouting, holy laughter, falling under the power of the Spirit . . . lifting hands, dancing, visions, dreams, physical sensations or feelings of warmth, fire or electricity, spontaneous vocal unison prayer, etc."[21] took place at the Gospel Tabernacle and early C&MA meetings. Simpson had taught for years that all the gifts of the Spirit and miraculous manifestations of God's power as found in the apostolic Church eventually would appear in the contemporary Church.

THE LONELY MIDDLE ROAD

As word of the Los Angeles events traveled across the nation and reached New York in late 1906, Simpson and his colleagues were initially overjoyed at what they felt were signs of the "Latter Rain" and precursors of the soon return of Jesus Christ. Throughout this whole period, from the first stirrings in the Midwest until the Pentecostal explosion at Azusa Street, Simpson strongly supported the move of the Spirit and persistently maintained a firm balance between the two extremes of the already polarized movement. One pole insisted on making the evidential experience of Pentecostal "tongues" the be-all and end-all for believers, while the majority of evangelical churches denied the validity of spiritual gifts in "the present dispensation," either labeling the experience as demonic or carnal hysteria.

In May 1906, a Prayer Conference on Truth and Testimony was led by Simpson at Nyack to bring "uniformity of testimony" to The Alliance.[22] Rejecting the idea of a "cast-iron creed," he wanted the leaders of the growing Alliance to agree on the essentials, while leaving open questions relating to church polity, baptism, Calvinism vs. Arminianism, etc. As an "alliance of believers" still rejecting denominationalism, the 1906 conference reaffirmed the essential beliefs of the centrality of Christ as expressed in the Fourfold Gospel: salvation by faith through grace alone; sanctification as a post-salvation blessing that includes the baptism and infilling of the Holy Spirit and the indwelling Christ; healing as part of Christ's atoning work; and the premillennial return of Jesus. While not specifically addressing Pentecostalism, the conference prepared The Alliance for the challenge to unity over the next several years.

Later that same year, with Simpson present, revival broke out at the Missionary Training Institute and the Gospel Tabernacle. Deep conviction of sin, confession, and repentance swept across the campus and the New York church. As time passed and the movement spread, Simpson continued to hold an open attitude toward the manifestation of the spiritual gifts, including tongues, which had occurred at Nyack and the New York Tabernacle as well as other Alliance branches in 1907. Simpson's later diary entries reveal that he earnestly sought and was open to all the gifts, including tongues. While some might interpret this seeking as a validation of the tongues evidence doctrine, implying that Simpson did not "press in" deeply enough to do so, the diary entries do not confirm that thesis.

Edith Blumhofer, author of *The Assemblies of God: A Chapter in the Story of American Pentecostalism,* significantly pointed out the wise stance of The Alliance in the first flashes of the movement: "Alliance spokespersons had an almost uncanny way of discerning potential difficulties that enthusiastic Apostolic Faith adherents seemed prone to overlook. Within several years, some Pentecostals would echo Alliance appeals for prudence and balance. For the moment, however, the cautions seemed to go largely unheeded."[23] The other spirit, Satan, who continually opposes the Holy Spirit, knows that counterfeit gifts exist only because there are "genuine golden" gifts of the Spirit.[24]

It became clear that A. B. Simpson was the only major evangelical leader of the early 20th ce.ntury who, though not Pentecostal, wholeheartedly accepted all the spiritual gifts mentioned in Scripture as valid for the present day, including tongues and interpretation. Spiritual phenomena such as holy laughter, spirit slaying, etc., were all part of the early days of the Gospel Tabernacle, more than 20 years before Azusa Street and the beginning of the Pentecostal movement. Some "Cessassionists," who previously had preached at the Gospel Tabernacle and had endorsed the Alliance message and mission, turned against him. They criticized him for not rejecting, outright, the whole movement. On the other hand, many pastors and colleagues who had been students of Simpson at the Missionary Training Institute criticized Simpson with equal energy for not being willing to "go all the way." Many left The Alliance and eventually became leaders of Pentecostal denominations that sprang up. The pain caused by the attacks on one side and the abandonment by former friends and allies deeply wounded Simpson. His daughter, Margaret, relates that "My father had a great heart, but an exceedingly lonely one. He was naturally sensitive, and though he had a number of great friends, he tended to be a lonely man. I never saw him angry either, though tears often came to his eyes."[25]

Over this period from 1907 to 1912, Simpson's diaries reveal his continual search for a deeper walk with Christ and all that God had for him. He noted times of "a baptism of holy laughter, . . . a distinct sense of warmth, at times a penetrating fire, . . . a mighty sense of rest, reality and joy," but no tongues experience.[26] There can be no doubt that God's

> "My father had a great heart, but an exceedingly lonely one."

purpose in the renewed acceptance of the spiritual gifts was to equip His church to evangelize the world and hasten Christ's return. However, what God meant for good, the enemy interferes with sufficiently so that this "God thing" became an instrument of division and confusion in the Body.

Many pastors and whole congregations withdrew from The Alliance, taking buildings and missionary support with them. Within a few years, as many as one-third of the adherents had abandoned The Alliance for the burgeoning Pentecostal movement. They included foreign missionaries, home workers, and thousands of members. Ohio sustained the heaviest losses. Ironically, the hotbed of the C&MA tongues movement was in the town of Alliance, Ohio. It was visited by one of Simpson's most trusted colleagues, Dr. Henry Wilson, at the founder's behest. From there Wilson filed his famous appraisal: "I am not able to approve the movement, though I am willing to concede that there is probably something of God in it somewhere."[27] At that time, as Paul King clearly points out in *Genuine Gold*, the C&MA did not have a branch in Alliance, Ohio. Wilson had visited Alliance branch meetings in Cleveland, Akron, and likely other congregations where he concluded "that this work is of God, and no man should put his hand on it."²⁸ Thus, the "God-is-in-there-somewhere" observation apparently referred to a non-Alliance Pentecostal gathering that Wilson visited while in Ohio.

TONGUES—REAL AND NOT SO MUCH

While most of The Alliance overseas navigated the change and strain resulting from Pentecostalism sweeping the world and C&MA missions, the West China/Tibet field became a serious test case. The two Alliance pioneers of the Tibet field, William Christie and W. W. Simpson (no relation to A. B.), had gone out to the field during the missionary explosion of the early 1890s. Through their faithfulness in the face of persecution, sickness, and sacrifice, a solid work eventually developed in this stronghold of animistic Buddhism. In 1908, W. W. Simpson reported that his Chinese prayer partner had prayed in perfect English, despite knowing very little of the language. As a result, W. W. began to seek the "Spirit baptism" with tongues. Later that same year, an article appeared in *The Alliance Weekly* written by Christie and W. W. describing a Chinese believer who had a spurious "baptism," accompanied by tongues, prophetic utterances, trances, and impersonation of Jesus.²⁹ Both men concluded that this man had received a lying, false spirit, giving positive proof of the possibility of demonic imitation of the real thing. The editorials in the official Alliance magazine reported these developments in Tibet, recognizing that God was at work in Tibet, as well as the enemy, counseling candor and caution.

In 1912, W. W. received the baptism in the Spirit with tongues, as did Mrs. William Christie, W. W. Simpson's wife and children, and some local pastors and believers. William Christie was supportive and actively sought the same experience and at one point felt close to receiving the gift. However, after two months of seeking, he concluded that what he was experiencing was not of the Spirit, but from an "evil spirit." Meanwhile, W. W. was teaching to one and all necessity of tongues-speaking as the initial evidence of Spirit baptism and infilling, while Christie rejected the position as unbiblical. Confusion and controversy resulted from the impasse.

W. W. Simpson and his family eventually left the C&MA when the foreign secretary, Rev. Robert Glover, visited the field and presented W. W. with the official C&MA position on the question, which stated that speaking in tongues is not the essential evidence for Spirit baptism.

W. W. replied that he could not and would not sign the statement, thus resigning from The Alliance and returning to America. *The Alliance Weekly* announced his resignation from the Tibet field, noting that "we are sure that separation of this kind should be accomplished in the spirit of mutual love, confidence and consideration."[30] W. W. and his wife later returned to his former station in Tibet and led dozens of Tibetan pastors and believers into the Pentecostal tongues experience, thus causing division and damage to the still-young national church.

About the same time, A. B. Simpson responded to a letter requesting more information regarding W. W.'s resignation. In reply, he explained the Board of Manager's decision: the presentation of the policy to W. W. by the foreign secretary and his refusal to sign the letter, and W. W.'s subsequent resignation. Simpson wrote from memory, and in his usual irenic fashion, he spared the nitty-gritty details of the meeting between W. W. and Glover. This letter was shown subsequently to W. W. Simpson, and he penned a stinging letter to Simpson accusing him of "great discrepancy" regarding his account with what occurred in West China when Glover visited the field. W. W. charged A. B., the Board, and Glover with deception and "Tammany Hall politics."[31] The resulting fallout from this incident, as well as the long-term consequence of Pentecostalism, the attacks on his character and integrity, and the ensuing splintering of the Alliance work abroad and at home saddened Simpson, leading to occasional emotional valleys in his last years.

What is amazing in this difficult period of growing pains is that Simpson produced one of his most important and least-known books, *The Old Faith and the New Gospels,* published in 1911. From his experience and observations made 40 years previously, while on his European health tour, Simpson detected the sprouting seeds of secularism, rationalism, and unbelief being taught in schools, where once "the just shall live by faith" was the core course in the classroom. What he sensed, almost intuitively, while on that tour was the spiritual coldness of those lands so powerfully impacted by the Reformation. Where grace and faith had been Luther's watchwords, the same schools and seminaries founded by the Reformers now mocked belief in the Scriptures, questioned the historicity of Jesus Christ, and generally made unbelief their creedal statement.

Four decades later, these seedlings had grown into mighty oaks. Simpson, sensing the danger of Continental Liberalism coming to

America, wrote a book, that, while accessible to the average Alliance believer and worker, clearly predicted the wave of "modernism" that was about to devastate Protestant denominations in Canada and the United States. The slender volume of 161 pages dealt with evolution and creation, higher criticism and biblical authority, the "New Theology" and the Person and work of Jesus Christ, a Christ-less ethical life, divine healing and its counterfeits, and socialism and Christ's coming Kingdom. Succinctly and clearly, Simpson, like a good father, presented to his "Alliance family" straightforward teaching that stood his spiritual offspring in good stead when the Fundamentalist vs. Liberal Modernists controversy exploded on the scene just a few years later. While firmly adhering to the fundamentals of the Christian faith, Simpson steered the Alliance ship away from the upcoming battle. No doubt, this book provided a theological road map for the Alliance's educational pioneers at Nyack and other schools, blazing a trustworthy trail in the coming decades.

The years 1907 to 1912 were difficult, following almost 25 years of continued growth and blessing. Due to issues such as the need to grow the homeland base to support overseas expansion, criticism regarding the organization and supervision of the rapidly growing worldwide ministry, the divine healing controversy, and more importantly, the fallout from the Pentecostal crisis and conflict, the Alliance movement stalled and slowed somewhat. To regroup and recover forward momentum, the Boone, Iowa, Council of 1912 envisioned a major reorganization of the home and foreign work founded by Simpson. Its effects of this Council's decisions lasted for decades to come.

There came into his eyes and upon his frame more than a suggestion of deep fatigue. He had done five men's work, and he was feeling the weariness of five men.

CHAPTER 11
LENGTHENING SHADOWS

On Wednesday, April 18, 1906, *The Los Angeles Times* printed in bold-face type, "Weird Babble of Tongues," as front-page news.¹ Meeting in a rough-wood hall, the Azusa Street Apostolic Faith Mission introduced what many called heresy and hysteria, while others deemed it a "heaven-quake." At 5:12 a.m. that same day, a few hundred miles up the California coast, two massive tremors, one registering an estimated 7.9 on the Richter scale, devastated San Francisco, killing more than

> For 25 years, A. B. Simpson followed the contours of his God-given vision to reach the neglected masses in New York.

3,000 people and destroying 80 percent of the city. San Francisco was mostly restored in less than 10 years, but "aftershocks" of the Azusa Street Revival still ripple throughout the world today.

For 25 years, A. B. Simpson followed the contours of his God-given vision to reach the neglected masses in New York, where he pastored the unique Gospel Tabernacle ministry, as well as the ever-growing, worldwide Alliance missionary movement. From its first faltering steps, Simpson's ministry saw God's stamp of approval. However, with the arrival of the new century and the mushrooming Pentecostal wave sweeping the nation, as well as the world, those halcyon earlier years were followed by times of testing.

Due to the challenges coming from the rapid growth of The Alliance and the need for basic agreement in testimony and teaching, a pre-Council "Conference on Prayer and Testimony" was held in late May 1906. At the meeting, discussion revolved around the open question of what Alliance people would agree to disagree upon. Made up of men and women from Reformed, Wesleyan, Mennonite, and even Episcopal backgrounds, Simpson's leading such a diverse group was rather like herding cats. A major issue was the definition of sanctification as a distinct post-salvation experience, understood as the indwelling of "the living Christ Himself, who is the Source and Substance of all spiritual life."[2] The conference did not deal specifically with the tongues issue that was sweeping overland to the east, touching branches across the land. However, the Nyack meeting clearly laid down a broad outline of what was considered the "Alliance message."

Deep sorrow gripped A. B. Simpson in 1907, when his second son, James Gordon, succumbed to tuberculosis in an upstate New York sanatorium. He was 36. His older brother, Albert Henry, also passed

Simpson concluded that the gift of tongues was one manifestation of the Holy Spirit's indwelling, but neither necessary nor the sole evidence of such an experience.

under similar circumstances in 1895 at age 30. Both sons had been part of Simpson's early ministry. Albert Henry had been organist at the Tabernacle and managed the Alliance Publishing Company owned by his father, while James Gordon worked as secretary of the C&MA weekly publication. Unfortunately, the temptations of the big city and the lure of alcohol took root in their hearts as growing boys, and eventually, the effects took their toll. Before death, both sons restored their relationship with the Lord, but Simpson and Margaret deeply grieved the loss of their sons. Added to their pain was the fact that James Gordon left behind a widow with five children. His wife, Anna, 30, kept her baby daughter, Anna, while A. B. and Margaret raised the other four children in their Nyack hillside home for almost 10 years until their mother was able to support and care for them.[3]

James Gordon's grieving father faced more loss that year. Because the "tongues" phenomenon had become prominent in many Alliance fellowships, especially in the Midwest, the issue became divisive, resulting in many pastors and congregations leaving The Alliance and joining ranks with others to birth several Pentecostal denominations. The loss of close personal friends and longtime associates, as well as the deep financial losses toward the support of Alliance missionaries around the globe, weighed heavily on Simpson. Nights were spent in prayer and pleading to the Lord to heal this rift and restore the fellowship.

SOMEONE, NOT SOMETHING

At the same time, Simpson asked God to give him all that He desired, including the gift of tongues. Many of his associates who remained in The Alliance had received the manifestation at revivals at Nyack, the Gospel Tabernacle, and in branches across the land. God's answer to him was to be content with what he had received. While his sporadic diary entries indicated that he asked more than once for the tongues experience, he never received it. Simpson knew that God had given him deep experiences of great joy and peace, as well as worked through the resident gifts that he had received. He did not receive the sought-after manifestation, as Robert Nicklaus makes clear in *All for Jesus:* "He [Simpson] concluded that the gift of tongues was one manifestation of the Holy Spirit's indwelling, but neither necessary nor the sole evidence of such an experience."[4] His settled position regarding the baptism and infilling of the Spirit viewed Him as the giver of the gifts. The Spirit is "Someone, not something," the Giver of the gifts, to be received by faith, accepted and rested upon as an accomplished reality, in the same way that God's other gifts are received.

In 1908, one of Simpson's oldest and dearest friends, Rev. Henry Wilson, the Episcopal clergyman who was part of the Gospel Tabernacle's pastoral staff for years, died in Atlanta, Georgia, following his participation in the Atlanta missionary convention. He had traveled south despite leaving home not feeling well and preached in the Sunday service but soon took a turn for the worse, was hospitalized, and died a few days later.

The loss of this godly man, who combined a scholarly background with a childlike simplicity, was great. He had become the children's pastor of the whole Alliance movement, calling himself "B. B. B." (Big Baby Brother). The passing of this close friend was deeply felt by Simpson, since he saw change coming as the years passed. Wilson was the first of

Dr. Henry Wilson

many of Simpson's most trusted friends and colleagues who "graduated" to the Father's House. Their deaths became a reminder of his own mortality, even though he continued to have amazing energy and capacity for work and ministry, undiminished despite his many years of active service as pastor, preacher, teacher, writer, publisher, missionary mobilizer, and executive, not to mention husband and father.

PENANCE OR PENITENCE?

In 1910, Simpson took an extended tour in South America to visit Alliance missionaries in Brazil, Argentina, Chile, and Peru. He went on to Panama, crossing the isthmus where the Panama Canal was under construction, then on to Central America, Cuba, and Key West. He arrived back in Nyack after more than three months of travel.

Coincidently, Simpson's trip was made shortly before the famous Edinburgh Council for World Missions in June 1910, where it was determined that South America was already sufficiently "evangelized" by the Roman Catholic Church, not requiring Protestant missionary activity.[5] This reality-blind statement collided with the facts: South

America had been "missionized" by Catholic missionaries for almost 400 years, resulting in a grossly immoral Catholic clergy that promoted ignorance of the Bible, syncretic practices with animism, and a message that preached "penance" rather than penitence, i.e., repentance for sins. William Azel Cook, pioneer missionary and adventurer who served in Brazil with the C&MA in the late 1890s and early 1900s during the first attempt at establishing an Alliance mission in Brazil, described this

> This second tour of the Alliance fields revealed Simpson's total dependence for daily health on that same Spirit who raised Christ from the dead.

situation in his book, *Through the Wildernesses of Brazil by Horse, Canoe and Float*.[6] This long-term spiritual influence contributed to the endemic corruption and dictatorial governments that sprang up following independence from the Spanish and Portuguese colonizers. Across South America, evangelical mission agencies loudly protested the declaration, which betrayed either a total lack of knowledge of the situation "on the ground," or an attempted "diplomatic solution" to appease unhappy Vatican observers who attended the Edinburgh Conference.

Simpson's visit brought great encouragement and benefit to the missionary staff as well as leaders of the infant national churches being planted and nurtured. Still robust and adventurous at 67 years of age, he traveled solo for more than three months, navigating the many ocean voyages and trips by rail without mishap. This second tour of the Alliance fields revealed Simpson's total dependence for daily health on that same Spirit who raised Christ from the dead. Except for a couple of cases of *"derangement"* as he colorfully termed it, brought on by some unsavory foods at a few local restaurants, he enjoyed excellent health. However, traveling from Callao, Peru, north to Panama, he faced a challenge. His original plan had called for a visit with the Alliance missionaries in Guayaquil, Ecuador. But they cabled to tell him that the torrid port city "had much epidemic disease and bubonic plague, and that it was not a proper place either for us or them at that season of the year."[7]

Thus, Simpson and his shipmates steamed north to the quarantine station in Panama Harbor where their sanctification and patience were tested. Simpson's ship, the *SS Huallaga,* had carried a passenger with yellow fever the previous month; however, the ship had not been properly fumigated. Then, the sanitary team came aboard, vividly described as producing "from some plutonian pit an immense coil of hose, charged with sulfur and brimstone smoke and pumped it into every cabin, saloon, and corner for nearly an entire day, and then pasted up the cracks and keyholes of the cabins to keep the foul stuff in until it had saturated with its suffocating smell every mattress, pillow, sheet and carpet with a stifling odor that did not vanish for days."[8] Most of the passengers slept on the deck until they reached the port in Panama.

TRUSTING HIM IN TRIALS

After arriving at the port of Porto, they were detained at the quarantine station where doctors examined them daily for six days, looking for anyone with a sign of yellow fever or high temperature. Simpson had already experienced some short-lived mild fevers; yet despite being counseled to take quinine to avoid malaria, he declined and "simply trusted Him on the strength of whose definite promise we had undertaken this trying journey."[9] He was about to lean heavily on those promises. In Simpson's words:

> *The very day of our arrival at the quarantine station, the feverishness that had been creeping over us for days struck us with a sudden power, and we went to bed that night, literally on fire with a high pulse. Naturally the enemy pressured us sorely, knowing that if that fever should continue until the doctor's examination next morning, it would mean our detention in that pest-house and perhaps the holding of all our fellow passengers.*
>
> *Well, the battle raged that night for hours, and the Lord gently and gradually breathed His peace and His cooling and quieting life until we fell into fitful sleep in His loving arms, and the morning found the fever broken and just a trace of temperature on the doctor's thermometer, but not enough to constitute fever . . . But that did not end the conflict. Night after night all through those dreadful six days, did the enemy return and the battle rage again always to end in the same way before the dawn with a broken fever. A few hours of*

sleep, and just a trace of temperature, but not enough for the doctor to mark it. The last night was perhaps the hardest and most glorious.

At last that Monday morning came, the doctor's thermometer for the seventh time had passed into our mouth, and we were free. The little tender drew up to the shore, and the baggage was rushed on board and as we steamed to Panama, the shout inside reached to heaven, and we almost felt it could be heard in New York.[10]

Thus, Simpson ended his epic trip of almost 8,000 miles by ship, rail, car, and assorted conveyances. An account of his tour was found in weekly installments of *The Christian and Missionary Alliance Weekly*, from March through the end of May. This trip, like his earlier one taken in 1894, helped Simpson take stock of important issues such as field conditions, growth of the missions, the state of the missionary staff's

> **Doubtless, his presence was encouraging, inspiring, and a sign that their leader loved and cared for them.**

hearts and minds, and local religious situations and factors relating to opposition, challenges to ministry, health conditions, and availability of medical facilities. Doubtless, his presence was encouraging, inspiring, and a sign that their leader loved and cared for them.

One interesting sidebar relating to his time in Chile concerned Simpson's meeting Rev. Willis Hoover, a Methodist missionary who had been baptized in the Holy Spirit and had spoken in tongues. Simpson met with him, and despite The Alliance's painful experience with Pentecostalism, he encouraged Hoover and commended him on his sane position of seeing tongues as a gift but not the gift *sine qua non* required as evidence of Spirit baptism.[11] Hoover founded the Pentecostal movement that continues today in Chile.

Returning to New York, Simpson immediately plunged into his normal summer of activity at camps and conventions all over the country, the major conference being held in Nyack. By this time, the furor stirred by the Pentecostal wind settled some, and the C&MA continued to gradually evolve from a deeper-life, healing, missionary movement into a church that maintained those same emphases on the Fourfold

Gospel for all people everywhere. As a result, resistance arose on the part of some denominational leaders who previously had been strong supporters of The Alliance as it developed. They now saw it as a threat to their churches and membership. They saw the gradual development of The Alliance into an organized church, despite Simpson's protests, but the steady growth in number, organization, and distinct identity spoke louder than its leader's words.

Open criticism of Simpson and the Alliance position on tongues brought on attacks by Pentecostals on one side and "Cessationists" on the other. This balanced but uncomfortable posture made it necessary to publish in an April 1910 editorial the official Alliance position:

> *The statement is made that The Alliance and its leaders are opposed to the manifestation of the Gift of Tongues in this age. This is wholly false . . . But we are opposed to the teaching that this special gift is for all or is the evidence of the baptism of the Holy Ghost. Nor can we receive or use to edification in our work and assemblies those who press these extreme and unscriptural views.*[12]

This statement became "the line in the sand" that defined the Alliance position and continues to be the guiding principle regarding the gifts of the Spirit today. No doubt, Simpson's heart was grieved to see how Satan managed a kind of spiritual "jujitsu," taking the force and intent of the sovereign move of God and using it to cause such damage and division in the Body of Christ.

THE 1912 BOONE, IOWA, COUNCIL

When the two "Alliances" were formed in 1887, Simpson was the president of each of the "societies" and Margaret was a member of both boards. The Alliances grew and merged into The Christian and Missionary Alliance (the C&MA) in 1897,[13] with the administrative arrangement continuing; both Simpsons remained on the Board of Managers until their deaths. Simpson as founder, was the unquestioned leader, administrator, and guiding light for at least three decades. Margaret served as mission treasurer and on the missionary candidate committee. Because of their desire to keep overhead to a minimum, they basically controlled the growing Alliance organization. A. T. Pierson's criticism of this state of affairs in *The Missionary Review of the World (1899–1900)*, doubtless was very painful. However, the pointed assessment from a close friend, as well as the painful attacks from former friends who had abandoned Simpson, revealed a growing need for the reorganization of The Alliance and greater delegation of responsibility and authority.

Thus, the tongues controversy, the growing Alliance movement, and the headaches that come with growth and change, determined the need for a revision of the Alliance constitution, which took place in 1912 at the Boone, Iowa, Council, at which the Board of Managers became an executive body with the power of decision rather than acting as a sounding board. The various departments established to oversee the

> " . . . but we are opposed to the teaching that this special gift is for all or is the evidence of the baptism of the Holy Ghost."

work of The Alliance (Foreign, Home, Education, Finance, Publications, etc.) were led by "secretaries" with distinct responsibilities and authority. Simpson was not power hungry, but the accumulation of an ever-increasing workload had hindered Alliance growth by his inability to effectively keep all of the "balls in the air."

Consequently, at the 1912 Council, a revised constitution was adopted with the preamble, "The C&MA, owing to providential developments, finds itself called to readjust itself to a larger fellowship."[14] Much policy and practice that was understood and left for Dr. Simpson's discretion was codified, organized, and approved. Atlanta-based attorney Ulysses Lewis, honorary vice president for years, was the chief architect of the constitution. At the Boone Council, he was elected vice president, having a functional role in the Society. For the next 60 years, this constitution would be the governing document of The Alliance.

The new constitution recognized the need for the sharing of executive responsibilities, taking from Simpson's shoulders the weight of many duties accumulated over the years. Simpson continued as president until his death, but clearly the Alliance leadership had recognized the need to begin a process of transition. By this time, the overseas worker staff had grown to 259 missionaries in 16 countries. On the home front, there were 239 branches and affiliated churches in 35 states and 4 Canadian provinces. One hundred eighty-two workers led these "home works," of which 107 were ordained and 36 unordained men, with another 39 women credentialed and recognized as women in ministry. Missionary conventions held at Alliance summer camps and in local branches provided prayer and financial support, as well as being fertile ground for recruiting new workers.

Another policy adopted at the 1912 Council was the "reversion clause,"[14] which required Alliance schools, branches, and affiliated churches to include in their legal documents a clause stating that, "in the event that such property should cease to be used as originally intended, 'it shall revert to and become the property of the C&MA, as incorporated under the laws of the State of New York.'"[15] The inclusion of this clause resulted from the serious loss of properties caused through defections to the Pentecostal movement. However, it suggested to many that The Alliance was assuming a clear denominational stance, and this was troubling to those who wanted the movement to remain a fraternal fellowship. Doubtless, this addition to the constitution was painful for Simpson to accept.

THE GREAT WAR

With the outbreak of World War I in 1914, people across the United States and Canada were swept up in "The Great War" against Germany and its allies. So strong were the feelings against Imperial Germany regarding its war atrocities, use of poison gases, and indiscriminate submarine attacks on neutral ships that Simpson, now a naturalized U.S. citizen, attempted to bring balance to the emotions of his followers while urging the defeat of Kaiser Wilhelm II and his armies. His youngest son, Howard, joined the Canadian Army and shipped out to France to join his comrades-in-arms from the far-flung British Empire.

One of Simpson's closest associates was Albert E. Funk, a German Mennonite leader who enrolled in the Missionary Training Institute. He served on the pastoral staff of the Gospel Tabernacle and was part of the leadership of the growing Alliance movement. Funk led German-language services at "The Tab" for years for the large German immigrant population in New York. Some of the German members and friends of the Gospel Tabernacle were bothered by Simpson's language regarding Germany and the terrible war in Europe. In the December 5, 1914, issue of *The Alliance Weekly*, Simpson wrote on the opening editorial page:

> *Most of our readers are already familiar with the daring theories so widely exploited by General von Bernhardi in his famous book, "Germany and the Next War," which almost reads like a prophecy of the things that are now coming to pass. The Boston Transcript recently reviewed another volume by a distinguished continental scholar, in which he deprecates . . . the spirit of meekness and . . . weakness inculcated by Christian ethics as enervating to national vigor and pleads for "the religion of valor" and the old ideas represented by Odin and Thor. Surely human nature without Christ reverts to type, and instead of "the Ascent of Man" descends to the brute, and in accordance with the law of evolution "the survival of the fittest" would replace the law of right with the law of might.[16]*

When he first published *The Fourfold Gospel*, Simpson clearly stated his opinion as to what happened to the land of Luther, the cradle of the Reformation, the just-shall-live-by-faith movement that shook Rome and changed the political and religious climate of Western Europe:

> *Many Christians are converted and stop there. They do not go on to the fullness of their life in Christ, and so are in danger of losing what they already possess. Germany brought in the grand truth of justification by faith through the teachings of Martin Luther, but he failed to go on to the deeper teaching of the Christian life. What was the result? Germany today is cold and lifeless, and the very hot-bed of rationalism and all its attendance evils.[17]*

Years before, Simpson had helped bring reconciliation between the Protestant churches of Louisville. Now he was thrust into the role of champion of the United States' involvement in helping England and its allies against Germany's insatiable hunger for land, resources, and power, while trying to maintain good relations with these hard-working German immigrant members.

THE WEARINESS OF FIVE MEN

Over the next several years, the Alliance body of believers became increasingly aware of the new organization brought about by the 1912 constitution. Simpson was entering his 70th year, still strong and vigorous, but no longer a young man. While maintaining a full calendar of preaching at conventions and the Gospel Tabernacle, writing and publishing, teaching at MTI, and trying to care for his businesses, it was clear that the years were taking their toll on the "great man," even if he didn't recognize it.

Tozer describes it in *Wingspread:*

> *There came into his eyes and upon his frame more than a suggestion of deep fatigue. He had done five men's work, and he was feeling the weariness of five men.*[18]

The blows that came from the death of his two sons, the deep heart hurts felt as a result of the Pentecostal exodus, the death of old friends and colleagues, concerns for his youngest son, Howard, now fighting in France, and the financial pressures of his unprofitable business ventures were pressing down on him like the beams of an old barn struggling to

> **He had done five men's work, and he was feeling the weariness of five men.**

support tons of hay bales and grain in the loft. Simpson, ever an oak among the "jack pines," began to bend under the weight of years of unrelenting service to His Lord and The Alliance.

Ever the dapper dresser, his appearance became dated and old fashioned. Legendary Alliance missionary to Japan, Mabel Francis, was a young student under Simpson at Nyack. She described him as having "a pleasing, melodious voice, and the meetings were permeated with a sense of joy." However, she noted that Simpson "always looked cleanly dressed with tie, clean collar, but with a suit not always in the latest fashion for the men of his day. I do remember that he wore a shirt which was shiny to the point of being green—you know how black can get when it is worn—but it was pressed, and he didn't care about things. He was all out for God."[19] Long-suffering wife Margaret kept a close watch on his choice of tie, and often demanded he remove "that tie" and wear one more suitable for the occasion. Simpson was getting old.

During the next several years, important leadership figures began arising from the ranks to assume major roles with the C&MA. The Board of Managers now had the responsibility of appointing the department heads, a responsibility previously held by Simpson. Longtime Gospel Tabernacle member and businessman, David Creare, was reappointed treasurer. Tabernacle associate pastor, A. E. Funk, became the first foreign secretary and E. J. Richards took over as home secretary over the Alliance branches in North America. A gradual transition of leadership was underway, and a few of the leaders began to emerge as potential successors to Simpson.

Rev. Robert Glover became deputation secretary and later was appointed foreign secretary. As a pioneer missionary to China, he was noted for his administrative ability and experience. John E. Jaderquist, former missionary to Africa and Alliance superintendent for several years, was asked to take over as publications secretary in 1912 to reorganize the Alliance print ministry. He made some difficult decisions that were unpopular at first but, ultimately, proved to be correct. Like Glover, Jaderquist became a respected voice to the Board of Managers. A third potential leader, Walter Turnbull, previously a missionary to India, eventually took over the dean's position at the Missionary Training Institute. He assumed the reins of the Institute at a difficult time, following the departure of Dr. William Stevens and Dr. Hudson Ballard, both very capable educators and leaders who left MTI after the 1914 Alliance Council decided against their plans to make Nyack into a full-fledged university. Upon the death of Dr. George Pardington, longtime colleague of Simpson, Turnbull became a major figure among Alliance leaders.

Walter Turnbull and wife with A. B. and Margaret

During this time of transition, Simpson invested a great deal of time traveling about the United States and Canada, speaking at Alliance conventions in major cities as well as visiting dozens of branches along the way. Through his speaking, publications, and participation in healing and deeper life conferences, he continued to promote the growing ministry of the C&MA in North America. On his travels, Simpson met a man who soon stood tall among his peers in The Alliance in physical as well as ministerial stature.

THE COWBOY PREACHER

Daniel Paul Rader, born in Denver, Colorado, was raised by his Methodist pastor father in a pious "holiness" home. He was a "sickly" child and spent much of his early years as an invalid. He accepted Christ as Savior at age nine in one of his father's evangelistic services. As a boy singer, he traveled with his father to small ranches and mining towns, where his father preached to the rough crowds. At 16, the tall youth began to do solo evangelistic work and soon became well known as "the cowboy evangelist."[20] He quickly gained notoriety for his powerful preaching and commanding presence. Rader eventually grew to a towering six feet four inches by the time he entered the University of Denver in 1897. For the next two years, his Bible-based faith learned from his father was assaulted by his philosophy professor who introduced the bright but unlearned freshmen to evolution, higher criticism of the Scriptures, and a course in comparative religion. He went from being a simple believer to finally rejecting the old-fashioned gospel. Rader's faith was shaken to its roots, and he essentially abandoned his belief in Christ as Lord and Savior, the authority of Scripture, and life eternal with God.

Rader decided to change schools and went to the University of Colorado in Boulder in 1899 where he majored in football as a talented fullback and learned the fine art of fisticuffs. After one year, he left Colorado for Central College in Missouri. There, he starred in football, sharpened his boxing skills, and sparred with heavyweight contender, Bob Fitzsimmons. They often fought exhibition matches in Western towns for easy money. In 1901 he entered Hamline University in St. Paul, Minnesota, where he played football and became the school athletic director. He still thought about entering the ministry despite his departure from the faith of his father. While there, he took courses in theology to prepare for the pastorate. Like a nomad ever seeking a home, Rader moved from Minnesota to Tacoma, Washington, where he became an instructor at the University of Puget Sound and met the daughter of a prominent member of his father's church. The woman, Mary Caughran, eventually became his wife.

Still unsettled, he received an invitation to cross the country to the East Coast, where he was ordained as a Congregational clergyman in Boston, complete with liberal theology and lifestyle. He did postgraduate work at Harvard University, where he received generous doses of liberal theology. Making the acquaintance of wealthy friends, he was invited to travel abroad, visiting major libraries, galleries, and cultural centers in Europe. Growing more urbane and worldly wise, he couldn't stomach the pastorate and left Boston in 1906, returning to the West Coast where he married his sweetheart.

In 1907, Rader again accepted a pastorate at a Congregational church in Portland, Oregon, where he also coached and played football at a local athletic club. By 1909, despite his success as a temperance

Rader became well known as "the cowboy evangelist."

promoter, convincing his county to vote "dry," the attraction of do-good liberalism left him empty. Thus, he abandoned the pastorate and decided that he needed to embark on a new career in business. Lacking capital, he fell back on the one ability that he still had and believed in—his fists and fast feet. There was always money in prize fighting, accepting exhibition bouts with local fighters. Being surprisingly quick and agile for a big man, he usually avoided the ponderous pounders, defeated them quickly, and made off with the purse.

Because of his earlier reputation as a boxer while in Colorado, he leveraged his notoriety and sparred with, "Gentleman Jim" Jefferies, a contender for the heavyweight title. On July 4, 1910, Rader sat ringside and watched the great African American boxer, Jack Johnson, beat Jefferies like a junk-yard dog for 15 rounds.[21] Rader claimed that boxing promoters, looking for a "Great White Hope" to take the title from Johnson, invited him to step into the ring as an eventual contender. Rader wisely decided against the move but continued his lucrative role as an exhibition boxer, taking on the local roughnecks, all the time using a pseudonym to protect his father's name.

Deciding that he wanted to make his fortune on Wall Street, Rader went to the Philadelphia gym of Jack Johnson to raise capital for his new career. Consequently, he and Jack fought an exhibition match. Light of feet, a smart boxer with a good punch, Rader fared well enough that he walked away with a healthy purse. For the next several weeks, he earned from $250 to $300 per match, always looking for more lucrative fights. Knowing his godly father wanted to see him pounding the pulpit rather than another man's jaws, Rader finally gave up the square ring and left for New York City with enough money to gamble on the stock market.

After the death of his father in 1911, Rader began investing his prize-fighting purses in the booming petroleum industry. He soon did very well on Wall Street and eventually sent a wire to his wife telling her that he was "fixed for life." When she wired back, the telegram read, "Fixed for <u>what</u>?" Unknown to him, his telegram had arrived garbled and read, "Fixed for like." She didn't understand and wanted clarification from his telegram. However, that mixed message caused Rader to realize that he didn't know what kind of life he had fixed for himself.

It was in New York, near Times Square and 44th Street, that Rader encountered God and his life's calling. Struck by the question in his wife's telegram, Rader spent three days in prayer and Bible study in his room, where he regained trust in the Word of God and returned to the faith of his parents. The next day, he left his room, went to his office, turned over his keys, correspondence, and stock portfolio to his dumbfounded partners, and walked out of the office a "free man" in Christ. Soon he was preaching on the streets.[21]

He decided to reunite with his wife who was living on the West Coast. Accordingly, he took the train west, and at a stop in Harrisburg, Pennsylvania, he met a Mr. Rossiter, head of the local branch of the C&MA. Recognizing the potential in Rader, Rossiter gave him a letter of introduction to Rev. E. D. "Daddy" Whiteside of Pittsburgh. Having only heard about The Alliance by name, Rader soon was introduced to the teaching of the C&MA. Regarding The Alliance position on healing, the role of the Holy Spirit in sanctification and infilling, the mandate to take the gospel to all peoples everywhere, and the simplicity of the Fourfold Gospel presentation, Rader declared that this was the "outfit" for him. When he learned that his three-day battle to return to the faith took place just a few blocks from the Gospel Tabernacle in

Manhattan, Rader was convinced that this was the sign from God for him to join ranks with Simpson and The Alliance.

By 1914, the dynamic young Rader, only 35, was quickly recognized as a powerful evangelist, and soon he was on the road with Simpson, preaching, singing, and becoming a close companion to the founder. Perhaps he was Simpson's "Joshua?" Time would tell.

"LAST DAYS" COUNTDOWN

In 1915, Simpson continued to support every possible effort to reach the Jews in America, as well as giving continued emphasis on the work in Palestine. That same year, he joined 16 leading evangelical pastors to form the Hebrew Christian Alliance[22] as a follow up to the "Conference on Behalf of Israel," held at Moody Church, then pastored by Paul Rader. These leaders worked together to form an "alliance" that would specifically target the largest Jewish population in North America.

> **Despite his 74 years, Simpson had a very full year in 1917.**

Simpson gave two addresses: "The Jew and the Nations" and "Spiritual Lessons from Israel's History." At the same conference, Rev. A. E. Thompson, the head of the Alliance mission in Palestine, a Canadian like Simpson and his future biographer, also spoke twice on "Modern Palestine and the Jews" and "The Restoration of Israel."

Despite his 74 years, Simpson had a very full year in 1917. He spoke from coast to coast. He was away from his Gospel Tabernacle more than half the year. While still listed as a teacher at the Missionary Training Institute, his classes were sporadic and highly valued by the students who could see that he was in his best and last years. With the 1917 entrance of the United States into the "Great War" in Europe, Simpson and many other prophetic teachers felt that this war, later to be called World War I, was somehow directly related to the return of Christ. Many felt that they were in the "last days" countdown.

As Germany and her Turkish Ottoman allies were being defeated in the Middle East, Simpson became increasingly excited by the prospects of the end of the "days of the Gentiles" and Jerusalem becoming a home for the Jews again. The Zionist movement, begun in 1897, had raised the cry for the Jews to have a national home freeing them from pogroms and prejudice across Eastern and Central Europe. On November 2, 1917, Sir Arthur Balfour, in his famous declaration, stated that the British government officially supported the idea of "the establishment of a national home for the Jewish people."[23] That statement, made by the Foreign Minister of the most powerful nation in the world at that time, was viewed as a major step in the fulfillment of prophecy and the "budding of the fig tree."

On December 11, 1917, General Edmund Allenby walked into Jerusalem[24] like a pilgrim through the Jaffa Gate, as opposed to Kaiser Wilhelm who had ridden into the Holy city in 1898 on a white charger. Allenby's respectful attitude contrasted with the haughty German king's demeanor, and the victorious British general was received by cheering

> **They had never heard him speak better on life in Christ.**

crowds of Jews, Palestinian Muslims, ex-patriate Christians, and soldiers. Katherine Brennen wrote in her booklet, *Mrs. A. B. Simpson—The Wife or Love Stands*,[25] that Simpson was so emotionally elated by the event, seeing it as another box checked before the return of Christ, that he suffered a mild stroke. He had just finished an Alliance Convention in St. Paul, Minnesota. One of his Nyack colleagues, W. C. Stevens, reported on Simpson's speaking at the convention: It was commented that he was in great form. They had never heard him speak better on life in Christ for the soul and the body, Christ's glorious return, and telling the story of The Alliance and the missionary appeal on the closing Sunday of the convention.

Weary in body, Simpson left St. Paul for Chicago, where "he picked up an extra [newspaper], telling of the capture of Jerusalem. He immediately hurried to his hotel and, falling on his knees by the bedside, burst into tears of joy because of the culmination of his life-long hope. He wired the New York Alliance headquarters to tell them that he would preach on "The Fall of Jerusalem in Light of Prophecy," which he did as soon as he arrived, despite his weariness. *The Alliance Weekly* noted that "he delivered his marvelous address, which has been an inspiration to thousands."[26]

It is difficult for the contemporary reader to understand the impact that Allenby's entrance into Jerusalem had on Simpson. He had been influenced by the prophetic conference movement for many years.

The Approaching End of the Age by H. Grattan Guinness, 1878, had been read and assimilated by Simpson. By means of an in-depth study of Ezekiel, Daniel, and Revelation, as well as developing complex soli-lunar computations for calculating the "end times," Guinness had established himself as one of the leading prophetic teachers and authors of his day. Simpson promoted Guinness' book and followed his eschatological hermeneutic. One of the key prophecies related to "the time of the Gentiles," when they would no longer tread on Jerusalem. The triumphal entry of British General Allenby, a Christian who walked into the Holy City through the Jaffa Gate, symbolized to students of prophecy the fulfillment of that long-awaited promise, one step closer to the return of Christ the Coming King. For this reason, after watching and waiting for so many years, Simpson was overwhelmed with emotion and suffered the mild stroke. Guinness had already passed away, but his influence was still strong, even in death.

Now nearing the end of his public ministry, Simpson shared a revealing story from his early ministry as an independent pastor in New York:

> *In the beginning of this life of faith God gave me a vision which to me was a symbol of the kind of life to which He had called me. In this dream a little sail boat was passing down a rapid stream, tossed by the winds and driven by the rapids. Every moment it seemed as if it must be dashed upon the rocks and crushed, yet it was preserved in some mysterious way and carried through all perils. Upon the sails of the little ship was plainly painted the name of the vessel in one Latin word, Angustiae, meaning "Hard Places." Through this simple dream the Lord seemed to fortify me for the trials and testings that were ahead, and to prepare me for a life's voyage which was to be far from a smooth one but through which God's grace would always carry me in triumph.*[27]

Now at the end of his long and fruitful ministry, Simpson was going through another difficult and "narrow passage" that would eventually lead to heaven's wider planes. Simpson's daughter, Margaret, likely his favorite child, gave her recollections of her father in a document, "My Father—What a daughter thought about A. B. S." This was written years after his death. She describes a scene with her parents sometime in early 1918:

> I remember in January 1918, an incident in the old "690" [44th Street] boardroom, as my mother and I sat beside him at the long table, when he penned a small check, and to our surprise, he wrote a strange name in place of his own signature. Suddenly he put his hand on his brow with the words, "Where am I? I cannot think clearly." Soon after this, he went with my mother to Clifton Springs Sanatorium, where he had gone in his earlier life. Then after some weeks of quiet rest he returned to Nyack and tried to again take up his work. Twenty or so long, trying months followed. These were days mixed with hope and fear, doubt and faith, strength and weakness, battles won and battles lost, times of depression and times of refreshing. But at last God closed the book and called my father home.[28]

In McKaig's "Simpson Scrapbook" are "The Recollections of a Secretary," Miss Emma F. Beere, who wrote the following about Simpson:

> One of the outstanding characteristics of Mr. Simpson was his desire to be conscious of the Lord's presence, and any break in this relationship sent him to his knees. When his health broke [in early 1918], he seemed to be especially tempted by Satan to believe this fellowship broken. He always recognized it, however, as a temptation of the evil one. One afternoon he called me to his office, and placing a hymn book in my hand, asked me to read the hymn, "O Thou, in Whose presence my soul takes delight, On Whom in affliction I call . . ."
>
> As I began to read it, he placed his head in his hands, and, leaning over his desk, began to cry and sob like a child. That was the only time I had ever seen him cry. It was with difficulty that I finished reading the hymn. A few minutes later, raising his head, he thanked me, adding that the Lord had met him, and that he was feeling better. [29]

Miss Beere continued her recollection, describing when she and the other Alliance workers at Alliance Headquarters "first realized that he was beginning to fail physically." It was in the Baptist Tabernacle in Harrison, New Jersey, where he was conducting the funeral service of the pastor, a friend of many years. Mr. Simpson prayed a rather long and eloquent prayer, and when he should have stopped, he began all over again and re-prayed with practically the same words he had just uttered. We all sensed at once that something was wrong, and in the following days we saw other evidences of his failing powers. It seemed hard to believe that his ministry would end; but, of course, it did.[30]

It was soon after this incident that Simpson and Margaret went to Clifton Springs for several weeks of rest, his first vacation in 30 years. It is ironic that such a godly and biblically-oriented man should have

> **Now at the end of his long and fruitful ministry, Simpson was going through another difficult and "narrow passage."**

missed so glaringly the basic rule of the "Sabbath rest." Since so much of Simpson's "Christ in Me" theology derived from the principle of resting in Christ, it is hard to understand how he preached divine health and healing yet did not recognize the need to come apart and rest awhile.

Understanding that transition of leadership was underway due to his failing health, *The Alliance Weekly* was reorganized with an editorial committee named by the Board of Managers. Simpson's last major project, the Correspondence Bible Course, was turned over to Nyack MTI under the direction of the school's dean, Walter Turnbull.[31] During this period, the Board took over Simpson's financial burdens, failing businesses, and outstanding debts, giving the Simpsons a monthly stipend of $250, the first compensation ever received from the C&MA since its founding. While Simpson was at Clifton Springs, two of the Board members visited him "to seek his advice and views about the coming Council." Already the question of succession forced its resolution on The Alliance.

During this period, Simpson struggled with the old enemy of his earliest days of spiritual quest. *All for Jesus* describes the long battle that Simpson had with depression:

For many crises of his life he had known the loneliness of a leader, but not this time. One by one, his friends would "drop by" or even come openly to converse with him along quiet paths or on the porch swing. They knelt with him in prayer at the close of day, gently urged him to sleep when the hour grew late, and kept a prayerful vigil throughout the menacing night hours that mocked his faith.

One or two of his friends, especially burdened to pray for his deliverance, knelt with him in the library. Alternating storming the ramparts of heaven and assailing the powers of darkness in Jesus' name, they petitioned God for his recovery.

Before they rose from their knees, their beloved friend said, "Boys, I do not seem to be able to take quite all that you have asked. You seem to have outstripped me—but Jesus is so real." From that day forward, his biographer observed, no one ever heard Dr. Simpson speak again of the Enemy he had fought for so many years.[32]

As the light of Christ's presence came back into his life, Simpson attended Easter Sunday service at the Missionary Training Institute, to the surprise and delight of the students. There he led in prayer where it seemed that "the very gates of heaven were ajar as he led us in prayer, talking with God face to face. His ardent thanks for prayer on his behalf made such intercession seem a wonderful privilege."[33] Later that year, he participated in the opening of the fall semester of MTI, when he preached and later led some of the faculty members in prayer "to press the battle against student infestation" from the great influenza epidemic of 1918. A. B. and Margaret attended the Old Orchard Convention, and a few weeks later, the Nyack Convention, where he "brought a special message in great power and blessing."[34] At year's end, Simpson wrote his last Christmas message for *The Alliance Weekly*.

The following year, 1919, Simpson spent most of the year at his Nyack home, only spending a few weeks at Alliance Headquarters while it was remodeled by Levi Keller Brubaker and his wife. The Brubakers, former farmers from Lititz, Pennsylvania, and graduates of the last class of MTI, were devoted aides of the Simpson family. Brubaker was the business manager of the Nyack MTI campus. Simpson missed attending the 1919 Annual Council at Toccoa Falls, Georgia. That spring and summer he remained in Nyack with Margaret, and Brubaker was always nearby as a watchful attendant to Simpson's every need.

Margaret Simpson had been raised to the manor-born, served by domestic help from her birth till she married. Even though she was a pastor's wife, she didn't always have domestic help for her and her brood of children. After their move to Nyack, two African-American women served in the Simpson home. Katherine Brennen mentions "Augusta, who served us, dusky of face but greatly loved by us all . . ."[35] Near the end of Simpson's life, one of his helpers spoke of a small building near the Simpson home on the hillside. "Asked where he went to get away from people and talk with God, this was the place, A. B. S. said. Anne was [a] black lady in [the] A. B. S. home, cook and helper."[36] Likely both ladies, part of the family, had moved to Nyack from New York in 1896. Their godly service and quiet presence were a blessing to the aging couple.

By the end of the summer of 1919, Howard, the youngest of the family, returned home from two years of military service in France. He spent several months with the Simpsons in their Nyack home. As summer eased into fall, Simpson missed the Old Orchard Convention for

Bert and Maggie, circa 1918

the first time since 1885. A. E. Thompson, in *The Life of A. B. Simpson*, describes his last day:

> On Tuesday, October 28, [Simpson] spent the morning on his veranda and received a visit from Judge Clark, of Jamaica, conversing freely, and praying fervently for Rev. and Mrs. George H. A. McClare, our Alliance missionaries in Jamaica, and for the missionaries in other fields, who were always in his mind. After the judge left him, he suddenly lost consciousness and was carried to his room. His daughter, Margaret, and a little group of friends watched by his bedside with Mrs. Simpson till his great spirit took leave of his worn-out body and returned to God who gave it, early on Wednesday morning, October 29, 1919.[37]

On the Sunday following Simpson's death, Judge Clarke spoke at the chapel service of MTI:

> "How our hearts were thrilled as we listened to Judge Clark of Jamaica tell how, about an hour before he was stricken, Dr. Simpson poured out his heart to God for the missionaries of that island, Mr. and Mrs. McClure."[38]

So, at the age of 76 years, Albert Benjamin Simpson slipped into unconsciousness and awoke in the presence of Jesus Christ, Himself. His companion and attendant, Levi Brubaker, was with him, as were the "Margarets," mother and daughter. Brubaker, assisted by another Simpson admirer, George Ferry of Ohio, prepared Simpson's body for burial.

The Simpson family had decided to bury Simpson at the family burial ground in Canada but agreed with the Board's request that his final burial place should be at the Missionary Training Institute. Begun back in 1882, it was one of Simpson's most lasting legacies. Consequently, after a funeral service in Nyack and another at the New York Gospel Tabernacle, his coffin was laid to rest temporarily at the Woodlawn Cemetery in New York. The next year, Simpson's coffin was buried in the concrete vault built on the site of what had been the outdoor Nyack Tabernacle built in 1897, now next to Pardington Hall, where wife Margaret's remains later were also placed.

Almost immediately, it was decided to have a biography written, *The Life of A. B. Simpson,* penned by Alliance missionary to the Holy Lands, Rev. A. E. Thompson. He, a Canadian like Simpson, was an able writer who had the full cooperation of the Simpson family and the Alliance leadership. By the end of 1920, a handsome bound volume with Simpson's signature embossed in gold on the cover, was published by Christian Publications but printed by the Revell Publishing Company.

> So, at the age of 76 years, Albert Benjamin Simpson slipped into unconsciousness and awoke in the presence of Jesus Christ, Himself.

A run of 5,000 copies was printed and sold for $2.50 each. Mrs. Simpson was paid 10 percent royalties of the sales. A great man of God who lived in Christ and Christ in him, A. B. Simpson left a legacy that has produced the fruit of a life of prodigious labor and service to His master that continues today the world over.

Simpson's funeral procession at Missionary Training Institute, Nyack, New York

He learned to still his heart and tune into the quiet voice of the One living within.

CHAPTER 12
THE MEASURE OF THE MAN

World War I, optimistically termed "The war to end all wars," was the first modern global conflict, ending on November 11, 1918, with Germany signing the Armistice agreement. The following year, the Treaty of Versailles was signed by the major powers involved in the war, imposing severe war reparation debts on Germany, which sowed seeds of bitterness that eventually birthed the National Socialist Party, led by Adolf Hitler, and the inevitable "second round," World War II. In this year of international debt settling, a new global reality emerged—and A. B. Simpson died. The reality of Simpson's passing caused the Alliance family to take stock of the great man's legacy, looking back from where he started and looking ahead to where God was taking them.

Dating back to the years of the Tabernacle wanderings, Simpson demonstrated what close colleague and noted Simpson biographer Rev. Kenneth Mackenzie called "a life of naked faith." Seemingly destroying a promising career in a settled pastorate, he stepped off the cliff into the arms of His Lord. "Renouncing a Christian fellowship where he enjoyed affection and confidence, a stated salary of $5,000, which few men enjoyed, and having a large family depending upon him, even his most intimate friends were staggered and predicated a calamitous ending to this incomprehensible action."[1]

Coupled with Simpson's faith was his "innate modesty." Mackenzie tells the story of Simpson's "doctorate," the DD behind his name:

Recognizing his scholastic attainments, his worldwide leadership, and sterling character, a certain seat of learning conferred upon him the honorary degree of Doctor of Divinity. After due thought, and no doubt much prayer, Simpson returned the parchment and the doctor's hood, with an appreciative expression of his recognition of the kindness. His letter of explanation made clear to the faculty and trustees that his only plea, that of the restraint he felt in being in any measure exalted above the lowliest of his brethren; and as well, lest in accepting this distinction, he might fail of the Lord's benediction, and his work lose the divine approval.²

Whichever "certain seat of learning" offered and then received back the proffered degree is still a mystery. Despite his nonacceptance, most of his followers and friends "conferred" the degree on him and proudly called him Dr. Simpson out of respect and recognition of his role as a pioneer and leader.

Although Simpson was not "to the manor-born," his Canadian upbringing and excellent education made him genteel and gentle in manner. At a special event held on the Nyack campus, dinner was being served to Simpson and his guests. The nervous student waiter, attempting to pour a cup of coffee, managed to slosh it down the front of Simpson's snow-white dress shirt. The mortified student apologized as Simpson mopped off the boiling brew. After a few moments, he calmed the flustered student. At the end of the meal, he left a dollar tip for the young man. Such was his grace under fire, even when burning and black.

NEW DOCTRINE

As Simpson's notoriety spread, so did the "new doctrine" that he championed as expressed in the unusual term, "Fourfold Gospel." Simpson first introduced the novel doctrinal catchphrase in the September 1, 1886, issue of *The Word, The Work and The World*, on which he wrote, "There is the gospel of salvation, the gospel of indwelling Christ, the gospel of the risen Christ, and the gospel of the coming and reigning Christ." The "healing fold" was missing. However, the next time the term appeared in the March 1, 1887 magazine issue, some scorn arose regarding healing in the Atonement.

Some found fault with much of the "new-fangled" Fourfold Gospel. Few had a problem with the first "fold," the truth of Christ as the only and all-sufficient Savior, freely received by faith as a grace gift from God. The second "fold," Christ our Sanctifier, was and is deeper and more difficult to comprehend. As Simpson taught it, sanctification meant separation, not only alone from sin and the "things of this world" but also

> As Simpson's notoriety spread, so did the "new doctrine" that he championed as expressed in the unusual term, "Fourfold Gospel."

separation unto God Himself, just as clearly as marriage brings a man and woman together into an enduring bond and separates them from all others. "Christ in Me" meant just that: by the Holy Spirit, Jesus is present and lives in the heart of the redeemed. All who are totally yielded and full of His Spirit may live holy, victorious lives. This presentation of truth regarding sanctification as "habitation" differed from Wesleyan "annihilation" and Keswickian "suppression," but it was not so outrageous as to cause outright rejection by those who disagreed.[3]

THE "HEALING FOLD"

The most "scandalous charge" against Simpson by former clergy friends was his strong belief in "Divine Healing," i.e., that physical healing was included in Christ's atoning work. At that time, such teaching, labeled "Faith Cure," was looked upon with disdain by most respectable, educated clergy. Nevertheless, Simpson knew that God had miraculously healed him in the summer of 1881, and that settled it. Thus, he firmly proclaimed that God's power was sufficient to minister to every arc of the circumference of the faithful believer's need. In a sermon preached following his 1893 trip to the Middle East and Orient, Simpson clearly declared: "God has given to us, in the living and indwelling Christ, a secret of power which He wants us to test and prove in everything that comes within its range, and the more fully we can penetrate and pervade the whole circumference of our life with God and His All-Sufficient grace and power, the greater glory will redound to our victorious Christ."[4]

Despite the attacks on his reputation and teaching on healing, Simpson maintained his position and did not back down, even when attacked by erstwhile friends. It seems clear that the criticism leveled at

Simpson for his conviction regarding healing and the use of medicine came from the early days of the Gospel Tabernacle's missionary initiatives and the lessons learned from those painful experiences. In reality, Simpson's settled teaching was similar to the maxim taught by fellow healing advocate Rev. Rees Howells: "man's extremity is God's opportunity."[5] Where medical resources are available, part of God's "common grace," the believer is free to use them, trusting in the guidance of the Holy Spirit. When those resources ultimately face incurable infirmities, God's healing touch is available to those who believe and receive by faith.

BRING BACK THE KING

The last "fold" for which Simpson longed and lived for emphasized Jesus Christ, the Coming King. He early understood and taught Matthew 24:14 as the linchpin of his eschatology and missiology. We do missions, he taught, to "bring back the King." Back in the day, Alliance folk sang their theology. Tozer said it well: "As long as the church can sing her great hymns, she cannot be defeated; for hymns are theology set to music."[6] As his hymn "Missionary Cry" affirms in the fourth verse:

> *The Master's coming draweth near;*
> *The Son of Man will soon appear;*
> *His Kingdom is at hand.*
>
> *But ere that glorious day can be,*
> *The gospel of the kingdom we*
> *Must preach in every land,*
> *Must preach in every land.*

Departing from his postmillennial position learned at Knox College, Simpson became an ardent adherent of the premillennial doctrine of the visible, personal return of the Lord Jesus Christ to earth to reign for 1,000 years. Simpson never believed that the Church would Christianize the world and, according to Mackenzie, he saw the Tribulation as occurring before the judgment.[7] Over the years, Simpson's conviction of the premillennial Second Coming of Christ deepened while the details of the Rapture, Tribulation, and Parousia demonstrated an admirable Simpson trait of being able to rethink his theology and change.

Enthralled at the capture of Jerusalem by General Allenby in late 1917, Simpson preached one of his most powerful sermons, "The Fall of Jerusalem in Light of Prophecy," given as the fulfillment of biblical prophecies relating to Christ's return. The surge of emotion that accompanied this long-awaited moment precipitated his first stroke in early 1918. This was the first of the body blows that, over the next two years, gradually incapacitated the tireless leader. As to the timing of Christ's return, Mackenzie shared a surprising recollection in his *Alliance Weekly* series: "He [Simpson], once and only once, ventured the opinion that the Lord might come about 1930; but he was ever guarded in any opinionated stand as to the time and conditions."[8]

THE WHOLE GOSPEL FOR THE WHOLE WORLD

Mackenzie dedicated one chapter of the *Alliance Weekly* series on "My Memories of Dr. Simpson" to point out the great heart of the founder of the C&MA who preached the whole gospel for the whole man. And that good-news message for the whole person meant that there was a practical side, a recognition of human suffering and the need for

> "The glory of Dr. Simpson's conventions lay in his largeness of heart."

its relief. Either under his administration or with his blessing and encouragement, a cornucopia of ministries issued forth from the Gospel Tabernacle: rescue missions, orphanages, homes for "fallen women," trade schools, healing homes, Bible and missionary conventions, summer camp meetings, Bible institutes, and more. As Mackenzie observed: "The glory of Dr. Simpson's conventions lay in his largeness of heart."[9]

In time, as the scope of The Alliance's worldwide work grew with burgeoning financial obligations, coupled with the gradual proclamation of the "social gospel" by the increasingly liberal mainline Protestant denominations, Simpson's enthusiasm tempered. He raised warning flags regarding the danger of a man-centered gospel that sought to meet society's temporal needs while ignoring the transformational dimension of "Christ-in-me" that heals people's hearts and enables them to live as whole members of their families and communities.

Mackenzie recalled that "[Simpson] lived with his Lord and the enrichment of spirit which that fellowship ensured."[10] And he enumerated various facets of this deep relationship.

FLAWED HUMANITY

When recounting the life story of the founder of The Christian and Missionary Alliance, one of the leading evangelicals of the late 1800s and early 1900s, equal in stature with D. L. Moody, A. J. Gordon, and A. T. Pierson among others, one needs to tread carefully. To write a hagiography of Simpson would not be honest and would detract from a fully developed picture of the man. To appraise only his obvious strengths without recognizing his shortcomings would be unworthy of his memory. Such an exercise, while not comfortable for his spiritual offspring, better honors and explains the worldwide legacy that continues to grow a century after his death.

Looking at Simpson's family life, one can observe an area of weakness in the home. For years, he apparently did not include Margaret in major decisions that affected the family. When he decided to leave Louisville for New York, and just three years later, to resign from 13th Street Presbyterian, he made these moves despite Margaret's opposition. When she found out what her husband was planning and reacted against them, the decision had already been made; the die was cast and cold. Since Simpson felt he was following God's leading, often only a next step, he wasn't able to share what he was thinking or hearing from God. If he had managed to share his growing burden for the lost and where it was leading them, possibly there might have been less anger and pain in their home.

North American society during the late 1800s and early 1900s witnessed the emergence of the women's suffrage movement, the Women's Christian Temperance Union, and other feminist organizations, which risked questioning the traditional role of women to bear the children, care for the home, and not dare to challenge her husband's decision. Bert and Maggie reflected this growing struggle for the woman's voice to be heard.

Once Simpson threw himself into reaching the "neglected masses," an almost inevitable imbalance between ministry and family emerged. He led nightly evangelistic meetings for weeks, arriving home late at night. This practice started in Louisville during the extended Whittle-Bliss campaign and went on until the family moved to New York. Arriving at 13th Street Presbyterian, he held nightly evangelistic services for several weeks. After founding the Gospel Tabernacle, he again embarked on multi-week campaigns. Eventually, Margaret joined him at the evangelistic services. Because of this "work" focus and frequent absence from the home, the older sons, Albert Henry and James Gordon, discovered the lure of alcohol, gambling, and other temptations that crippled their Christian walk and led to their early graves. Youngest son Howard also struggled with alcohol throughout most of his life before returning to the Lord. Like others who have sensed God's call and passion for the lost, the drive to follow the call can result in failure to pastor the family, the minister's first responsibility as head of his home.

Another area that clearly was not Simpson's forte—and a challenge for his wife—was money. A. E. Thompson wrote that he could have been highly successful if he had dedicated himself to his business af-

> **To appraise only his obvious strengths without recognizing his shortcomings would be unworthy of his memory.**

fairs. However, his many enterprises (the Alliance Press, the Christian Alliance Publishing Company, the Nyack Highlands Development Company, as well the 8th Avenue Christian bookstore, and a restaurant-dairy), had one thing in common—red ink. In the early years of the Gospel Tabernacle, Simpson had mixed success on real estate ventures, losing thousands on one occasion and making a substantial profit on another purchase and resale. It was his decision to live a life of "naked faith" that posed such a great challenge for his wife, who was accustomed to her husband receiving an ample, steady monthly salary as a Presbyterian pastor.

Simpson later admitted that not accepting a salary from the Gospel Tabernacle or The Alliance was a good school of faith for him. However, it set a bad precedent for the Tabernacle that he pastored and led the growing Alliance movement. His commercial ventures provided the Simpson family income from 1882 on. In 1912, the C&MA began to lighten some of the financial burden, taking over his publishing company, clearing up his debt, and putting his interests in the black. Eventually in 1918, the Board took complete control of all his business ventures, freeing him from the weight of his financial affairs, with friends settling the outstanding obligations. For the first time in more than 35 years, A. B. and Margaret Simpson were given a modest monthly allowance by The Alliance.

HASTY LAYING ON OF HANDS

Another shortcoming in Simpson's administrative practice came from what Mackenzie called his "boundless enthusiasm." It sometimes resulted in an overly optimistic assessment of newcomers, giving responsibility before being assured of their abilities. An early example of this tendency manifested itself in John Condit, appointed leader of the 1884 Congo Band by Simpson, after knowing him in the first class of the missionary training school.

Another example of a questionable choice of a field leader occurred when Simpson met Emílio Olsson in 1887. In less than three years after first meeting Simpson, Olsson was dismissed from the mission because of poor leadership and financial malfeasance.

> **It must be recognized that Simpson, an intelligent, faith-filled man, was not afraid of risk.**

In his defense, it must be recognized that Simpson, an intelligent, faith-filled man, was not afraid of risk. He possessed clear vision for what God wanted him to do. When The Alliance began, there were no veterans and no proven leaders to head the missions that quickly opened overseas. Most choices for field leadership proved to be very capable. William Christie of Tibet, R. A. Jaffray of China and Vietnam, and many others were godly, proficient field chairmen who grew into their roles. The same held true for those who became district superintendents in the homeland. Not all worked out, but the majority had time to show their potential before he "anointed" them for a leadership role. Those early examples of "hasty laying on of hands" were soon forgotten as the constant stream of graduates from the Missionary Training Institute went out to serve and eventually provided a strong and experienced leadership pool.

A TROUBLED MYSTIC?

One last concern proved to be an aspect of Simpson's long life that brought him under the unfriendly fire. One detractor described him as suffering "from severe bouts of emotional depression, psychosis and psychosomatic illness. Out of his difficulties, he created a distinctive theology, eventually left the Presbyterian Church and founded his own sect, The Christian and Missionary Alliance . . . ."[11]

While intending to present an honest, fully developed "picture" of a man admired by evangelicals worldwide and revered by the Alliance global family, one should question such a caustic critique considering the long-lasting fruit of his life. Considering that dealing with the story of a man whose death occurred a century ago, when terminology describing psychological states and mental health was far from precise or uniform, it would be presumptuous to try to "clinically diagnose" A. B. Simpson today. What can be ascertained from the record is that Simpson, before his healing in 1881, was a very gifted man of high emotional intelligence, acutely sensitive and deeply spiritual. Consequently, when subject to severe pressure, due to his meager physical resources and sensitive soul, he experienced occasional physical and emotional breakdowns for the first half of his life.

Was Simpson a an emotionally unstable person who founded his own cult? Or was he a passionate, intelligent, and keenly sensitive man whose emotions ran strong? The latter is the truth: Albert Benjamin Simpson was a man of God who felt deeply and reacted holistically—his entire being responding in times of stress and joy. From his early years, he had always been "sickly" and in "delicate health" and continued to be so until age 37. But under the stress of excessive workloads, battles

Albert Benjamin Simpson was a man of God who felt deeply and reacted holistically—his entire being responding in times of stress and joy.

with church leaders unwilling to follow his vision, and the strain of dealing with an unhappy wife, Simpson would collapse like an overloaded wagon with a broken axle. Then he would have to stop and rest to restore his health before taking up his load again. When he was unmistakably healed, everything changed.

Once he learned the secret of "Christ in Me" as not only the eventual hope of glory but also a day by day inpouring of health and help for his daily walk, the dark valleys of depression were filled with the presence of the Abiding Lord. He learned to still his heart and tune into the quiet voice of the One living within. Simpson found relief as he learned to abide in Christ as Christ abided in him.

To sum up the measure of a man, one must step back and look at the body of work produced by God through his life. It's like looking at a very large mural painted over time, or the final exposure of a panoramic photograph. The obvious is seen easily. Yet as one lingers over the total picture, a fuller appreciation of the complete portrait appears, as is the case when considering the whole of Simpson's life and the many facets of the man's ministry.

POET PREACHER

A. B. Simpson was one of the most notable preachers of his era. A. E. Thompson tells how, during his first Christmas holiday after entering seminary, the 17-year old Simpson, not long off the farm, preached in his "family church" in Tilbury, near his home in Chatham. He had spent days preaching to the squirrels and rabbits in the woods on the farm, committing his message to memory.

> *The greatest trials of all these days was my preaching for the first time in the church in which I had been brought up and in the presence of my father and my mother. In some way the Lord helped me to get through, but I never once dared to meet their eyes. In those days, preaching was an awful business, for we knew nothing of trusting the Lord for utterance. The manuscript was written in full and the preacher committed it to memory and recited it verbatim.*[12]

His greatest fear was that by failing to recall one word, he might forget the whole sermon, and be forced to start over again. Or worse yet, he might end up like one of his contemporaries who got stuck vainly trying "to recall his sentences and murmuring over and over again, 'My brethren, my brethren,' finally [he] stuck his fingers in his hair and tearing, like one half mad, fled from the pulpit in the church and was never seen in those parts again."[13]

It soon became apparent at Knox Church in Hamilton that their young pastor was an exceptional preacher, and that reputation grew as he gained experience and maturity. His invitation to pastor both at Louisville and New York City came about largely because of his growing reputation as a gifted preacher. By the time he stood behind the 13th Street Presbyterian pulpit, he no longer had to write out his sermons. His remarkable memory and full "sermon barrel" enabled him to carry on the extensive visitation and missions magazine writing load, while still packing the church out on Sundays. Eventually, he was considered a master pulpiteer among his peers. D. L. Moody once told Dr. A. E. Pierson, "Pierson, I have just been down to hear A. B. Simpson preach. No one gets at my heart like that man." No less a great preacher, Paul Rader, future Alliance president and outstanding evangelist, remembered: "He was the greatest heart preacher I ever listened to. He preached out of his own rich dealings with God. The Word was ever new and fresh in his own experience and messages."[14]

Mackenzie judged Simpson to be secure in his beliefs, writing simply and directly, in the style of his time. His preaching, equally, was straightforward and to the heart. "His sermons rang with the appeal of deity," added Mackenzie. "They were not worked up by a studious

> "Preaching was melodious and musical when it fell from his lips; it was full, resonant, and triumphant. He was a poet preacher."

plan to capture the admiration of the people. I have often come across his notes, left lying where he had forgotten to pick them up. Simple outlines, a track upon which to run his train of thought. The rest he left with his Lord."[15]

From his first time in the pulpit and throughout his preaching career, he had an exceptional pulpit manner. Dr. W. Leon Tucker paid Dr. Simpson this tribute: "Preaching was melodious and musical when it fell from his lips; it was full, resonant and triumphant. The very sway of his body was poetic and passionate. He was a poet preacher."[16]

SERVANT MENTOR

Simpson's desire to see the MTI graduates and many lay preachers serving local Alliance branches and becoming effective preachers led him to begin a "Preacher's Column" in the Alliance magazine. Practical tips on sermon preparation and preaching gave those called but not trained helpful suggestions for their pulpit responsibilities. This kind of desire to help other preachers even extended to his closest colleagues.

Rev. W. T. MacArthur, who a short time before had spent two or three days with Simpson, returned unheralded. Dr. Simpson met him at the door and said:

> *"Well, Mac, you have come to pray for me again?"*
>
> *"No, Brother Simpson, I have come to ask you to pray for me."*
>
> *"That is a very gracious way of putting it,"* he replied.
>
> *"Not at all; it is the truth. I have carried my old sermon barrel till I am sick of it. I must have a fresh anointing."*
>
> *"Oh, then, if that is so,"* said Dr. Simpson, *"we will go right into my study."*

That night a series of messages was born in the preacher's soul and those who heard him that summer [of 1918] knew that fresh oil had been poured upon him.[17]

PROLIFIC WRITER

Because of Simpson's prowess as an unusually clear and compelling speaker, his secretary, Emma Beere, or his 16-year-old daughter, Margaret, would record his sermons in shorthand and type them for Simpson to review and edit—thus producing final drafts for the output of books he authored, covering missions, divine healing, the sanctified or deeper life, prayer, the Second Coming of Christ, the "Christ in the Bible" series, and many more. Of Simpson's 101 titles printed, 67 were transcribed sermons.[18]

In addition, Simpson wrote dozens of pamphlets and gospel tracts for use in local Alliance branches. He wrote poems and hymns, produced several hymnals, and taught The Alliance to sing their Fourfold theology. His publishing ventures produced hundreds of books, tens of thousands of pages, and a torrent of publications poured out from his printing business for more than 30 years—the major source of Simpson's personal income. He also had a well-stocked Christian bookstore located at 692 8th Avenue, conveniently located for Tabernacle members. Because of this extensive literature ministry, his name and The Christian and Missionary Alliance became well-known throughout the evangelical world.

TRAIL-BLAZING EDUCATOR

Simpson was involved in education for most of his life. During his first pastorate in Hamilton, Ontario, he served on the local Presbytery's Committee for the Examination of Students, for seminary graduates who sought licensure or ordination. His reputation while at Knox and outstanding scholastic record made him a natural choice. For the next several years, he proved himself a strong supporter of Knox College and worked hard to support the school's administration and faculty. In 1872, he was appointed to the college's board of managers, concerned with the physical and fiscal operations of the college, as well as hiring teachers and making curriculum changes.

While pastoring in Louisville, Kentucky, Simpson became active in the Louisville Synod of the Presbyterian Church. In 1874, he was "appointed a trustee of Center College, the denomination's liberal arts college in Kentucky. He was also appointed, with one other colleague, to act as a consultant to review and report upon the operations of Danville Theological Seminary."[19] When he later focused on the need to evangelize "the neglected masses" near and abroad, he became impatient with the laboriously slow pace of preparation that produced graduates overqualified to reach the majority of the unreached around the world. He questioned the effectiveness of an education process for ministry candidates with little spiritual vitality and even less experience in gospel ministry that prepared them for the real world.

Simpson envisioned an "army of godly men and women, the consecrated layman, the earnest business man, the humble farmer boy, the Spirit-filled maiden whom the Master has called and fitted to follow in the footsteps of the lowly fishermen of Galilee and create a new battalion in the army of the Lord, the volunteers and irregulars of whom we have no cause to be ashamed, and who but for this movement might never accomplish their glorious work."[20] He compared them to the famed volunteer "Rough Riders" of the Spanish-American War of 1898:

> . . . they are the brave volunteers and Irregulars in the army of Christ and of missions, and they go forth to regions where others have not ventured and fields where others have not scattered the precious seed. If there is a hard place, if there is a lonely spot, if there is a neglected soul, that is the place that is the work for which these brave hearts are first to volunteer.[21]

By the time Simpson had spent a few years at 13th Street Presbyterian Church in New York and had observed the major denominational mission agencies and their practices, he became convinced that doing the same thing the same way would produce the same mediocre results. Simpson was ready to try something new, never before done on the North American continent. He asked:

> "Is there not room for a missionary training college in every great Church in this land? . . . [To] study the history of missions, the methods of mission work, and the languages in which they expect to preach the Gospel to the heathen? . . . [To include a] college and school of technology, the printing press and medical mission, as well as the preaching, of the evangelist and the teaching of the pastor . . . A good Missionary Training College would prevent many a subsequent mistake; it would save future years of preparation, and it would cherish into mature and abiding impulses many a transient dream of missionary enthusiasm. Mr. Guinness superintends two such institutions in England . . ."[22]

Simpson's personal experience and observations of contemporary theological institutions led him to believe that a missionary training school of shorter duration, more focused and practical, would produce an army ready to fill in those vast blank regions on the missions map where few or no missionaries were present. In the January 1, 1882, issue of *The Word, The Work and The World*, Simpson wrote about such training. Missionary schools are mentioned, including three European schools in Berlin, Germany, Upsala, Sweden, and the "one in London under the charge of Mr. [Henry Grattan Guinness], from which most of the laborers of the Inland missions have gone forth."[23]

In the February issue, he included a two-page article about the East London Training Institute for Home and Foreign Missionaries, describing the school's philosophy, aim, and methods. In closing, it reads:

> It is one of the most serviceable and successful [Institutes]. It has been in existence only a little more than eight years, but during that time more than a thousand candidates have applied for admission, and about two hundred and fifty have been received, and of these about one hundred are at present laboring in the gospel.[24]

The result of these observations led to his beginning classes for a Missionary Training College in 1882. Even before it had a permanent home, it was the first Bible school in North America and a pioneer educational institution for the training of missionaries. The aims, methodology, and educational philosophy were similar to the East London Institute, which provided a successful workable model. The result was the rapid growth of the school in New York City, which soon had to move to Nyack for space to grow. It produced thousands who were sent around the world—thus speaking for the success of this venture.

SOCIAL ISSUES ADVOCATE

Simpson was a passionate evangelist who loved people of all classes and color. He believed that the "Whole Gospel for the Whole World" included good news for the "whole man," body, soul, spirit, as well as social concerns for people everywhere. The early years of the Gospel Tabernacle and the subsequent beginning of The Alliance saw Simpson

> **Simpson was a passionate evangelist who loved people of all classes and color.**

lead a movement of men and women deeply committed to reaching the "Samaritans" of Acts 1:8, which he understood as the "outcasts" of the city. George Reitz, in "A. B. Simpson, Urban Evangelist" states: "Simpson went on to identify these outcast thieves as the drunkard, harlot, thief, convict, foreign population, and the multitude 'struggling in the dark underworld of poverty.'"[25]

Like Moody and other popular evangelists of the day burdened with a concern for social outcasts, "Simpson was primarily concerned with the condition of people's souls. His great focus was with the spiritual, but he did not let his focus on the spiritual aspect blind him to the physical needs of those to whom he was ministering. This was essential to the perspective of all the evangelicals who worked among the poor and needy in the urban centers."[26]

Donald Dayton wrote in *Discovering an Evangelical Heritage*, "Out of Simpson's work grew The Christian and Missionary Alliance, a movement that originally understood itself to have a special call to serve the 'neglected masses' both at home and abroad."[27]

John Dahms added, "Due to the influence of the Alliance and its leadership, the ministry in 'hospitals, almshouses, and charitable institutions' in New York City was so considerable by 1894, that it was said that even A. B. Simpson would have been at a loss to tell 'how much the Alliance was doing for all [such] agencies of Christian work in that city.'"[28]

FORGOTTEN MAN

Despite such significant contributions to modern evangelism and the cause of Christ, A. B. Simpson has been largely forgotten by the greater evangelical world. It would seem that even in The Alliance, he has become a distant, bearded figure in a framed picture in the pastor's office. By far, A. W. Tozer has a much higher name recognition for the vast majority of C&MA members today. Tozer's books and recorded sermons still "sell," while no recordings of Simpson's preaching exist, since the recording industry was still in its infancy at the time of his death. Most Alliance church members have probably read little or nothing from his vast literary production. Yet the fact remains that Simpson "built his ministry upon both evangelistic outreach in the urban setting of the United States as well as an international mission emphasis. He was one of the leaders in the holiness movement and the related healing movement. He was well known at the time in evangelical circles and played an important role in the Third Great Awakening."[29]

But Simpson wasn't just a historical figure whose contributions and influence affected the events of a time gone by. His spiritual posture is worthy of emulation today. Simpson was a man of God, simple and direct in appealing to others to know that same Lord. He knew God and reverently revealed Him both to audiences and readers. He was a man of prayer who often spent hours at night in conversation with his Master. At camps and conventions, he could be heard praying in his room at all hours of the night softly saying, "Yes, Lord; yes, Lord; yes, Lord." As a man who lived by "naked faith," he lived in expectancy for the "things hoped for" and expected to see the "evidence of the unseen" soon become reality.[30]

In knowing God, Simpson also knew people. Often, he had to walk alone and be guarded in the use of his time and attention since he was constantly sought after. The scene at his Tabernacle funeral service illustrated the magnitude of his influence on people. As Mackenzie recalled, "All about me were men who as young fellows had come under the spell of his own dedication; and now, mature and dynamic in their ministry, formed a great company of well-trained and responsible servants of God. It was a sight never to be forgotten."[31] Simpson's legacy included the hundreds of men and women already spanning the globe with the gospel of Christ—a legacy that continues today.

A. B. Simpson was an organizer, innovator, risk taker, missions mobilizer, and founder of a worldwide missionary movement. He synthesized and popularized the Fourfold Gospel. He was an accepted peer of the giants of the late 19th and early 20th century, such as D. L. Moody, A. J. Gordon, A. T. Pierson, R. A. Torrey, C. I. Scofield, F. B. Meyer, Andrew Murray, and others—and with them played a major role in the Third Great Awakening. Pentecostal and charismatic churches the world over trace their theological roots to Simpson's teaching on divine

> **Simpson's legacy included the hundreds of men and women already spanning the globe with the gospel of Christ—a legacy that continues today.**

healing and prayer for the sick, the post-salvation experience of Spirit baptism and infilling, and the validity of the operation of the gifts of the Holy Spirit in this present church age.

To understand A. B. Simpson is to understand The Alliance. To know and appreciate Simpson the man is to embrace his flawed humanity as well as his spiritual genius. His message and mission in life was to lift up "Jesus Only," inspiring a vision and movement to reach the "neglected masses" that is as clear today as it was in 1881. The fact is that all The Alliance's work today, as a Christ-centered, Acts 1:8 family, reaching the unreached around the world with the hope and saving power of the gospel, is owed to God's guiding hand through A. B. Simpson's life and legacy. Because of Simpson's faithfulness and submission to his Lord, thousands of people—from the largest cities to the most remote villages and hardest places—have heard the gospel and received eternal life through Jesus Christ.

There could be no greater tribute to this mighty man of God, his life, and his work than for those living out his legacy within The Alliance today to fix their eyes on Jesus and continue to go, with Simpsonian determination and confidence of the Lord's full provision, to the ends of the earth until all have heard the good news of their salvation in Him.

Young Mrs. Simpson

APPENDIX 1

MARGARET SIMPSON—A MOTHER IN ISRAEL

*O*N THAT FATEFUL DAY when second-year seminary student, Bert Simpson, knocked on the door of John Henry, the prosperous Presbyterian layman in Toronto, he had no idea that he would meet his future bride. Bert and his older brother, Howard, were looking for a place to board while studying for the ministry at Knox College. When the Simpson boys set their eyes on the vivacious daughter of the home, Cupid's arrows were loosed and hit the hearts of both brothers. Howard was older and more serious, but there was something about the younger brother that caught Margaret's eyes. Not that she let the gawky country boy get too sure of himself; she let him pursue her for almost three years before they formally became engaged—one month before they married in September 1865.

LIKES REPEL AND OPPOSITES ATTRACT

It is doubtful that either Bert or Margaret could have specifically said what drew them together, since their backgrounds and personalities were unalike socially and financially, but God brought together a couple that man may have counseled differently. She was high born and high strung, two years five months older than "Bertie," the name that she gave him that might have driven away a young man less sure of himself.

Their long years of marriage and ministry saw them grow and mature, but not necessarily at the same pace. As Bert grew in spiritual stature, God expanded and broadened his vision as to what God was asking of him. Margaret did not follow her husband's lead easily, since he often seemed unable to share much of what God was saying until after an important decision had already been made. Their time in Hamilton, where Simpson pastored the Knox Presbyterian Church, was pleasant, and Margaret spent most of her time having and caring for four babies. The move from Canada to Kentucky pleased Maggie, since it meant a warmer clime, a significant pay increase, and opportunity to raise her children with more freedom. She loved the years in Kentucky and enjoyed the gracious community of their well-to-do congregation, even though her husband's growing impasse with the church leadership caused them stress. The two-year struggle over the design of the Broadway Tabernacle made it clear that Simpson increasingly sensed a need to move on while Margaret felt a mother's need for security for her family.

After Bert's crazy "China vision" and missionary call in 1878, he was compelled by an even more outrageous leading of the Lord—a move to New York City. At this, Maggie revolted. Her anger at being asked to leave the safe city of Louisville to move to New York was beyond understanding. Enraged and fearful, she ripped the pages out of her husband's diary after reading that he sensed God moving "the cloud" from Louisville to New York. This decision to go despite her unwillingness to follow wreaked havoc in their home life.

HERS WAS FIRST A SEGREGATED LIFE

Dr. Kenneth Mackenzie, one of Simpson's closest associates during the early years of the C&MA, wrote perceptively and compassionately about Mrs. Simpson, a woman often viewed as selfish and shallow. Margaret had eventually become comfortable in the new circumstances at 13th Street Presbyterian Church, when her husband announced a new step of obedience. Mackenzie wrote about the next major battle in the Simpson home after moving to New York and settling down.

> *Do you realize that when a man starts out on a life of faith, he has much to give up and has much to expect? When this was the case with our beloved brother [A. B. Simpson], the test that came to his*

wife must have been one well-deserving of her thought. It was no easy thing for her to renounce the comforts of a settled home with a growing family to care for . . . and to submit to the exigencies which a life of faith necessarily brings. But you will appreciate that she lacked what he most naturally had had, a clear vision of the call of the Lord, the constant contacts that rewarded his venture, the enjoyment of the divine romance of trust. He was exhilarated, day by day, in beholding the fruits of his sacrifice, while she, confined to home—and it must have been a very much humbler home than she had previously enjoyed—meeting the necessities of daily life, bearing the toil and the complexities of the nurture of children, had to feed her faith upon God alone. Hers was first a segregated life.[1]

Set in the traditional social and familial setting of the late 1800s, the expectation that the wife would meekly follow her husband's leading reigned supreme, even though the earliest glimmers of the feminist movement were appearing on the horizon. Margaret wasn't a "women's libber"; she was a mother concerned about how to feed, clothe, and care for her five children when her husband had just given up a princely salary at a fashionable church to live by faith and reach the "lost." Worse yet, due to the sudden stop in their cash flow, she had to dip into her personal savings that had come from her father's estate to pay the bills when the offerings dried up. It is not surprising that such a state of affairs was galling to her, since those funds had been marked for "a rainy day," or their golden years. No doubt in her heart, she cried out, "Bertie, what about our family? Where do we go from here? What's going to happen next?"

More than a century later, one is in the uncomfortable place of looking objectively at the revered founder of a worldwide movement of God—the Christ-centered, Acts 1:8 family that seeks to be faithful to the mission and message that God gave him. Mackenzie's eulogy that he gave at Margaret's funeral proved to be the most accurate and astute of the many wise words given. "To her, the change [leaving 13th Street Presbyterian] was traumatic, like stepping out on the aching void. But after the initial plunge, her bravery and endurance grew with the years. Remember, it was he who had the clear vision and call of the Lord, not she."[2]

THAT BRAT OF A BERTIE

At one point, A. B.'s older brother, Howard Simpson, an ordained Presbyterian pastor in the Midwestern United States, came to New York when he heard of his younger brother's new-fangled doctrine and crazy resignation from the Presbyterian Church. Granddaughter Katherine Brennen describes his visit as he tried to convince Margaret to leave her faith-daring husband:

> *That brat of a Bertie—never knew his place; always bobbing up, can't keep him down—two years younger even than his own wife.*
>
> *And so, during those days of battle came Uncle Howard. Such an overwhelming gospel was bound to seem revolutionary—new—because it was so old. Inevitably there would be amazed comment. Saviour, Sanctifier, Healer—this angle could only be discussed behind closed doors, in whispers, with hands over the lips and with bated breath. Then spake the Oracle, Great Uncle Howard.[3]*

From this scene, it seems clear that the rivalry between the brothers had been on a low boil for years, at least in Howard's heart. All of his frustration at "that brat of a Bertie" came out with his brother's sudden resignation from their Presbyterian church family. Margaret, who he still held in esteem, was suffering for her husband's harebrained "heresies," but Margaret would have none of that, firmly stating, "He is my husband—with great gifts and powers given him by God." Love stands—So spake the Wife.[4]

THE WATERSHED MOMENT

Apparently, this was the watershed moment in Margaret's life, as she had to decide whether to throw her life and lot in with her soaring husband or leave him for safer ground with the children. And as Dr. Kenneth Mackenzie pointed out, once Margaret "took the plunge," she became the most loyal champion of her husband, whose vision and passion she increasingly understood and shared. One interesting note regarding her commitment to the new life to which God had called her relates to her lack of preparation for pastoral ministry. She had graduated from Toronto Model School and attended "Mrs. Brown's Finishing School" before marrying and becoming a pastor's wife. She was to be an accomplished hostess and keep an elegant home; that was the role of the pastor's wife. At that time in the Presbyterian Church in Canada, Margaret would have been considered sufficiently prepared to be a pastor's wife. Later in New York, she sensed her lack of ministerial training. Consequentially, she enrolled in the Missionary Training Institute while still in New York and later proudly referred to the fact that she was an alumnus.

She gave testimony in Simpson's periodicals to the healing power of God that she witnessed in her husband's life in 1881, as well as daughter Margaret's healing from a deadly attack of croup, Mabel's deliverance from an attack of diphtheria, and Gordon's miraculous recovery from scarlet fever. She gave testimony to the amazing care of the Lord regarding their temporal needs. At Old Orchard in 1892, she gave an address on sanctification and shared her own experience of how she was filled with the Spirit. She became a founding member of the "two Alliances" and financial secretary of the mission for many years. In addition, she was on the board of examination of missionary candidates, as well as carrying on a heavy load of correspondence with Alliance missionaries around the world.

At her funeral, she was called "a true mother of Israel," the "mother of the missionaries," a loving, maternal figure who blessed the burgeoning ministry of the Gospel Tabernacle. Following the founding of the two Alliances in 1887, she became part of the original leadership team and a member of the Board of Managers of the C&MA. She was notable for her keen sense of humor and discernment, for speaking plainly to missionary candidates of the fledging Alliance Mission. Her blunt question, "Is it the LORD you seek—or a husband?" seemed to effectively cull out those whose missionary motivation was suspect. Other Board of Managers members spoke of her insight and incisive ability to cut to the chase and get to the heart of the matter. She served on the Board till her death in 1924.

BAH, BERTIE, THAT WAS NO DOVE

Margaret's wit and ready humor livened the home conversation. She always had a way of keeping her ebullient Bertie from soaring too high. Once the aging Dr. Simpson regaled dinner guests with a long-ago experience at Old Orchard Camp. He described how the service ended with a powerful sense of the presence of God. He described how a white dove lit on his shoulder as he was praying. Into this hallowed memory came the voice of Margaret, as always in the kitchen preparing something delightful for her guests. She called out, "What was that about Old Orchard?" Simpson responded, "The dove, Maggie, remember the dove that landed on my shoulder while I prayed?" She replied, "Bah, Bertie, that was no dove, it was a pigeon!"[5] The crowd burst into unholy laughter and Simpson just smiled and shook his head.

As a mother, she endured grief, first with the death of little Melville, not yet four years old, on the same day that her beloved father passed away. Her heart was torn by the desire to be with her

> **The steel in the little woman was tempered by the fires of life.**

father and her equal need to be with her son. This first deep challenge to her growing faith threw her into God's goodness and care. Her husband's periodic breakdowns with the accompanying depressions had left her with the children while he traveled to Europe or to a health spa to recover.

The steel in the little woman was tempered by the fires of life. When her husband was miraculously healed after a lifetime of weakness and ill health, her growing faith was challenged by her husband's insistence on trusting God for their children's health. Gordon, Mabel, and Margaret were all "prayed through" major health crises by Simpson, while Margaret anguished. Her road was not easy, but she ran as hard as her short legs of faith would take her to catch up to her sprinting husband. If she never flew as high as he did, neither did she sink as low as he when battling another valley experience. She was eulogized for her youthfulness, cheerfulness, tact, and joy. One of Simpson's poems published posthumously in The Songs of the Spirit, called "My Secret," explains what made this once-flighty socialite such a woman of God:

> *Shall I tell you what it is that keeps me singing,*
> *Never minding whether it be shade or shine?*
> *'Tis because His own glad song is singing in me,*
> *'Tis because the Saviour's joy is always mine.*[6]

ABIDE IN ME

Margaret testified that the last phrase of her dying little boy, Melville, "Abide in me," began her walk into what her husband called, "the deeper life." The same "Christ-in-me" life that Bertie had been trying to explain to her, describing the abiding presence of Christ by His Spirit, became the secret of her Christian life. In an *Alliance Weekly* article, she gave this succinct summation of what happened that brought about such change in her life:

> *It seemed it [being filled with the Spirit] must be a special gift for some but not for me. There was a mistake. I kept my eyes on myself and others, forgetting to ask God to open my eyes and heart, letting me see Himself in all His love, then I could without doubt believe and obey his Word.*[7]

She became an incessant intercessor for her "dear missionaries." After her death, eight steamer trunks were found in her Nyack attic full of letters from missionaries abroad and people from all over North America. When asked how many had been answered, she replied: "All of them."[8] She was known for prayer, wise words, encouragement, and never-failing good spirits. Her keen mind outlasted her worn out body. On her last days, she was writing letters and receiving guests in her hillside home. To the end, she refused to answer any name but "Mrs. A. B. Simpson." She suffered a heart attack on January 1, 1924, died within an hour, and was buried next to her husband.

Margaret Simpson, circa 1918

One can only imagine the challenge of being a son or daughter of Rev. A. B. Simpson.

APPENDIX 2
PREACHER'S KIDS

Anyone born into a minister's family knows the weight of the cross for being a preacher's kid; the expectations placed on that child may be burdensome. The size of the parent's shadow seems to be in direct proportion to their notoriety and effectiveness. Too often the son or daughter reacts against the higher standards of conduct and accomplishments out of sheer frustration or anger. This can lead them down a path of sorrow and pain, and often to a life of sinful excess, as though subconsciously trying to discard the PK (preacher's kid) badge by their rebellion and independence.

This phenomenon of disappointing behavior can be seen in Old Testament accounts. Aaron's two sons, Nadab and Abihu, defiantly offered "strange fire" and were destroyed by God. Eli's sons, Phineas

> The size of the parent's shadow seems to be in direct proportion to their notoriety and effectiveness.

and Hophni, appeared to vie with one another in outrageous acts while serving in the tabernacle. They were destroyed and the ark captured. Even Samuel, a much more noteworthy example of a godly father in ministry, saw his sons, Joel and Abijah, corrupted in their role as judges by receiving bribes. And there is no need to look at King David's sons. Happily, the New Testament spares us the chagrin of reading about another "bad" PK.

One can only imagine the challenge of being a son or daughter of Rev. A. B. Simpson. Knowing their father first as a respectable Presbyterian minister, the oldest children had observed their father gradually morphing into an increasingly unconventional evangelist and missions champion. They lived through the shock of his eventual abandonment of their secure life in a fashionable New York pastorate and his launching out on the frail lifeboat of faith to fulfill God's calling on his life to reach the unchurched and unreached masses of lost men and women everywhere. Because of their father's miraculous healing in 1881, doctor's visits to the Simpson home ceased, and on different occasions three of the children were later at death's door while their father held on to God's promises and prayed them back to health.

Once, one of the siblings grew very sick and no amount of prayer brought about healing. Simpson later intimated that one of the other family members had sinned and hidden it. Once it was confronted and confessed, the younger child was instantly healed. Such were the challenges of the children of Albert and Margaret Simpson.

ALBERT HENRY SIMPSON

The first son, Albert Henry Simpson, born June 27, 1866, was named after his father and his mother's surname, arriving in the Simpson home nine months following his parent's marriage in Hamilton, Ontario. As a little boy, he grew up in the friendly Knox Church family under the ministry of his young but effective pastor father. What is known about their relationship indicates that Simpson loved his son, who, like his father, devoured books and study. Like his father, he was considered "cultured and scholarly." When young Albert was about eight and a half, his father accepted the call which moved him, younger brother James Gordon, and baby sister, Mabel Jane, from the cold winters of Western Ontario for the milder weather of Louisville, Kentucky.

There, he and his siblings lived in a comfortable parsonage of the Chestnut Street Presbyterian church, and their busy mother, Margaret, soon organized the Simpson household. Over the next few years in Louisville, young Bert saw his father evolve as a pastor and preacher. While probably not understanding the impact of his father's deepening relationship with God following his 1873 experience of sanctification, the growing boy could not help but see that his father had embraced a new ministry model of mass evangelistic meetings. Doubtless, he accompanied his father to some of the amazing Whittle-Bliss evangelistic meetings that shook the city of Louisville in 1875. The two evangelists were not as cultured and refined as his father, but young Bert could see that they had a power and passion for lost people that soon infected his father.

The family's move to New York City in November 1879 brought radical change. Young Bert, now 13, likely sensed the strain between his parents because of this sudden move from the cultured and calm life

> As Albert grew, he struggled between the pull of the gospel and the push of Gotham.

in Louisville to the big city that Simpson had once called the "godless Gotham" of America. Moving from Main Street Kentucky to Big Apple Broadway resulted in massive culture shock for the family. Suddenly the tree-shaded streets, the grassy playgrounds and parks, were replaced by cobbled streets of a city undergoing massive infrastructure construction, electrification, and a city administration struggling to deal with massive immigration and the consequent social problems: alcoholism, gambling, and Irish gangs that fought turf wars to control the vice industry.

As Albert grew, he struggled between the pull of the gospel and the push of Gotham. Within two years of his family's arrival in New York, he witnessed another major struggle between his parents as his father sensed God's leading to leave the 13th Street Presbyterian Church and begin a "free church" that soon would be known as the Gospel Tabernacle, where young Bert eventually became the church's first organist. Sometime after finishing high school, he began to work at his father's Alliance Publishing Company. At age 19, he traveled to England and attended the Bethshan Conference with his parents. It appears young Bert was finding his way in the big city. A few years later, he married, and eventually the couple had three children. His wife managed the Alliance Bookstore on 8th Avenue for many years.

Sadly, the strain of being the eldest of the Simpson family, the temptations of "sin city," his lack of success managing his father's printing company, as well as his own family responsibilities, got to Albert. At the age of 30, he died of tuberculosis in a sanitarium. "The cultured and scholarly young man, his body wracked and worn by overstrain and certain dissipations of youth, went Home", as described by his cousin,

Katherine Brennen. She later narrated that at his death "Simpson prayed with him. He sighed at the thought of wasted years. 'The Master knows all, forgives all, and I shall be with him.'"[1] One can only wonder at the pain his parents and wife felt at his loss and the bewilderment of the Gospel Tabernacle as they saw the son of their beloved leader taken so early in life.

MELVILLE JENNINGS SIMPSON

Melville Jennings, was born two years after Albert Henry, in June 1868. While on his four-month European tour in 1871, Simpson sent little funny messages in his letters to "Bertie, little Melville and baby

> As he was put into her arms, the baby lips had only strength to whisper, "Abide in me."

Gordon." His father dearly loved and missed them terribly. Just a few months after Simpson returned from Europe, Melville became sick with "membranous croup" and died on a cold January day in 1872. His mother had traveled to Toronto to be at her dying father's side when a telegram arrived with the words, "Melville very low." Frantic, Margaret returned home. Katherine Brennen recounts: "As he was put into her arms, the baby lips had only strength to whisper, 'Abide in me.' The baby head drooped—and he was still."[2] Margaret had been teaching her three-year-old the verse from John 15. He was buried at the Henry

Melville Jennings Simpson, age 2

family plot in Hamilton. The unexpected tragedy darkened the home, and Margaret had a serious spiritual crisis as she questioned where God was in this or if He even existed. Such was the dark night of her grief-stricken soul. For her husband, those days required his deepest devotion and pastoral care for his wife's anguished heart. Eventually, the pain eased; baby Mabel was born, Margaret's broken mother's heart slowly healed, and life went on.

JAMES GORDON SIMPSON

The third son, James Gordon, also was born in Hamilton, Ontario, on August 31, 1870. Like his brother Albert, he loved life in Louisville and enjoyed a good education and a refined home where his mother could exercise her taste and fine upbringing. At the same time, his father's concern for the lost led him to lead the churches in a united citywide campaign of mass evangelism. Likely, Gordon and brother Bert attended those exciting citywide events with their parents. Later, he and his older brother may have sensed their ambitious father's attention being drawn toward New York City. Whether or not Gordon and Bert ever witnessed their parent's heated discussions about the pros and cons of moving there, they no doubt were excited by the prospect of the move

> **Gordon had a special propensity for getting in trouble.**

when announced by their father in November of 1879. On the long train ride from Louisville to New York, they stayed with their mom and little sisters, Mabel Jane and Margaret Mae. During most of the train ride, their Dad kept to himself, immersed in prayer and thought, while Maggie did her best to keep her two energetic sons out of trouble and care for the little girls.

Despite being totally different from the Louisville home, the new home in downtown Manhattan had its "charms." Their neighborhood was populated with well-off New Yorkers, while just down the block were poor city kids and the offspring of the teeming immigrant population. Gordon had a special propensity for getting in trouble; on many occasions, he learned the dictum that a spared rod would spoil the child. So, his loving but firm father did not let the dust gather on the "rod," as he sought to keep him from the "broad way that leads to destruction."[3]

As a boy, Gordon was tender toward the gospel and gave his heart to Christ. However, like his older brother, he struggled with the enticements of the city. After his father left 13th Street Presbyterian Church and began his new faith venture, his time and attention were consumed by the newly opened Gospel Tabernacle and its multiple ministries. On most occasions, mother Margaret accompanied her husband to the nightly meetings. More likely than not, the boys escaped their home and experimented with life on the wild side. As an "ornery growing boy," Gordon tried out these newfound pleasures and developed a taste for alcohol, much to the chagrin of his teetotaler father, who was a well-known backer of the Women's Christian Temperance Union. Gambling also sank its tentacles into his young soul. His eventual misadventures and scrapes with the law and the lawless caused his father embarrassment on more than one occasion.

After finishing high school, he settled down sufficiently to study medicine for several years, but never graduated. He followed his older brother working for his father's Alliance Publishing Company and apparently had more success than Albert. He eventually managed the Alliance Press in Nyack and superintended the construction of the open-air Nyack Tabernacle in the summer of 1897. It was used for camp and conventions on the MTI campus. Later, the wooden tabernacle was razed to begin construction of Pardington Hall in 1909.[4]

In 1891, Gordon, 21, married Anna Widmay, 14-year old daughter of an American father and German-born mother. Their first child, Joyce Ann, was born on October 25 of that same year. Anna was talented, beautiful, and came from a well-to-do Staten Island family. She became a strong Christian woman and wrote a few hymns that found their way into the early editions of *Hymns of the Christian Life*. Eventually the family left Nyack for Connecticut, where Gordon found employment. Like Albert, Gordon struggled under the grip of alcohol, and tragically like his brother, also succumbed to tuberculosis at age 37 in a sanatorium in Liberty, New York, in 1907. His funeral was held at the Gospel Tabernacle where many of the congregation remembered the lovable rascal son of their revered Pastor Simpson.

Thankfully, as did his brother, he returned to Christ and recommitted himself to Christ and his parents. With his last breath, he entrusted Anna and their five children to his parents. Thus, his aging parents suddenly received into their Nyack home the four children, Albert,

Joyce, Ruth, and William, while Anna kept the youngest daughter and lived on a small allowance. By 1915, she came into a trust fund set up by her parents and was able to take the four children and care for them. Anna and Gordon's children eventually moved on, one of whom, Albert William Simpson, the oldest child, later became a bombardier in World War II and police chief of Miami, Florida, in the 1950s.

Gordon's daughter, Ruth, remembered sitting on the stone wall in front of the Simpson's hillside home as a young girl. In the evenings, she and her siblings and friends from the Wilson Academy would watch the Hudson steamboats as they ran from Albany to New York City. The captains would shine the ship's spotlight toward the hillside to illuminate the Simpson home for the passengers; such was Simpson's fame as a leading pastor and nationally known figure. The kids on the wall would merrily wave back to the steamship passengers as they went by.

MABEL JANE SIMPSON

Mabel Jane, the last of the Simpson children born in Hamilton in 1872, was also the first daughter. She and her mother were very close, and doubtless the added responsibility of caring for a little girl, not yet eight years old when they moved to New York, was a major concern to Margaret. Katherine Brennen, Mabel's daughter, describes how Margaret insisted Mabel receive a good education in the finer

> At age 17, Mabel was swept off her feet by the 34-year-old suitor.

things of life. Thus, when the Simpson family moved to Nyack, Mabel attended a "finishing school" for young ladies, called "The Castle," a short ferryboat ride to Tarrytown on the opposite bank of the Hudson River. Mother Margaret and Mabel regularly took tea together and enjoyed conversation at the three-story Simpson home built on the lower slope of the hillside site of the newly opened Nyack Missionary Training Institute in Nyack.

At age 17, Mabel met a young man from Canada, Hugh Brennen, son of the owner of a large lumber company. The teenage girl was swept off her feet by the 34-year-old suitor and struggled with the age difference, being so young and unsure of committing to marriage. A thousand thoughts crowded her young mind, and her mother was not at all convinced that it was a good idea. As Simpson's granddaughter, Katherine Brennen wrote that Simpson encouraged his unconvinced wife: "Maggie, dear, Hugh is a good man. The world abounds with many other types. If Mabel loves him . . ."[5] Despite her husband's counsel, Margaret did not approve of her daughter marrying a grown man while she was at such a tender age. However, within a year, there was a beautiful wedding held at the Gospel Tabernacle on 8th Avenue. Wanting a quiet wedding, her father had insisted: "No, Mabel, you belong to our people. They would feel hurt and could not understand." So, the Simpson children were a part of the Tabernacle and would continue to be so till their father's death. Margaret wasn't the only one opposed to Mabel's marriage. Little brother Howard is described in Katherine Brennen's book as saying, "I hate Hugh Brennen—he's stolen my sister."[6]

Mabel moved to Canada and began her new life with Hugh, who proved to be the good Christian husband that Simpson had perceived. Because of mother Margaret's attitude, she was denied entrance in the Brennen home for two years until she finally accepted the *fait acompli*, when she and Hugh finally reconciled. Mabel almost died following the birth of her first child. She lingered between life and death for weeks, cared for by four nurses at St. Luke's Hospital in New York, and eventually regained her strength. A few years later, their second daughter, Katherine Alberta Brennen arrived and completed the family. Katherine's quirky little book, *Mrs. A. B. Simpson—The Wife or Love Stands,* was published in the 1940s, about the time of Tozer's *Wingspread.* The 31-page booklet provides a wealth of Simpson family lore about which neither Thompson nor Tozer wrote. Mabel visited her parents yearly in Nyack, and on one of the trips, she fell while scaling the Nyack hillside. Her kneecap was broken and did not mend well, requiring her to use a crutch or cane till she passed away in Toronto in 1923, just a year before her mother's death.

MARGARET MAE SIMPSON

The year before her family moved to New York City, Margaret Mae was born in April 1878 in Louisville. Consequently, the baby girl arrived at a time when her father was already contemplating a move to New York that was dreaded and opposed by her mother.

Nicknamed "Tot," by Simpson, Margaret grew up with The Alliance, attending the early meetings of the "traveling Tabernacle."

She was converted at the age of 12 and sensed a missionary call to China, where she wished to go as a missionary nurse. She became a talented musician, pianist, and song writer, as well as her Dad's personal

> She was "daddy's girl" and remained very involved in the life of the Gospel Tabernacle during the heady early years of the C&MA.

secretary in 1894. In her words, she typed up "miles of his sermons from dictation on the gelatin-coated records of the phonograph on which he would [record] his sermons."[7] She was "daddy's girl" and remained very involved in the life of the Gospel Tabernacle during the heady early years of the C&MA. Like her father, she had a sensitive,

Margaret Mae Simpson, age 20

romantic streak, and was sometimes subject to melancholy and sickness. Twice before age 30, she suffered "nervous prostrations" due to her tendency to "work too intensely and long in the days when I ran his publishing business and became Editorial Assistant."[8] From her personal memoir, it is apparent that she idolized her father and sorely missed him after his death.

As a young woman, Margaret wrote the music for many of Simpson's hymns, including "To the Regions Beyond." On many occasions, her father would write a poem to close his Sunday Tabernacle message. He would ask "Tot" to meet him at the piano in their Nyack home. There he would pound out a tune and read the just-written poem for tomorrow's sermon. She would organize the melody, then harmonize and transcribe it to sheet music for use the next day.

At age 26, after the strain of 10 years of work with The Alliance, she became a Salvation Army "lass" and spent the next year working in the slums of Whitechapel in London. She returned home "in a state of decline" and needed a year to get back her health.[9] She then worked with her father's *Living Truths* publication, where she did editorial work and wrote articles under the pen name, "El Kalil." In 1906, her father sent her to medical school in Philadelphia where she studied for five years before dropping out of school due to a serious knee injury. Returning home, she leveraged her medical knowledge and experience and worked with a noted specialist on Park Avenue.

In 1912, she married George Buckman and had their only son, George Jr. in 1914. She described her marriage as "a few brief years [which] spelt disillusionment and tragedy."[10] She was widowed when George Jr. was only two and a half, and then she went to work to provide for him. She eventually became a businesswoman of some success for 10 years. This was followed in 1929 by a very serious bout of infectious arthritis, which left her bedridden and penniless in St. Luke's Hospital in New York for four months. She managed to get out of the hospital and make her way back to Nyack. In 1932, she attempted to transform the old Simpson home on the Nyack hillside into the "Simpson Memorial Home," similar to the healing and rest home model of Berachah Hall. However, she was not successful in this venture.[11]

Apparently, due to the harsh winters in Nyack and Margaret Mae's continued problems with arthritis and need for a warmer climate, she and George Jr. moved to Berkley, California, and remained there till 1956, when aging and alone, she returned to Nyack. There she provided valuable recollections preserved in McKaig's *Simpson Scrapbook*. She passed away in 1958 at the age of 80 years, leaving son George as sole survivor. Margaret had a difficult life on her own, living with the memories. However, unlike her brothers, she remained faithful to the Lord and was grateful to be alive and see the founding of the Simpson Memorial Church in Nyack under McKaig's pastoral leadership.[12]

HOWARD HOME SIMPSON

The last of the Simpson clan was born on September 19, 1880, in New York City. He was named Howard Home, after A.B.'s elder brother. He is the least known of the Simpson siblings. At his birth, the attending doctor arrived drunk, botched the delivery, and seriously injured Margaret during childbirth, causing a major hemorrhage. Margaret, exhausted and in great pain, had no desire to suffer more. Alone, Simpson prayed by her bedside and pleaded, "Stay with me, Margaret." "So – tired – Bertie." Katherine Brennen wrote: "But once again, by a hair's breadth, he fought, and inch by inch, regained possession of her will—forced her for his sake to step back from the River Jordan and take her place once more by his side."[13]

Howard grew up during the amazing years following Simpson's miraculous healing and headlong plunge into independent ministry at the Gospel Tabernacle, the opening of the Missionary Training Institute, and the founding in 1887 of what became The Christian and Missionary

Howard Simpson and his mother

Alliance. Howard went with his parents to the multiple venues of the Gospel Tabernacle until its permanent home was built on 8th Avenue with the mission headquarters and Missionary Training Institute around the corner on 44th Street. He witnessed the move from gaudy "Gotham" to the calmer hills of Nyack in 1897. He saw his father's God-given vision grow from the first humble meetings of the Gospel Tabernacle to a movement of God that spanned the globe and crisscrossed North America before Simpson's death.

The few cryptic references in John Sawin's massive archive of notes, pose more questions in relation to Howard than they provide answers. Howard, born in New York City, was a United States citizen. The United Kingdom declared war on Germany on August 4, 1914, the same day as Hugh Brennen's death. Thus Howard, already 34 years of age and nearly beyond the age of military service, volunteered as a U.S. citizen to fight with the Canadian Expeditionary Force (CEF) following the death of Hugh. While the United States did not enter World War I

> **Howard grew up during the amazing years following Simpson's miraculous healing and headlong plunge into independent ministry at the Gospel Tabernacle.**

until 1917, many Americans enlisted with the CEF because of their Canadian or British family ties. By God's grace and the prayers of A. B. and Margaret, he survived the horrors of war in the trenches of France in the "Great War." At war's end, he returned to Nyack and lived with his parents for a time and was present when his father died. Eventually he left home and returned to Montreal.

The highpoints of Canadian military achievement during the Great War came during the Somme, Vimy, and Passchendaele battles and what later became known as "Canada's Hundred Days," which counted 67,000 killed and 250,000 wounded, out of the 620,000 soldiers mobilized. It is very possible that Howard fought during the horrific trench war, experiencing gas attacks as well as the suicidal "over-the-top" charges on an enemy with a highly efficient mechanized army that mowed down the allied troops like ripe wheat on a hot August afternoon. "Shell shock," now understood as post-traumatic stress disorder (PTSD), plagued the emotionally shattered survivors.

John Sawin's notes in *The Life and Times of A. B. Simpson,* tell a poignant story about the wayward youngest son. George Ferry of Hamilton, Ohio, who worked at MTI, often walked to the train station just down the hill from the founder's Nyack home to carry Simpson's heavy briefcase. On the nights when Simpson taught Bible in Chapel Hall, George would walk with him to class up the long flight of steps to the campus. During Simpson's final years, Howard worked in New York City but lived at home. Like his brothers, he had become a heavy drinker. On several occasions, George accompanied the aging Simpson to the station to help get Howard home, sometimes going alone to bring him home.

It is possible that the months that Howard spent in the quietness of his parent's Nyack home were his opportunity to regain emotional footing before making his way in life. Alcohol, often the temporary solace of the soul-shattered, apparently was his constant companion for most of his life. According to the Sawin files, Howard came to Alliance headquarters on 260 West 44th Street some time in 1940 and asked for a room in the "missionary hotel." As the last living son of the founder, he was taken in but was dismissed a few days later, apparently for unruly behavior.

Simpson had seen a gifting in Howard not seen in his brothers and urged him to become a preacher of the gospel, but Howard refused. Sawin's *Life and Times of A. B. Simpson* relates a sad story: "Simpson's son (Howard) came to Tozer's church when [he] was pastor, looked at the large audience that came to hear a son of Dr. A. B. Simpson, [and] sobbed as if heart would burst and told them how his father . . . had wanted him to go into the ministry and he had always refused. He realized now he had made a mistake."[14] Howard was childless. It is not known whether he was reconciled to God before he passed in 1949.

HOME AND HARVEST—THE BATTLE FOR BALANCE

So, ends the rather sober story of the Simpson children, four sons and two daughters. Three of the four sons battled alcoholism their whole lives, while Melville had died years before at age three. The Simpson daughters spared their parents the sorrow they experienced from their prodigal sons. What is one to conclude from such a sad account?

One could hardly dare to condemn the Simpsons for their sons' bad choices and wandering ways. However, Simpson likely recognized that he struggled with balance between his home and the world as his parish. Before he was "Dr. A. B. Simpson of the Gospel Tabernacle," he was Albert Simpson, devoted husband and doting daddy to his growing brood. Somehow, after gaining a vision of the lost and his compelling burden to take the gospel to them, Simpson must have lost sight of the fact that part of God's calling on his life was to disciple and raise up world Christians in his home. The boys apparently were left to their own devices while their parents were preaching, teaching, and serving the lost—while losing their sons.

A. B. Simpson was a great man of God, a towering figure on the late 19th and early 20th century evangelical scene in North America. Yet as great as he was as a man and leader, hindsight reveals his shortcomings as a father and husband. The world blesses his memory, and it is comforting to know that most, if not all the family, were reunited with their

> **Simpson likely recognized that he struggled with balance between his home and the world as his parish.**

parents in "the Father's House." No one would ever accuse him of being a lenient Eli, whose sons profaned the house of God with their behavior. Samuel, the last judge and Israel's great prophet, had sons who did not follow their father's godly example. Scripture also provides examples of bad fathers who had good sons in the Chronicles of the kings of Judah and Israel. As a result, hasty judgment of a man based on his son's life is unwise and unwarranted.

However, the reader should take away from this account the fact that family comes first, not in terms of Kingdom priority, but in terms of chronology. Before being a pastor and leader, Simpson first was a husband and a father. At the same time, he became a pastor and eventually the leader of a worldwide movement. The call to serve the family of God the world over is never a call to forget the family already at home. Happy is the one who can maintain the balance needed to minister to all across this continuum of relationships.

APPENDIX 3
TRANSITION

*O*FTEN, THE SUCCESSOR OF A VISIONARY LEADER struggles to implement his sense of where the organization's future lies, and so it was upon the death of A. B. Simpson. For some years, his advancing age and declining health clearly indicated that the C&MA needed to prepare for his inevitable homegoing. It was only natural that the Society begin to think about a possible future leader, and gradually a few natural candidates came to the fore.

THE CANDIDATES

A few younger Alliance leaders had already shown their potential. Rev. Robert Glover, former field director in China, served as The Alliance's foreign secretary from 1912 to 1921, displaying remarkable wisdom and ability. Rev. John Jaderquist, a former missionary to Africa, also displayed outstanding administrative gifts. At Simpson's request, he assumed the post of publications secretary and associate editor of *The Alliance Weekly*, where he made difficult decisions which returned the troubled enterprise to financial health, thus gaining recognition as a decisive leader. Rev. Walter Turnbull, dean of the Missionary Training Institute at Nyack, also served as an Alliance missionary in India. When two of the MTI's leaders, Dr. J. Hudson Ballard and Dr. William C. Stevens, left after the 1914 General Council disagreed with their aim of turning the Institute into the "Nyack Missionary University," Turnbull was asked by Simpson to take over. He proved to be an able leader, eliminating Nyack's debt over the next few years.

THE NEWCOMER

The year 1912 proved to be a watershed year in Alliance history, and onto the scene strode an unknown and unproven newcomer, Rev. Paul Rader. Working under E. D. Whiteside's mentorship in Pittsburgh, Pennsylvania, Rader was just 35 years old and larger than life at six

Young Paul Rader—street preacher

feet four inches and 225 pounds. A former college football star and heavyweight boxer, Rader was a dynamic preacher and charismatic figure who soon confirmed his ability as an evangelist and occasional traveling companion of the founder. Rader towered over Simpson, who was still a robust six-footer in his later years. Like the founder, Rader stood out, first of all, as an impassioned evangelist who preached for decisions. He came to love the Alliance message, experienced the deeper life, and like the founder, became one of its most effective advocates.

Simpson saw something in Rader early on and encouraged broader roles for him in The Alliance. "Rader appeared to manifest the vision and passion that Simpson had in organizing the Alliance more than 30 years earlier."[1]

> *Liberated from a deadening liberal theology like a revolutionary freed from prison, Rader embraced the Fourfold Gospel with a zeal born of personal discovery. Profoundly influenced by Simpson, Rader placed him above others in esteem: "My outstanding impression of*

Dr. A. B. Simpson is that he was the foremost world man of our generation . . . Here is a man who, single-handed, started and carried forward a movement to 'the regions beyond.' He planted his workers in sixteen mission fields of the earth and did it in twenty-five years."[2]

Just four years later, Rader was elected honorary vice president at the 1916 General Council. While more figurative than administrative, this position revealed his growing stature in The Alliance. Recognizing that

Rader embraced the Fourfold Gospel with a zeal born of personal discovery.

Simpson would be gone sooner than later, the natural question arose: "Who will God raise up to lead the Society to reach those without access to Christ's gospel?" At the 1919 Toccoa Falls Council, Rader was elected vice president and became heir apparent. He had led the "Forward Movement" beginning in 1917 for two years, resulting in dozens of new Alliance branches opening and a resurgence in missionary candidates and support.

Simpson and Rader—circa 1918

In the months preceding the 1919 Council, Rader had been approached by several Board of Manager members, urging him to let his name be placed in nomination for the vice president position. Rader went back and forth on this momentous decision. In Chicago, his home base of ministry, he pastored the non-denominational Moody Church

> Historians believe that by maintaining his churchman role, Rader helped restore the movement's evangelistic fervor.

and soon led them to build a 5,000-seat tabernacle that was quickly filled with new converts. He divided his time between the growing demand for his role in the C&MA and his involvement with Moody Church.

In early 1919, the Board was divided, most seeing Rader as the answer to growing the home base to support the growing overseas work, while a minority had reservations. Glover and Jaderquist questioned Rader's administrative abilities and his willingness to take the torch from Simpson and lead The Alliance. At the same time that the Board was divided, Rader would not "express clear readiness to accept the responsibilities that accompany the office."[1] Even today, it is not clear if Simpson saw Rader as heir apparent or simply the logical choice to pastor the Gospel Tabernacle. Jaderquist, Glover, and Canadian Alliance leader, Rev. Peter Philpott, pointed to Rader's relative youth, few years with The Alliance, lack of administrative experience, and his refusal to agree to dedicate himself fully to the role of future president as impediments against his nomination at the Council. Thus, Rader withdrew his name as a candidate.

Due to his weakened condition following a second minor stroke in January 1919, Simpson did not attend the Toccoa Falls Council. Rader preached there several times but left for Chicago before the elections. In his absence and despite his withdrawal as a candidate, his name was submitted by the nominating committee. Former C&MA Vice President Ulysses Lewis of Atlanta was nominated from the floor but declined to accept. By voice vote, Rader was acclaimed vice president of The Christian and Missionary Alliance. Six months later, Simpson spent his last conscious hours in prayer at his Nyack home, then sank into a coma. On Wednesday morning, October 29, 1919, he left this world to meet his Lord and Savior.

Rev. Paul Rader

OUT OF THE RUT

Consequently, with Simpson's death, Rev. Paul Rader became the second president of the C&MA. While he had shown ambivalence as to whether God wanted him to be president, he took over the reins of leadership and began to cast the vision that he believed would "get the Alliance out of the rut," as he had told John Jaderquist some months before. Rader's leadership style was considerably different than Simpson's. Dynamic and sometimes blunt of speech, the new president's charismatic personality contrasted with Simpson's gracious, never-ruffled demeanor. Simpson the sensitive poet contrasted greatly with Rader, the former pugilist. Where Simpson sought consensus, Rader's heavy hand held the rudder. While Simpson had dedicated his life to the ministry of The Alliance, Rader divided his time between presidential duties and his pastoral obligations at the Moody Church in Chicago. Some felt that by splitting his attention, Rader was compromising his commitment to each of these weighty positions; looking back, however, historians believe that by maintaining his churchman role, Rader helped restore the movement's evangelistic fervor, which had begun to wane with the deteriorating condition of its founder.

TABERNACLISM

Rader's answer for getting the C&MA "out of the rut" was to trace a new path. He was a strong believer in "tabernaclism." This strategy involved the construction of low-cost wooden buildings, simple and "unchurchy," where the non-religious urban masses could be introduced to the message of the gospel through strong evangelistic preaching, lively music, and up-to-date promotional methods. Those converted would quickly be organized into "new branches" and the gospel team moved on to another site while an appointed pastor would remain with the just-formed congregation. While the tabernacle model was successful when gifted evangelistic teams were available to barnstorm the country and raise up new, vibrant works, there simply weren't enough teams.

RED FLAGS

Rader suggested that The Alliance be reorganized with local branches placed under the tabernacles in major cities under his direct supervision. He proposed that the C&MA headquarters be moved to Chicago or, minimally, an extension office be opened there with a qualified evangelistic team for holding mass meetings. All of the major proposals to change the C&MA's organizational structure, move the head office to Chicago, and tabernacle strategy under Rader's direct control raised red flags. In addition, Rader had resigned from Moody Church in 1921 and opened the Chicago Gospel Tabernacle "steel tent," a metal-frame structure, non-denominational and totally unrelated to the C&MA over which he presided.

By this time, Glover, Jaderquist, and Philpot had resigned from The Alliance due to Rader's leadership style. The biggest wedge issue between Rader and the Board was his refusal to commit himself to leading The Alliance. He agreed in principle but never fulfilled his pledge. He began ministries outside The Alliance that competed with the organization he presided. His theology of church contrasted sharply with Simpson's model since its earliest years. Consequently, his unwillingness to work within the structure that God had raised up constantly stressed his relationship with the Board.

Rader's aggressive personality and cavalier attitude toward his responsibilities with The Alliance forced things to a head. Increasingly, Rader identified himself with the "fundamentalist" movement then battling liberal "modernist theology." Rader's confrontational style contrasted with Simpson's goal to keep The Alliance doctrinally faithful to the fundamentals of the Christian faith while steering clear of the bitter debates between these warring wings of Protestantism. Rader's "come ye out from among them" attitude contrasted sharply with Simpson's vision of an "alliance of believers" in agreement with the basic mission and message of the church.

Eventually, it became evident that Rader's vision of the Alliance's future conflicted with the Body as well as the Board. His resignation, a foregone conclusion, was more a question of when rather than if. Since

> **The biggest wedge issue between Rader and the Board was his refusal to commit himself to leading The Alliance.**

Rader had not attended most Board meetings during his presidency, the members asked for his resignation, which Rader tendered in December 1923, and was accepted by the Board of Managers in January 1924.[4] Rader believed that he and the C&MA had similar goals but incompatible approaches. Apparently, there was a collective sigh of relief, both by the Board as well as Rader. He resigned graciously and maintained fraternal fellowship with Alliance leaders for the next several years. But his go-it-alone spirit, ambivalence regarding his leadership, and heavy-handed attempt to reorganize The Alliance proved unpopular, unworkable, and untenable.

Rader's presidency, from 1919 to 1924, was followed by Rev. Frederick Senft, Simpson's friend and colleague. Senft led for only 22 months; yet under him, tensions relaxed. As vice president, he proved to be a "bridge over troubled waters." Suddenly, he fell ill with pneumonia and died in November 1925. His short but significant role as leader brought a rather unsettling era to an abrupt end. He was followed by Vice President Rev. H. (Harry) M. Shuman, who assumed the office upon Senft's death. The following year, Shuman was elected at General Council and then for the next nine successive terms. For 28 years, he led as president and chair of the Board of Managers till 1954. Doubtless, the lessons learned from this difficult transition are still valuable whenever the issue of succession arises.

A. B. Simpson, age 22

APPENDIX 4
COVENANTS AND VOWS

A SOLEMN COVENANT
The Dedication of Myself to God

By Albert Benjamin Simpson

Saturday, January 19, 1861

"O Thou everlasting and almighty God, Ruler of the universe, Thou who madest this world and me, Thy creature upon it, Thou who art in every place beholding the evil and the good, Thou seest Me at this time and knowest all my thoughts. I know and feel that my inmost thoughts are all familiar to Thee, and Thou knowest what motives have induced me to come me to Thee at this time. I appeal to Thee, O Thou Searcher of hearts, so far as I know my own heart, it is not a worldly motive that has brought me before Thee now. But my 'heart is deceitful above all things and desperately wicked,' and I would not pretend to trust to it; but Thou knowest that I have a desire to dedicate myself to Thee for time and eternity. I would come before Thee as a sinner, lost and ruined by the fall, and by my actual transgressions, yea, as the vilest of all Thy creatures. When I look back on my past life, I am filled with shame and confusion. I am rude and ignorant, and in Thy sight a beast. Thou, O Lord, didst make Adam holy and happy, and gavest him ability to maintain his state. The penalty of his disobedience was death, but he disobeyed Thy holy law and incurred that penalty, and I, as a descendant from him, have inherited this depravity and this penalty. I acknowledge the justness of Thy sentence, O Lord, and would bow in submission before Thee. How canst Thou, O Lord, condescend to look on me, a vile creature? For it is infinite condescension to notice me. But truly, Thy loving kindness is infinite and from everlasting. Thou, O Lord, didst send Thy Son in our image, with a body such as mine and a reasonable soul. In Him were united all the perfections of the Godhead with the humility of our sinful nature. He is the Mediator of the New Covenant, and through Him we all have access unto Thee by the same Spirit. Through Jesus, the only Mediator, I would come to Thee, O Lord, and trusting in His merits and mediation, I would boldly approach Thy throne of grace. I feel my own insignificance, O Lord, but do Thou strengthen me by Thy Spirit. I would now approach Thee in order to covenant with Thee for life everlasting. Thou in Thy Word hast told us that it is Thy will that all who believe in Thy Son might have everlasting life, and Thou wilt raise Him up at the last day. Thou hast given us a New Covenant and hast sealed that covenant in Thy blood, O Jesus, on the cross. I now declare before Thee and before my conscience and bear witness, O ye heavens, and all the inhabitants thereof, and thou earth, which my God has made, that I accept the conditions of this covenant and close with its terms. These are that I believe on Jesus and accept of salvation through Him, my Prophet, Priest, and King, as made unto me of God wisdom and righteousness and sanctification and redemption and complete salvation. Thou, O Lord, hast made me willing to come to Thee. Thou hast subdued my rebellious heart by Thy love. So now take it and use it for Thy glory. Whatever rebellious thoughts may arise therein, do Thou overcome them and bring into subjection everything that opposeth itself to Thy authority. I yield myself unto Thee as one alive from the dead, for time and eternity. Take me and use me entirely for Thy glory. Ratify now in Heaven, O my Father, this Covenant. Remember it, O Lord, when Thou bringest me to the Jordan. Remember it, O Lord, in that day when Thou comest with all the angels and saints to judge the world, and may I be at Thy right hand then and in heaven with Thee forever. Write down in heaven that I have become Thine, Thine only, and Thine forever. Remember me, O Lord, in the hour of temptation, and let me never depart from this covenant. I feel, O Lord, my own weakness and do not make this in my own strength, else I must fail. But in Thy strength, O captain of my salvation, I shall be strong and more than conqueror through Him who loved me. I have now, O Lord, as Thou hast said in Thy Word, covenanted with Thee, not for worldly honors or fame but for everlasting life, and I know that

Thou art true and shalt never break Thy holy Word. Give to me now all the blessings of the New Covenant and especially the Holy Spirit in great abundance, which is the earnest of my inheritance until the redemption of the purchased possession. May a double portion of Thy Spirit rest upon me, and then I shall go and proclaim to transgressors Thy ways and Thy laws to the people. Sanctify me wholly and make me fit for heaven. Give me all spiritual blessing in heavenly places in Christ Jesus. I am now a soldier of the cross and a follower of the Lamb, and my motto from henceforth is "I have one King, even Jesus." Support and strengthen me, O my Captain, and be mine forever. Place me in what circumstances Thou mayest desire; but if it be Thy holy will, I desire that Thou give me neither poverty nor riches; feed me with food convenient, lest I be poor and steal, or lest I be rich and say, "Who is the Lord?" But Thy will be done. Now give me Thy Spirit and Thy protection in my heart at all times, and then I shall drink of the rivers of salvation, lie down by still waters, and be infinitely happy in the favor of my God.[1]

—A. B. Simpson

Three-fold vow regarding healing I made to God, as if I had seen Him there before me face to face, these three great and eternal pledges:

1. *As I shall meet Thee in that day, I solemnly accept this truth as part of Thy Word and of the Gospel of Christ, and God helping me, I shall never question it until I meet Thee there.*

2. *As I shall meet Thee in that day I take the Lord Jesus as my physical life, for all the needs of my body until all my life work is done; and helping me, I shall never doubt that Thou dost so become my life and strength from this moment, and wilt keep me under all circumstances until Thy blessed coming, and until all Thy will for me is perfectly fulfilled.*

3. *As I shall meet Thee in that day I solemnly agree to use this blessing for the glory of God, and the good of others, and to speak of it or minister in connection with it in any way in which God may call me or others may need me in the future.*

Written across this covenant are the following renewals; one of which was made during his third year in college and the other during his second pastorate.[2]

> "September 1, 1863. Backslidden. Restored. Yet too cold, Lord. I still wish to continue this. Pardon the past and strengthen me for the future, for Jesus' sake. Amen."

> "Louisville, Ky., April 18, 1878. Renew this covenant and dedication amid much temptation and believe that my Father accepts me anew and gives me more than I have dared to ask or think, for Jesus' sake. He has kept His part. My one desire now is power, light, love, souls, Christ's indwelling, and my church's salvation."[3]

NOTES

PREFACE
1 Battles, Robert and D. J. Fant, research gathered from recorded interview with John Sawin, June 2, 1978. Courtesy of C&MA Archives.
2 Colson, Chuck. "BreakPoint: Digging up Biblical History." July 2017. http://www.breakpoint.org/2017/07/breakpoint-digging-up-biblical-history/
3 Lonsinger, J., personal communication, October 27, 2016.

CHAPTER 1
1 McKaig, C. Donald, "A Surviving Diary," *Simpson Scrapbook*, 1971, p 153. (These entries begin near the end of his Louisville pastorate and continue to the early part of his New York ministry—November 10, 1879 through March 5, 1880).
2 Thompson, A. E., *The Life of A. B. Simpson* (Harrisburg, PA: The Christian Alliance Publishing Company, 1920), p. 84.
3 Niklaus, Robert L., John S. Sawin, and John J. Stoesz, *All for Jesus* (Camp Hill, PA: Christian Publications Inc., 1986, 2013), p. 66.
4 Evearitt, Daniel J., *Body and Soul: Evangelism and the Social Concern of A. B. Simpson* (Camp Hill, PA: Christian Publications, 1994), p. 5.
5 Simpson, A. B., "How the Church Can Reach the Masses," *The Word, The Work and The World*, January 1, 1882, p. 24
6 Wikipedians, Canada, https://books.google.com/books?id=X-mQ0TEnLBMC&pg=PA498&lpg=PA498&dq=St.+John+Island+became+British+colony&source=bl&ots=t4TcZuT-F0y&sig=Yb8ZE_uVzDCkWHU2dN2FGQo5ZQA-&hl=en&sa=X&ved=2ahUKEwjpoeS3goHdAhUEr1kKHei6CqQQ6AEwDnoECAQQAQ#v=onepage&q=St.%20John%20Island%20became%20British%20colony&f=false; pp. 5, 433, 498.
7 Reid, Darrell, *Jesus Only: The Early Life and Presbyterian Ministry of Albert Benjamin Simpson, 1843–1881*, (Ph.D. dissertation, Queen's University. 1994), p. 48.
8 Thompson, *The Life of A. B. Simpson*, p. 3.

9 Ibid, 118.
10 Reid, Darrell, *Jesus Only: The Early Life and Presbyterian Ministry of Albert Benjamin Simpson, 1843-1881*, p. 48; Thompson, *The Life of A. B. Simpson*, p. 118.
11 Thompson, *The Life of A. B. Simpson*, p. 4.
12 Wayne, Michael, "The Black Population of Canada West" Histoire Sociale/Social History, York University, Vol. 28, No. 56 (1995), pp. 466, 470, 476.
13 Tozer, A. W., *Wingspread* (Harrisburg, PA: Christian Publications, Inc., 1940), p. 14; Thompson, *The Life of A. B. Simpson*, p. 4.
14 Thompson, *The Life of A. B. Simpson*, p. 4.
15 Book of Mark 6:4.
16 Thompson, *The Life of A. B. Simpson*, p. 9.
17 Ibid, pp. 8, 34.
18 Ibid, p. 9.
19 Ibid, p. 9.
20 Ibid, p. 5.
21 Ibid, p. 5.

CHAPTER 2

1 Thompson, A. E., *The Life of A. B. Simpson*, (Harrisburg, PA: The Christian Alliance Publishing Company, 1920), p. 7.
2 McKaig, C. Donald, "A Surviving Diary," *Simpson Scrapbook*, 1971, p. 5.
3 Thompson, *The Life of A. B. Simpson*, p. 7.
4 McKaig, "A Surviving Diary," p. 5.
5 Thompson, *The Life of A. B. Simpson*, p. 8.
6 Ibid, p. 8.
7 Ibid, p. 8.
8 Ibid, p. 9.
9 Ibid, p. 10.
10 Ibid, p.11.
11 Ibid, p. 11.
12 Ibid, p. 11.
13 Simpson, A. B., *The Fourfold Gospel*, (New York: Christian Alliance Publishing Company, 1890), p. 14.
14 Ibid, p. 11–12.

15 Ibid, p. 11.
16 Ibid, p. 11.
17 Ibid, p. 13.
18 Ibid, p. 13.
19 Ibid, p. 13.
20 Conley, Joseph F., *Drumbeats that Changed the World* (Pasadena, CA: William Carey Library, 2000), p. 25.
21 Thompson, *The Life of A. B. Simpson*, p. 26.
22 Ibid, p. 26.
23 McKaig, "A Surviving Diary," p. 11.
24 Ibid, p. 11.
25 Ibid, p. 12.
26 Thompson, *The Life of A. B. Simpson*, p. 17.
27 *The Word, The Work and The World*, Vol. IX, No. 1, July 1, 1887, p. 2.
28 Thompson, *The Life of A. B. Simpson*, p. 23.

CHAPTER 3

1 Thompson, A. E., *The Life of A. B. Simpson* (Harrisburg, PA: The Christian Alliance Publishing Company, 1920), p. 31.
2 Ibid, p. 31.
3 https://www.bankofcanada.ca/wp-conte, pp.39–42 The Province of Canada changed from the British pound to the dollar in 1853, thus becoming the official currency of Canada. This was due to increasing trade with the United States, already using the decimal based dollar for many years. In 2018, $120 would be equivalent to $3,643.
4 McKaig, C. Donald, "A Surviving Diary," *Simpson Scrapbook*, 1971, p. 18; Thompson, *The Life of A. B. Simpson*, p. 37.
5 Ibid p. 19.
6 *The Christian and Missionary Alliance*, Vol. XXVII, No. 27, December 28, 1901, p. 357.
7 Thompson, *The Life of A. B. Simpson*, p. 33.
8 Ibid, p. 33.
9 Ibid, p. 36.
10 Ibid, p. 37.
11 Tozer, A. W., *Wingspread* (Harrisburg, PA: Christian Publications, Inc., 1940), p. 33.

12 Simpson, Harold H., *Cavendish—Its History, Its People*, (Amherst, Nova Scotia: Harold H. Simpson and Associates, Limited, 1973), pp. 188, 189.
13 Thompson, *The Life of A. B. Simpson*, p. 28.
14 Ibid, p. 35.
15 Brennen, Katherine, *Mrs. A. B. Simpson—The Wife or Love Stands*, n.d., p. 1.
16 Thompson, *The Life of A. B. Simpson*, p. 35.
17 Ibid, p. 41.
18 Ibid, p. 33.
19 Reid, Darrell, *Jesus Only: The Early Life and Presbyterian Ministry of Albert Benjamin Simpson, 1843–1881* (Ph.D. dissertation, Queen's University. 1994), p. 149.
20 Ibid, p. 150.
21 Thompson, *The Life of A. B. Simpson*, p. 42.
22 Ibid, p. 41.
23 Tozer, A. W., *Wingspread* (Harrisburg, PA.: Christian Publications, Inc., 1940), p. 39.
24 Brennen, *Mrs. A. B. Simpson—The Wife or Love Stands*, p. 5.

CHAPTER 4

1 Sawin, John, *Life and Times of A. B. Simpson* (Regina, Saskatchawan: Archibald Foundation Library, Canadian Bible College, Canadian Bible College/Canadian Theological Seminary), p.207; *Hamilton Spectator*, June 27, 1865, p. 2.
2 Brennen, Katherine A., *Mrs. A. B. Simpson—The Wife or Love Stands*, n.d., p. 8.
3 Thompson, A. E., *The Life of A. B. Simpson*, (Harrisburg, PA: The Christian Alliance Publishing Company, 1920), p. 44.
4 Niklaus, Robert L., John S. Sawin, and Samuel J. Stoesz, *All for Jesus, 125th Anniversary Edition* (Colorado Springs, CO: The Christian and Missionary Alliance, 2013), p. 43.
5 Brennen, *Mrs. A. B. Simpson—The Wife or Love Stands*, p. 8.
6 Ibid, p. 6.
7 Ibid, p. 7.
8 Ibid, p. 5–6.
9 Sawin, *Life and Times of A. B. Simpson*, p. 215.

CHAPTER 5

1. McKaig, C. Donald, "Biographical Highlights in the Life of the Founder," *Simpson Scrapbook*, (Ambrose University CBC/CTS Archives, 1971), p. 104.
2. Ibid, p. 90.
3. Ibid, p. 103.
4. Ibid, p. 116.
5. Ibid, p. 107.
6. Ibid, p. 107.
7. Simpson, A. B., *The Gospel of Healing* (Harrisburg, PA.: Christian Publications, Inc., 1915), p. 156.
8. Hartzfeld, David F. and Charles Neinkirchen, *The Birth of a Vision* (Beaverlodge, Alberta: Buena Book Services, 1986), p. 32.
9. McKaig, C. Donald, "Biographical Highlights in the Life of the Founder," *Simpson Scrapbook*, (Ambrose University, CBC/CTS Archives, 1971), p. 124.
10. Ibid, p. 128.
11. Brennen, Katherine A., *Mrs. A. B. Simpson—The Wife or Love Stands*, p. 6, n.d., n.p.
12. Thompson, A. E., *The Life of A. B. Simpson* (Harrisburg, PA: The Christian Alliance Publishing Company, 1920), p. 47.
13. Reid, Darrell, *Jesus Only: The Early Life and Presbyterian Ministry of Albert Benjamin Simpson, 1843–1881* (Ph.D. dissertation, Queen's University. 1994), p. 242; *Hamilton Spectator*, December 15, 1873, p. 3.

CHAPTER 6

1. Tozer, A. W. *Wingspread* (Harrisburg, PA: Christian Publications, Inc., 1944), p. 45.
2. Thompson, A. E., *The Life of A. B. Simpson*, (Harrisburg, PA: Christian Publications, Inc., 1920), p. 70.
3. Simpson, A. B., "A Personal Testimony," *The Alliance Weekly*, Vol. XLV, No. 1, October 2, 1915, p. 11.
4. Thompson, *The Life of A. B. Simpson*, p. 67.
5. Simpson, A. B., "A Personal Testimony," *The Alliance Weekly*, Vol. XLV, No. 1, October 2, 1915, p. 11.
6. Ibid, p. 11.
7. Ibid, p. 12.

8. Simpson, A. B. *Thirty-One Kings,* (Harrisburg, PA, Christian Publications, Inc.), p. 4, n.d.
9. Niklaus, Robert L., John S. Sawin, and Samuel J. Stoesz, *All for Jesus, 125th Anniversary Edition* (Colorado Springs, CO: The Christian and Missionary Alliance, 2013), p. 19.
10. Simpson, A. B., *The Alliance Weekly,* Vol. XLVI, No. 25, September 16, 1916, p. 395.
11. Ibid, p. 395.
12. Reid, Darrell, *Jesus Only: The Early Life and Presbyterian Ministry of Albert Benjamin Simpson, 1843–1881* (Ph.D. dissertation, Queen's University. 1994), p. 260. This reference cites Warren, E. L., *The Presbyterian Church in Louisville from its Organization in 1816 to the Year 1896* (n.pub., Chicago, 1896), p. 26.
13. Tozer, A. W. *Wingspread* (Harrisburg, PA: Christian Publications, Inc., 1944), p. 46.
14. Niklaus, et. al., *All for Jesus, 125th Anniversary Edition,* p. 10.
15. Thompson, The Life of A. B. Simpson, p. 55.
16. Simpson, A. B., *The Gospel of Healing* (Harrisburg, PA: Christian Publications, Inc., 1915), p. 161.
17. Thompson, A. E., *The Life of A. B. Simpson* (Harrisburg, PA: Christian Publications, Inc., 1920), p. 58.
18. Reid, Darrell, *Jesus Only: The Early Life and Presbyterian Ministry of Albert Benjamin Simpson,* p. 328, citing the Louisville *Courier-Journal,* January 9, 1876, p. 6.
19. *The Alliance Weekly,* November 20, 1915, p. 116.
20. Sawin, *The Life and Times of A. B. Simpson.* Pdf. Regina, Saskatchewan. Archibald Foundation Library Canadian Bible College/ Canadian Theological Seminary, p. 234.
21. Reid, *Jesus Only: The Early Life and Presbyterian Ministry of Albert Benjamin Simpson,* p. 333.
22. Brennen, *Mrs. A. B. Simpson—The Wife or Love Stands,* p. 11.
23. Reid, Darrell, *Jesus Only: The Early Life and Presbyterian Ministry of Albert Benjamin Simpson,* 218.
24. Ibid, p. 359.
25. Ibid, p. 359.
26. McKaig, C. Donald, "A Surviving Diary," *Simpson Scrapbook,* 1971, p. 149.

CHAPTER 7

1. McKaig, C. Donald, "A Surviving Diary," *Simpson Scrapbook*, 1971, p. 51.
2. Ibid, p. 152.
3. Ibid, p. 156.
4. Reid, Darrell, *Jesus Only: The Early Life and Presbyterian Ministry of Albert Benjamin Simpson, 1843–1881* (Ph.D. dissertation, Queen's University. 1994), p. 372, citing Burchard's The Centennial Historical Discourse, preached in the Thirteenth St. Presbyterian Church July 1876 (New York: Arthur & Bonnel, 1877), p. 7.
5. Reid, Darrell, *Jesus Only: The Early Life and Presbyterian Ministry of Albert Benjamin Simpson, 1843-1881,* p. 372.
6. Stoesz, Samuel J., *Understanding My Church* (Harrisburg, PA: Christian Publications, 1968), p. 105; Niklaus, Robert L., John S. Sawin, and Samuel J. Stoesz, *All for Jesus, 125th Anniversary Edition* (Colorado Springs, CO: The Christian and Missionary Alliance, 2013), p. 50.
7. Packenham, Thomas, *The Scramble for Africa: White Man's Conquest of the Dark Continent from 1876 to 1912* (New York: Perennial/Harper Collins, 1991).
8. Simpson, A.B. *The Gospel in All Lands,* Vol. III, No. 2, February, 1881, p. 188.
9. Ibid, p. 188.
10. Ibid, p. 188.
11. Niklaus, et. al., *All for Jesus,* p. 53.
12. Simpson, A. B., *The Gospel of Healing,* (Harrisburg, PA.: Christian Publications, Inc., 1915), p. 158.
13. Simpson, A. B., *The Christian Alliance,* Vol. 1, No. 1, January 1888, p. 12.
14. Simpson, *The Gospel of Healing,* p. 158.
15. "Ride on King Jesus", Negrospirituals.com, http://www.negrospirituals.com/songs/rıde_on_king_jesus.htm; https://watchfiremusic.com/lyrics/cantata-toccata; There is no known Negro Spiritual with the refrain, "No man can work like Him."
16. "Nothing is Too Hard for Jesus," *Hymns of the Christian Life, Nos. 1 & 2,* (Harrisburg, PA. The Christian Alliance Publishing Company, 1891), p. 163.

17 Niklaus, et. al., *All for Jesus*, p. 54.
18 King, Paul L., *Genuine Gold* (Tulsa, OK: Word and Spirit Press, 2006), p. 24; Neinkirchen, Charles W., *A. B. Simpson and the Pentecostal Movement* (Peabody, MA.: Hendrickson Publishers, 1992), pp. 13–16.
19 Thompson, A. E., *The Life of A. B. Simpson* (Harrisburg, PA: Christian Publications, Inc., 1920), pp. 75–76.
20 Simpson, *The Gospel of Healing*, p. 172.
21 Ibid, p. 163.
22 Ibid, p. 169.
23 Niklaus, et. al., *All for Jesus*, p. 57.
24 Ibid, p. 58.
25 Buckman, Margaret Simpson, *His Own Life Story*, n.p., 1953. A collection of documents written by the daughter of A. B. Simpson.

CHAPTER 8

1 Reid, Darrell, *Jesus Only: The Early Life and Presbyterian Ministry of Albert Benjamin Simpson, 1843–1881,* (Ph.D. dissertation, Queen's University. 1994), pp. 420–421.
2 Caledonian Hall was located two blocks west of Thirteenth Street Presbyterian Church, located on 143 West 13th Street, between 6th and 7th Avenues. This is now part of Greenwich Village.
3 Simpson, A. B. "A Story of Providence," *Living Truths,* Vol. VII, No. 3, March 1907, p. 152.
4 Ibid, pp. 151, 152.
5 Ibid, p. 153.
6 Ibid, p. 153.
7 King, Paul L., *Anointed Women: The Rich Heritage of Women in Ministry in The Christian and Missionary Alliance* (Tulsa, OK: Word & Spirit Press, 2009), pp. 19–37.
8 Simpson, A. B., "A Story of Providence," *Living Truths,* Vol. VII, No. 3, March 1907, p. 153.
9 Ibid, p. 153.
10 Ibid, p. 153.
11 Ibid, p. 153.
12 Ibid, p. 153.
13 *The Word, The Work and The World,* "The Gospel Tent," Vol. III,

No. 7, July 1, 1883, p. 267
14 McKaig, C. Donald, "A Surviving Diary," *Simpson Scrapbook*, 1971, p. 198.
15 *Christian Alliance Yearbook*, 1888, pp. 63–64.
16 *The Alliance Weekly*, "My Memories of Dr. Simpson," June 17, 1937, p. 453.
17 *The Word, The Work and The World*, "Evangelistic Meetings in New York," October 1, 1883, p. 154.
18 Ibid, p. 154.
19 Simpson, A. B., *Living Truths*, p. 154.
20 Ibid, p. 155; Thompson, A. E., *The Life of A. B. Simpson*, (Harrisburg, PA: Christian Publications, Inc., 1920), pp. 90–91.
21 Simpson, A. B., *Living Truths*, p. 155.
22 Ibid, p. 155.
23 "The Lost Proctor's Theatre—Nos. 139–145, @. 23rd Street.", p. 2;http://daytoninmanhattan.blogspot.com/2013/11/the-lost-proctors-theatre-nos-139-145-w.html.
24 "Oberammergau is the site of a "Passion Play" held since 1634 and is shown every 10 years. https://en.wikipedia.org/wiki/Oberammergau_Passion_Play.
25 "The Lost Proctor's Theatre – Nos. 139-145, W. 23rd Street.", p. 2. http://daytoninmanhattan.blogspot.com/2013/11/the-lost-proctors-theatre-nos-139-145-w.html.
26 Ibid, p. 2.
27 Ibid, p. 2.
28 Ibid, p. 2; Simpson, A. B., *Living Truths*, p. 155.
29 Simpson, A. B., *Living Truths*, p. 155.
30 Thompson, *The Life of A. B. Simpson*, p. 91.
31 Conley, Joseph F., *Drumbeats that Changed the World* (Pasadena, CA: William Carey Library, 2000), p. 42.
32 Jones, David P., *So Being Sent . . . They Went—A History of the CMA Mission in Cabinda: 1885–1957* (Newark, DE. PWO Publications, 2015), p.46.
33 *The Regions Beyond Magazine* was the missionary periodical for Guinness's mission, later called the RBMU (Regions Beyond Missionary Union).
34 Jones, David P., *So Being Sent . . . They Went—A History of the CMA Mission in Cabinda: 1885–1957*, p.46.

35 Neinkirchen, Charles W., *A. B. Simpson and the Pentecostal Movement* (Peabody, MA.: Hendrickson Publishers, 1922), p. 15.

36 Hartzfeld, David F. and Charles Neinkirchen, *The Birth of a Vision* (Beaverlodge, Alberta: Buena Book Services, 1986), p. 21.

37 Boardman, W. E., *Record of the International Conference on Divine Healing and True Holiness* (London: J. Snow & Co., and Bethshan, Drayton Park, Highbury, N. London, 1885), p. 41.

38 Van de Walle, Bernie, *The Heart of the Gospel* (Eugene, OR: Pickwick Publications, 2009), p. 93.

39 Simpson, Albert Benjamin, et al, *Hymns of the Christian Life, Nos. 1, 2 and 3 Combined.* "#445, Himself," (Harrisburg, PA.: The Christian Alliance Publishing Company, 1908).

40 Boardman, W. E., *Record of the International Conference on Divine Healing and True Holiness,* p. 58.

41 Brennen, Katherine Alberta, *Mrs. A. B. Simpson—The Wife or Love Stands.* Self-published, n.d., p. 10.

42 "A New Missionary Alliance," *The Word, The Work and the World,* June 1, 1887, pp. 365–368.

43 Guiness, H. Grattan, *The Approaching End of the Age: Viewed in the Light of History, Prophecy, and Science* (London: Hodder and Stoughton, 1879).

44 Simpson, A. B., *The Holy Spirit: Power from on High,* Vol. 1 (Harrisburg, PA: Christian Publications, Inc., 1894), p. 207.

45 *The Word, The Work and The World,* September 1, 1886.

CHAPTER 9

1 Neinkirchen, Charles W., *A. B. Simpson and the Pentecostal Movement* (Peabody, MA.: Hendrickson Publishers, 1992), p. 18.

2 "A Gross Misrepresentation," *The Christian Alliance and Missionary Weekly,* Vol. 3, No. 16, November 15, 1889, p. 241.

3 Jampolier, Andrew C. A., *Congo: The Miserable Expeditions and Dreadful Death of Lt. Emory Taunt, USN,* (Annapolis, MD: Naval Institute Press, 2013), p. 75.

4 *The Word, The Work and The World,* March 1883, Vol. III, No. 3. "Missionary Work," p.46.

5. Niklaus, Robert L., John S. Sawin, and Samuel J. Stoesz, *All for Jesus, 125th Anniversary Edition* (Colorado Springs, CO: The Christian and Missionary Alliance, 2013), p. 106.
6. *The Christian Alliance and Missionary Weekly*, "A Missionary Seal," Vol. V, Nos. 3-4; "The Old Orchard Convention," No. 3, July 17, 1890, p. 33.
7. Ibid, p. 33.
8. Ibid, p. 33.
9. King, Paul L., *Anointed Women: The Rich Heritage of Women in Ministry in The Christian and Missionary Alliance* (Tulsa, OK: Word & Spirit Press, 2009), pp. 19, 20.
10. Ibid, p. 19, 20.
11. *The Christian Alliance and Missionary Weekly*, Vol. VII, No. 3, July 17, 1891, p. 33.
12. Niklaus, et. al, *All for Jesus, 125th Anniversary Edition,* pp. 114, 115.
13. Simpson, A. B., *The Coming One* (New Kensington, PA: Whitaker House, 2014), p. 53.
14. Ibid, p. 54.
15. Simpson, Albert Benjamin, et al, "To the Regions Beyond," *Hymns of the Christian Life, Nos. 1, 2 and 3 Combined*. (Harrisburg, PA. The Christian Alliance Publishing Company, 1908), #834.
16. Niklaus, et. al., *All for Jesus, 125th Anniversary Edition,* p. 111.
17. Ibid, p. 114.
18. Thompson, A. E., *The Life of A. B. Simpson* (Harrisburg, PA: Christian Publications, Inc., 1920), pp. 128–130.

CHAPTER 10

1. Niklaus, Robert L., John S. Sawin, and Samuel J. Stoesz, *All for Jesus, 125th Anniversary Edition* (Colorado Springs, CO: The Christian and Missionary Alliance, 2013), p. 115.
2. *The Missionary Review of the World,* July 1899, p. 617. https://books.google.com/books?id=rttDAQAAMAAJ&pg=PA621&lpg=PA621&dq=Missionary+Review+of+the+World++Emilio+Olsson&source=bl&ots=DSTzqC1skz&sig=YuQY-NbxtV9aPOJsOZ9q430r5rU&hl=en&sa=X&ved=2ahUKEwjG7Oi23pXfAhUQk1kKHdnoBkQQ6AEwCXoE-

CAkQAQ#v=onepage&q=Missionary%20Review%20of%20the%20World%20%20Emilio%20Olsson&f=false.
3. Ibid, p. 620.
4. Ibid, pp. 620–621.
5. Ibid, p. 619.
6. *Christian Alliance and Foreign Missionary Weekly,* December 4, 1896, Vol. XVII, No. 23, p. 508.
7. Jones, David, *Roots and Branches* (Newark, DE: PWO Publications, 2018), p. 44.
8. *The Missionary Review of the World,* July 1899 to December 1900, Vol. XXII, No. 1, p. 617–619; Ollson, Emilio, "Rev. A. B. Simpson's Misstatements Refuted," (NY: s.p., 1899).
9. *The Christian and Missionary Alliance,* 1906, Vol. XXVI, No. 23, p. 369.
10. Ibid, p. 369.
11. Niklaus, et. al., *All for Jesus, 125th Anniversary Edition,* p. 126.
12. *The Christian Alliance and Missionary Weekly,* April 2, 1897, Vol. XVIII, No. 14, p. 324.
13. Thompson, A. E., *The Life of A. B. Simpson* (Harrisburg, PA: Christian Publications, Inc., 1920), p. 165.
14. Warfield, Benjamin, *Counterfeit Miracles* (New York: Charles Scribner's Son, 1918), p. 165.
15. Reynolds, Lindsay, *Footprints,* (Beaverlodge, Alberta: Buena Book Services,1981), p. 75.
16. Ibid, p. 66.
17. "John Alexander Dowie," https://en.wikipedia.org/wiki/John_Alexander_Dowie, n.d.
18. Tozer, A. W., *Wingspread* (Harrisburg, PA: Christian Publications, Inc., 1944), p. 134–135.
19. Ibid, p. 135.
20. Ibid, p. 135.
21. King, Paul L., *Genuine Gold* (Tulsa, OK: Word and Spirit Press, 2006), p. 13.
22. *The Christian and Missionary Alliance, March 31, 1906, p. 185; A Movement for God, An Introduction to the History and Thought of The Christian and Missionary Alliance,* National Church Ministries of the C&MA, Colorado, Springs, CO. pp. 8, 11.
23. Ibid, p. 8.

24 Blumhofer, Edith, *The Assemblies of God: A Chapter in the Story of American Pentecostalism* (Springfield, MO: Gospel Publishing House, 1989) p. 185.
25 King, Paul L., *Genuine Gold* (Tulsa, OK: Word and Spirit Press, 2006), p. 84.
26 McKaig, C. Donald, *The Simpson Scrapbook*, (Nyack, NY, 1971), p. 261.
27 Simpson, A. B., *Nyack Diary*, September 12–13, 1907, p. 5.
28 King, *Genuine Gold*, p. 76.
29 Ibid, p. 76.
30 "Demon Possession in our Mincheo Native Conference," *The Christian and Missionary Alliance*, January 1908, pp. 38–39.
31 "Annual Report of the President and General Superintendent of The Christian and Missionary Alliance," *The Christian and Missionary Alliance*, June 5, 1908, p. 155.
32 *The Alliance Weekly*, May 30, 1914, p. 130; Ekvall, Robert B., *Gateway to Tibet*, Harrisburg, PA: Christian Publications, Inc., 1938, pp. 62–63.
33 King, *Genuine Gold*, p. 171.

CHAPTER 11

1 "Weird Babble of Tongues," *The Los Angeles Times*, (Los Angeles, CA, April 18, 1906), p. 17, https://www.newspapers.com/clip/9928151/azusa_street_weird_babel_tongues/.
2 Niklaus, Robert L., John S. Sawin, and Samuel J. Stoesz, *All for Jesus, 125th Anniversary Edition* (Colorado Springs, CO: The Christian and Missionary Alliance, 2013), p. 136.
3 Brennen, Katherine, *Mrs. A. B. Simpson—The Wife or Love Stands*, n.d., p. 16; Sawin, *The Life and Times of A. B. Simpson*, p. 176.
4 Niklaus, et. al., *All for Jesus*, p. 139.
5 *The Christian and Missionary Alliance*, July 2, 1910, p. 224; August 6, 1910, pp. 298–299; September 3, 1910, pp. 369–370.
6 Cook, William Azel, *Through the Wilderness of Brazil by Horse, Canoe and Float* (New York: American Tract Society, 1909), pp. 6–7.
7 *The Christian and Missionary Alliance*, May 14, 1910, p. 106
8 Ibid, May 21, 1910, p. 122.

9 Ibid, p. 122.
10 Ibid, p. 123.
11 Ibid, April 2, 1897, p. 324.
12 *The Christian and Missionary Alliance*, June 8, 1912, pp. 145–146.
13 Niklaus, et. al., *All for Jesus*, p. 131.
14 Ibid, p. 142.
15 *The Alliance Weekly*, December 5, 1914, p. 145.
16 Simpson, A. B., T*he Fourfold Gospel* (New York: The Christian Alliance Pub. Co., 1890) pp. 44–45.
17 Tozer, A. W., *Wingspread*, (Harrisburg, PA: Christian Publications, Inc., 1944), p. 138.
18 Francis, Mabel, *One Shall Chase a Thousand* (Harrisburg, PA: Christian Publications Inc., 1968), pp. 30–31.
19 Snyder, James. *Paul Rader: Portrait of an Evangelist* (1879–1938) (Ocala, FL: Fellowship Ministries, 2015.), p. 22.
20 Ibid, p. 47.
21 Ibid, pp. 52.
22 *The Alliance Weekly*, October 9, 1915, p. 28.
23 Ibid, January 15, 1919, p. 98.
24 https://www.haaretz.com/jewish/.premium-1917-general-allenby-shows-how-a-moral-man-conquers-jerusalem-1.5343853.
25 Brennen, Katherine, *Mrs. A. B. Simpson—The Wife or Love Stands*, n.d., p. 25.
26 *The Alliance Weekly*, December 20, 1919, p. 220.
27 *The Alliance Weekly*, November 8, 1919, p. 220.
28 McKaig, C. Donald, *The Simpson Scrapbook*, (Nyack, NY, 1971), p. 265.
29 Ibid, p.267–268.
30 Ibid, pp. 268.
31 Niklaus, et. al., *All for Jesus*, p. 165.
32 Ibid, p. 165.
33 "Notes from Nyack," *The Alliance Weekly*, April 6, 1918, p. 11.
34 Ibid, September 7, 1918, p. 353.
35 Brennen, *Mrs. A. B. Simpson—The Wife or Love Stands*, p. 19.
36 Sawin, John, *The Life and Times of A. B. Simpson* (Regina, Sas-

katchewan: Archibald Foundation Library, Canadian Bible College/Canadian Theological Seminary, n. d.), p. 255.
37 Thompson, *The Life of A. B. Simpson*.
38 Ibid, p. 220-221.

CHAPTER 12

1 "My Memories of Dr. Simpson," *The Alliance Weekly*, May 22, 1937, p. 324.
2 Ibid, p. 324.
3 Van De Walle, Bernie A., *The Heart of the Gospel* (Eugene, OR: Pickwick Publications, 2009), p. 92.
4 *The Alliance Weekly*, September 15, 1893, p. 166.
5 Ibid, p. 160.
6 Tozer, A. W., *Warfare of the Spirit*, compiled by Harry Verplough (Camp Hill, PA.: Wingspread Publishers, 1993), p. 63.
7 "My Memories of Dr. Simpson," *The Alliance Weekly*, August 21, 1937, p. 535.
8 Ibid, p. 535.
9 Ibid, September 4, 1937, p. 581.
10 *The Alliance Weekly*, September 11, 1937, p. 580.
11 Elliot, David R., *Studies of Eight Canadian Fundamentalists*, (Thesis for partial fulfillment of Doctor of Philosophy requirements, 1989), p. 1, The University of British Colombia). https://www.csph.ca/assets/1998-elliot.pdf.
12 Simpson, A. B., "My Own Story," (Ambrose University, Readings, 1.2, https://online.ambrose.edu/alliancestudies/ahtreadings/ahtr_s1.html.
13 Ibid, Reading 1.2.
14 Sawin, John, *The Life and Times of A. B. Simpson* (Regina, Saskatchewan: Archibald Foundation Library, Canadian Bible College/Canadian Theological Seminary, n. d.), p. 270.
15 "My Memories of Dr. Simpson," *The Alliance Weekly*, May 22, 1937, p. 325.
16 Sawin, p. 270.
17 Ibid, p. 55.
18 Brandi, James, *Recapturing the Vision: A Study of the Vision of Albert Benjamin Simpson as Articulated in His Sermons*, Submitted to the faculty in partial fulfillment of the requirements

for the degree of Doctor of Ministry at Trinity International University, p. 141.
19 Reid, Darrell, *Jesus Only': The Early Life and Presbyterian Ministry of Albert Benjamin Simpson, 1843–1881* (Ph.D. dissertation, Queen's University. 1994), p. 261.
20 Sawin, p. 580.
21 Simpson, A. B., "Aggressive Christianity," *O Christian,* http://articles.ochristian.com/article6347.shtml.
22 Simpson, A. B., *The Gospel in All Lands,* March 1880, p. 55.
23 *The Word, The Work and the World,* January, 1882 p. 44.
24 *The Word, The Work and the World,* February, 1882, p. 94.
25 Reitz, George. "A. B. Simpson—Urban Evangelist." *Urban Mission* 8 (1991), pp. 22.
26 Yount, Michael G., *A. B. Simpson—His Message and Impact on the Third Great Awakening* (Eugene, OR: WIPF & STOCK, 2016), p. 133.
27 Dayton, Edward, *Discovering an Evangelical Heritage,* (New York: Harper and Row), pp. 113.
28 Hartzfeld, David F. and Charles Neinkirchen, *The Birth of a Vision* (Beaverlodge, Alberta: Buena Book Services, 1986), p. 52.
29 Yount, p. 180.
30 *The Alliance Weekly,* September, 11, 1937, p. 580.
31 Ibid, p. 581.

APPENDIX 1

1 *The Alliance Weekly,* February 24, 1924, p. 807.
2 Ibid, p. 807.
3 Brennen, Katherine A., *Mrs. A. B. Simpson—The Wife or Love Stands,* n. d., p. 11.
4 Ibid, p. 11.
5 Nienkirchen, Charles, *The Man, the Movement, and the Mission: A Documentary History of the Christian and Missionary Alliance,* p. 72.
6 Brennen, *Mrs. A. B. Simpson—The Wife or Love Stands,* pp. 19.
7 Simpson, A. B., *Songs of the Spirit* (Harrisburg, PA.: Christian Publications Inc. n.d.), p. 18.
8 *The Christian Alliance Foreign Missionary Weekly,* July 20, 1894, p. 67.

APPENDIX 2

1. Thompson, A. E., *The Life of A. B. Simpson,* (Harrisburg, PA: Christian Publications, Inc., 1920), p. 9.
2. Brennen, Katherine A., *Mrs. A. B. Simpson—The Wife or Love Stands,* n.d., p. 22.
3. Buckman, Margaret Simpson, *His Own Life Story,* unpublished typewritten manuscript, 1953, p. 7.
4. Ibid, p. 44.
5. Ibid, p. 8.
6. Ibid, pp. 8, 44.
7. Ibid, pp. 37–39; 47–54.
8. Brennen, Katherine A., *Mrs. A. B. Simpson—The Wife or Love Stands,* p. 7.
9. Sawin, *The Life and Times of A. B. Simpson,* p. 182.

APPENDIX 3

1. King, Paul, *Genuine Gold,* (Tulsa, OK: Word & Spirit Press, 2006), p.189.
2. Niklaus, Robert L., John S. Sawin, and Samuel J. Stoesz, *All for Jesus, 125th Anniversary Edition,* (Colorado Springs, CO: The Christian and Missionary Alliance, 2013), pp. 175–177.
3. Ibid, pp. 166–167.
4. Ibid, p. 187.

APPENDIX 4

1. Thompson, A. E., *The Life of A. B. Simpson* (Harrisburg, PA: Christian Publications, Inc., 1920), pp. 19–23.
2. Ibid, pp. 75–76.

ANNOTATED BIBLIOGRAPHY

C&MA HISTORY

Adams, Samuel Hawley. *Life of Henry Foster, M.D. Founder Clifton Springs Sanitarium.* Rochester, New York: Rochester Times-Union, 1921.
    Written by the longtime chaplain (1898 to 1915) of the Clifton Springs Sanitarium, where A. B. Simpson spent three extended periods of time recovering from physical and emotional collapses in his ministry, the book gives extensive background on Dr. Henry Foster, the godly Methodist founder of the sanitarium where Simpson regained his health and was influenced by Foster's wholistic approach in treating the soul in order to heal the body.

Bailey, Anita. *Heritage Cameos.* Camp Hill, PA: Christian Publications, Inc., 1986.
    This little volume was written on the occasion of the 100th anniversary celebration of The Christian and Missionary Alliance. Biographical sketches of more than 20 Alliance women, including Margaret Simpson. This is the only published source of information in many of the biographies.

Brennen, Katherine Alberta. n.d. *Mrs. A. B. Simpson—The Wife or Love Stands.* Self-published.
    Brennen's quirky little book is often hard to understand due to her cryptic remarks, written as though she was writing to family members who were "in" on the family secrets. Despite this shortcoming, she reveals many fascinating tidbits from the life of A. B. and Margaret and the Simpson family, from Knox College days till the death of Simpson and later his wife.

Brown, Ronald and Charles Cook, eds. *The God You May Not Know.* Toronto: The Christian and Missionary Alliance in Canada, 2016.
    This book tells the story of the earliest Alliance mission fields to which A. B. Simpson sent missionaries such as Congo, Ecuador, Indonesia, and Vietnam. Many of these now have

strong national Alliance faith communities. Included are also 12 autobiographies of Canadian Alliance international workers who worked in these fields.

Brown, Ronald and Charles Cook, eds. *The God Made Known.* Toronto: The Christian and Missionary Alliance in Canada, 2018
In this second volume of a trilogy on the Canadian Alliance global engagement we have the story of another twelve Alliance mission fields such as Guinea, Mali, Thailand, Irian Jaya, France, and Argentina, including a dozen autobiographies of Canadian Alliance international workers.

Carner, E. R. *The Life of Ed. D. Whiteside, the Praying Man of Pittsburgh.* Harrisburg, PA: Christian Publications, Inc., 1963.

Draper, Kenneth L. *Readings in Alliance Thought and History.* 2009. http://www.awf.nu/wp-content/uploads/2013/08/Reader-AHT-2009.pdf.
Ambrose University has excellent resources related to A. B. Simpson and the history of the C&MA.

Dys, Pat and Linda Corbin. *He Obeyed God—The Story of Albert Benjamin Simpson.* Harrisburg, PA: Christian Publications, Inc., 1986.
This is an intriguing biography of Simpson, written for children from the perspective of a young boy who is learning Simpson's story from an old man who knew Simpson. No new facts are revealed, but the emphasis on Simpson's walk with God from his youth forward is helpful.

Ekvall, Robert B. et al. *After Fifty Years.* Harrisburg, PA: Christian Publications, Inc., 1939.
Written on the occasion of The Alliance's 50th year anniversary, this is largely an overview of the C&MA's worldwide ministry, but does contain a few biographical details. It is useful as a way of measuring the effect of Simpson's life some years after his death in 1919.

Evearrit, Daniel J. *Evangelism and the Social Concern of A. B. Simpson.* Camp Hill, PA: Christian Publications, Inc., 1994.
Evearrit's book recounts Simpson's early commitment to the

social implications of the gospel, tracing the early years of the ministry of the Gospel Tabernacle and the fledgling Alliance missions movement. Ministry to the addicted, "fallen women," orphans, healing rest homes, outreach to African-Americans, and more were all part and parcel of those early years. However, by the early 1900s, Evearrit points out a marked decline in the C&MA outreach to North American society, as a reaction against the growing "social gospel" as preached by increasingly liberal mainline denominations.

Holvast, Rene. *The Big Surprise: A History of the Christian and Missionary Alliance in the Congo 1885—1908*. Calgary: Global Vault, 2018.
The Big Surprise tells the story of the first 23 years of missionary work of The Christian and Missionary Alliance in what is today the Democratic Republic of the Congo. It is the moving story of missionaries embarking on a work for which they had no practical experience or training. They had no idea of what was waiting for them. It was the very first C&MA mission field. It is a story of unwarranted optimism and unwarranted pessimism, of inspiring heroism and dispiriting failures, of some paralyzed by fear and of others rising to the occasion.

Hostetter, Dorothy M. *If These Walls Could Talk*. America Start Books, 2014.
Ms. Hostetter tells the history and the "stories" from inside the walls of Chapel Pointe, formerly known as The Alliance Home, in Carlisle, Pennsylvania. The home began under the ministry of Rev. Fred H. Henry, whose heart for retired Alliance pastors and missionaries drove him to bring that dream into reality. There are "Simpson snippets" here and there lauded in her little volume.

Jones, David P. *Roots and Branches: The History of The Christian and Missionary Alliance in Brazil*. Newark, DE: PWO Publications, 2018.
This volume that traces the first attempt by Simpson to send missionaries to the "sleeping giant" of South America, up to the final successful sending of Alliance missionaries in the early 1960s, relates some of the early difficulties that Simpson had

in selecting missionary candidates and leaders for this young mission undertaking that was springing into being.

Jones, David P. So *Being Sent . . . They Went—A History of the CMA Mission in Cabinda: 1885–1957* Newark, DE: PWO Publications, 2015.

This history traces the earliest mission work of A. B. Simpson, before the founding of the C&MA in 1887, and the disastrous first attempt to send a missionary team to the Congo in the Portuguese Enclave of Cabinda. The tragic story of John Condit and the other members of the Congo Band is told in detail, with previously undocumented detail.

McKaig, C. Donald. "The Simpson Scrapbook." Nyack, NY, 1971. Unpublished typed manuscript and notes.

McCaig, longtime teacher at Nyack College and eventual vice president, collected hundreds of items, articles, notes, stories, memorabilia and anecdotes, and depositions regarding A. B. Simpson's life and ministry. While roughly organized, it provides a wealth of information about the founder of the C&MA.

Niklaus, Robert, John Sawin, and Samuel J. Stoesz. *All for Jesus.* Colorado Springs, CO: The Christian and Missionary Alliance, 2013.

Written on the occasion of The Alliance's 125th anniversary, this is an update of an earlier edition written for the 1987 centennial. It contains some new information regarding the ministry of the C&MA worldwide and gives a brief biographical treatment of Simpson.

Olsson, Emilio. *The Dark Continent . . . At Our Doors: Slavery, Heathenism and Cruelty in South America.* New York: Me. E. Munson, Publisher, M. E. Bible House, 1899.

Written by a Swedish missionary sent out by Simpson to head up the whole South American field, Olsson describes his adventures and efforts in scripture distribution and evangelism across most of the South American continent. His association was short-lived, but in the book, he explains his strategy for evangelizing the Southern Continent with 100 men in just 4 years.

Pardington, G. P. *Twenty-Five Wonderful Years*. Harrisburg PA: Christian Publications, Inc., 1914.

Pardington's book traces the first quarter century of The Alliance as it grows from a fledgling, struggling missionary society taking its first steps to an established missions agency with a growing missions presence worldwide and an ever-widening support base in America. In that Simpson was still alive at the time of the book's publication, Pardington, a longtime associate and colleague of Simpson, gives at best a brief biographical treatment of Simpson.

Reynolds, Lindsay. *Footprints: The Beginnings of the Christian and Missionary Alliance in Canada*. Beaverlodge, Alberta: Buena Book Services, 1981.

Reynolds, Lindsey. *Rebirth: The Redevelopment of the Christian and Missionary Alliance in Canada*. Beaverlodge, Alberta: Evangelistic Enterprises, 1992.

Sawin, John. *The Life and Times of A. B. Simpson*. Pdf. Regina, Saskatchewan: Archibald Foundation Library Canadian Bible College/ Canadian Theological Seminary.

Without a doubt, this monumental collection of Simpson's life and work is a tremendous contribution to the study of Simpson as well as the global movement spawned by his vision and drive. Sawin's work is a "diamond mine" that requires the reader/ researcher to dig deep and carefully sift through the "tons of material" in order to find bits and bytes of biographical information.

Simpson, Albert B. *Michele Nardi, The Italian Evangelist: His Life and Work*. New York: Blanche P. Nardi, 1916.

This slim volume is the only book written by Simpson, at the request of Blanche Nardi, wife of Michele Nardi, an Italian-American pastor and friend of A. B., whose life Simpson impacted as his pastor and teacher in the early years of the Gospel Tabernacle. The book reveals much of Simpson's affinity for the growing immigrant population in New York.

Simpson, Harold H. *Cavendish—Its History Its People*. Truro, Nova Scotia: Harold H. Simpson and Associates Ltd, 1973.

Written by the son of A. B. Simpson's first cousin, this fascinating out-of-print book gives ample background and biographical material on Simpson, his early life on Prince Edward Island; the family's move to Western Ontario in 1847; and Simpson's childhood, adolescence, and years at Knox College. An entire chapter is dedicated to the Simpson saga by this obviously proud close relative to A. B.

Snyder, James L. *Paul Rader—Portrait of an Evangelist.* Ocala, FL: Fellowship Ministries, 2015.

Snyder's account of the life of this dynamic, cowboy prizefighter-turned-evangelist, pastor, and eventual leader of the C&MA before going into an independent, wide-ranging ministry is eminently readable and provides a fascinating picture of this larger-than-life man of God.

Tucker, W. Leon. *The Redemption of Paul Rader.* New York: The Book Stall, 1918.

A fascinating first biography of Rader, covering his early life, conversion, ministry with the C&MA, and beyond.

Thompson, A. E. *The Life of A. B. Simpson.* Harrisburg, PA: Christian Publications, Inc., 1920.

Written by Albert Thompson, an Alliance missionary to Palestine and disciple of Simpson, this is the first "official biography" of A. B. Simpson. The book's major virtue is that it was written just one year after Simpson's death. Because access was given to him by the Alliance leadership and the Simpson family, Thompson was able to give an accurate portrayal of A. B. Simpson's life. At the same time, the proximity of publication, just one year after Simpson's death, is also the book's major weakness. There is a lack of historical perspective regarding Simpson's life and work and its effect on The Alliance and the world at large. It couldn't be any different since historical perspective takes time. In addition, Thompson was an Alliance missionary to the Holy Lands and a student and disciple of the "great man." As a result, the rather reverential style of writing and obvious respect and high esteem held by the writer for his subject makes the book sound more like a hagiography than a biography. This impression has grown over the years, with the result that Thompson's book has largely been forgotten by most Alliance members, and for those who do read it, great difficulty arises among younger generations who find it almost impossible to identify with and relate to this bearded iconic figure of another era.

Tozer, A. W. *Wingspread*. Harrisburg, PA: Christian Publications, Inc., 1944.

Tozer's *Wingspread* was written 24 years after Thompson's *The Life of A. B. Simpson,* apparently as an attempt to humanize and "humorize" Simpson's life to new generations of Alliance people who did not know Simpson as personally as those from the first generation. As Tozer later admitted, he did not write a biography of Simpson, but rather an "interpretation" of the life of Simpson. John Sawin told Paul King of *Genuine Gold,* that his desire was to take *Wingspread* out of circulation but Christian Publications would not permit that to happen, since the book was selling well.

C&MA THEOLOGY

Foster, K. Neill and David Fessenden, editors. *Essays on Premillennialism.* Camp Hill, PA: Wingspread Publishers, 2007.

This important work by Foster and Fessenden gives a broad panorama of the thought of Simpson and the C&MA as relates to the Millennium, perhaps as a response to a perceived move toward amillennialism in the Alliance. Emphasis is given to the hermeneutical foundation to the "pre-mil" position and the need to honor and expect the fulfillment of Old and New Testament prophecy as relates to Christ's thousand-year reign on earth following His return.

Hartzfeld, David F. and Charles Neinkirchen. *The Birth of a Vision.* Beaverlodge, Alberta: Buena Book Services, 1986.

Hartzfeld and Nienkirchen's excellent volume, written for the occasion of The Alliance Centennial celebration of 1987, is a festschrift of writings by C&MA writers on various aspects of Simpson's theology, missiology, educational philosophy, social concern, hymnody, literary production, etc. It contains a wealth of material regarding A. B. Simpson and the C&MA's history and ministry.

Keisling, Gary. *Relentless Spirituality: Embracing the Spiritual Disciplines of A. B. Simpson.* Camp Hill, PA: Wingspread Publishers, 2004.

Keisling's book examines the role that spiritual disciplines played in the life of Simpson, providing an in-depth look into the essential elements of his spiritual formation and development.

King, Paul L. *Anointed Women: The Richard Heritage of Women in Ministry in The Christian and Missionary Alliance.* Tulsa, OK: Word & Spirit Press, 2009.

King presents an excellent historical documentation of the "complementarian/egalitarian" position regarding women in ministry held by Simpson and the early Alliance for at least 75 years. Later revisionists attempted to replace this balanced view with a complementarian perspective, but that does not stand up in light of the extensive research done by King.

King, Paul L. *Genuine Gold.* Tulsa, OK: Word and Spirit Press, 2006.

Paul King's invaluable contribution to a better understanding of early Alliance theology and practice also contains tidbits of biographical material regarding Simpson's life and work. This book is a "must read" for all interested in understanding the roots and reasons of the C&MA.

McCrossan, T. J. n. d. *Speaking with Other Tongues, Sign or Gift—Which?* Harrisburg, PA: Christian Publications, Inc.

McCrossan, a scholarly former Presbyterian minister and teacher and early president of Simpson Bible Institute, gives in-depth teaching on the gift of tongues. The "Pentecostal question," which so strongly impacted the early C&MA, resulted in a final parting of ways between those who held that speaking in tongues was the "evidence" of the baptism of the Holy Spirit and those who felt that it was one of the gifts but not the "sign" of spirit baptism.

Neinkirchen, Charles W. *A. B. Simpson and the Pentecostal Movement.* Peabody, MA: Hendrickson Publishers, 1992.

Neinkirchen's book stirred controversy due to his thesis that Simpson was a frustrated tongues seeker who later felt that he had erred in positioning the C&MA as advocating all of the Pentecostal manifestations of the Spirit, including tongues, while refusing to accept the evidence of doctrine. The research and insight of this book, regardless of one's opinion regarding the book's thesis, is impressive and helpful.

Van de Walle, Bernie. *The Heart of the Gospel.* Eugene, OR: Pickwick Publications, 2009.
This work, showing how Simpson's Fourfold Gospel was at the heart of modern Pentecostalism, provides a close observation of the doctrinal themes of select and renowned American evangelical leaders, including A. J. Gordon of Boston, D. L. Moody of Chicago, A. T. Pierson of Philadelphia/Detroit, and A. B. Simpson of New York.

Yount, Michael G. *A. B. Simpson—His Message and Impact on the Third Great Awakening.* Eugene, OR: Wipf & Stock Publishers, 2016.
Yount's book deals with Simpson's life and ministry and his impact on the Third Great Awakening. It provides an in-depth analysis of Simpson's theological perspective and effect on the larger evangelical world.

EVANGELICAL HISTORY

Arrighi, Antonio Andrea. *The Story of Antoni—The Galley Slave.* New York: Fleming H. Revell Co., 1911.
A fascinating autobiographical work by Arrighi, *The Story of Antonio,* tells of his life as a slave in Italy, his migration to the U.S., his conversion, and ministry back in Italy and later in New York City.

Boardman, W. E. *Record of the International Conference on Divine Healing and True Holiness.* London: J. Snow & Co., and Bethshan, Drayton Park, Highbury, N., 1885.
This is the actual "Report as nearly verbatim as possible" of the five-day conference also known as the Bethshan Conference. All of the speakers' addresses are recorded, as are many testimonies from attendees the world over. A very interesting historical record.

Conley, Joseph F. *Drumbeats that Changed the World.* Pasadena, CA: William Carey Library, 2000.

Drumbeats brings the stories of the Regions Beyond Missionary Union and the West Indies Mission together in an intriguing manner, casting a bright light to the genius of Henry Grattan and Fanny Guinness, who began the East London Missionary Training College. This innovative school spawned a multitude of ministries, including the two missions mentioned above, and provided a working model that A. B. Simpson copied when he began the Missionary Training Institute in New York City, which later moved to Nyack. Guinness exerted a profound influence on the life of A. B. Simpson from his critical teen years and for most of Simpson's lifetime.

Grubb, Norman. P. *Rees Howells Intercessor.* Fort Washington, PA: Christian Literature Crusade, 1964.

This biography of Howells' life relates how Simpson's teaching on divine healing influenced Howells as he and his wife prepared for their years of missionary service in South Africa.

Guinness, Michele. *The Guinness Legend.* London: Hodder & Stoughton, 1989.

Written by one of the amazing Guinness clan, this book relates the history of the Irish family famous for brewers, bankers, and preachers. Henry Grattan Guinness, one of the most illustrious members, was the fiery young preacher whose hell-fire sermons brought teenage Albert Simpson under deep conviction. His influence continued during Simpson's life, informing his theology, missiology, philosophy of Christian education, and even his writing.

Hankins, Barry. J*esus and Gin—Evangelicalism, the Roaring Twenties and Today's Culture Wars.* New York: Palgrave McMillan, 2010.

This is Hankins's popular treatment of the history of the rise of fundamentalism and evangelicalism in the period immediately following Simpson's death in 1919. The book is important, since it provides a fuller account of Paul Rader's life and ministry with the C&MA and following his departure from Alliance ministries.

Magnuson, Norris. *Salvation in the Slums: Evangelical Social Work 1865–1920.* Eugene, OR: Wipf & Stock Publishers, 1977.

Magnuson's research concerning the social work of such evangelical leaders as A. B. Simpson, A. J. Gordon, F. B. Meyer, and many others, as well as the amazing work of the Salvation Army, urban rescue missions and, in particular, The Christian and Missionary Alliance from its earliest years, puts this wholistic ministry into perspective over and against the early proponents of the "social gospel." Led by Walter Rauschenbusch, this more optimistic theology saw the rise of society by enlisting the church in a program to feed, clothe, train, and educate the poor and neglected, thus raising them to be better citizens. This horizontal approach with a de-emphasis on the need for personal salvation caused many evangelicals to eventually reduce their efforts in social work.

FICTION

Montgomery, L. M. *Anne of Green Gables.* New York: Bantam Books, 1992.

A best-seller in the early 1900s and a classic in its day, this book is set on Prince Edward Island, the birthplace of A. B. Simpson. Through *Anne of Green Gables,* one sees this beautiful little redoubt of Scottish immigrants and the powerful influence of the local Cavendish Presbyterian Church, where Simpson's parents took him for his baptism. Local color and a heightened understanding of the culture of those Reformed stalwarts gives insight to Simpson's early years and personality development.

GENERAL HISTORY

Annbinder, Tyler. *Five Points: The 19th Century New York City Neighborhood . . .* New York: Simon and Schuster, 2001.

Annbinder's tome on the infamous lower Manhattan neighborhood, describes in detail the colorful criminals, struggling immigrants, black freedmen and women from the south, and a host of other denizens of this neighborhood that put the word "slum" on the map. It was in this in notorious area of lower New York City that Simpson began some of his earliest outreaches to the "neglected masses" of America's Gotham.

Breese, Dave. *Seven Men Who Rule the World from the Grave.* Chicago: Moody Press, 1990.

Breese's book is a popular treatment of seven major figures from the 19th and early 20th centuries whose writings and philosophies have had a profound impact on the world. Four of them, Darwin, Marx, Freud, and Wellhausen, deeply influenced the church in Simpson's day.

Jampolier, Andrew C. A. *Congo: The Miserable Expeditions and Dreadful Death of Lt. Emory Taunt,* USN. Annapolis, MD: Naval Institute Press, 2013.

A recent volume that contains fascinating and heretofore unmentioned criticism of A. B. Simpson and the first missionary venture of the "Congo Band" in 1885, Jampolier cites the caustic comments and attacks against Navy Lieutenant Emory Taunt. He was sent out by the U.S. Navy to investigate the Congo River in 1896 for information about navigation, commercial opportunity, and much more. In his travels, he met Frank Gerrish, the only member of the Congo Band who stayed on the field as a missionary. Taunt severely criticized Simpson in his report to the U.S. Navy Secretary as well as to the U.S. press, regarding the lack of preparation for this missionary venture. Much of what Taunt pointed out was accurate but totally lacked the perspective of the new missions society. A fascinating read with a sad finale.

Johnson, Paul. *Modern Times—The World from the 20s to the Nineties.* New York: Harper Collins, 1991.

This is another amazing work by Johnson, revealing his breadth of knowledge and insight into the forces and personalities that forged events and profoundly impacted world affairs and the intellectual milieu of Simpson's day and beyond.

THEOLOGY

King, Paul L. *Only Believe—Examining the Origin and Development of Classic and Contemporary Word of Faith Theologies.* Tulsa, OK: Word and Spirit Press, 2008.

Only Believe is considered "the definitive study of the teaching and practices of faith throughout church history. Thoroughly documented with classic and contemporary citations, it breaks new ground." (Mark E. Roberts, Director, Holy Spirit Research Center, Oral Roberts University.)

Marshall, Walter. *Gospel Mystery of Sanctification* (reprint). Hertford, Great Britain: First Evangelical Press edition, 1981.

This reprint of the book that was critical in Simpson's salvation story was written by a Puritan pastor in the 1600s. For a young boy steeped in Calvinistic theology and uncertain as to his election for salvation, Bert Simpson relished Marshall's simple words about the simple gospel message, which led the teenager to Christ's feet for forgiveness and peace of heart and mind.

DISSERTATIONS

Glass, Clyde M. "Mysticism and Contemplation in the Life and Teaching of Albert Benjamin Simpson." Milwaukee, WI: Marquette University, 1997.

This dissertation was presented by Glass to the faculty of the Marquette Graduate School, part of his PhD requirement. In it, Glass traces Simpson's spiritual journey and the various sources for Simpson's mystical and contemplative thought. The section of "Spiritual Journey" is especially helpful in sketching out his spiritual development.

Bedford, William. "A Larger Christian Life: A. B. Simpson and the Early Years of The Christian And Missionary Alliance." A Dissertation presented to the graduate faculty of the University of Virginia in Candidacy for the Degree of Doctor of Philosophy, 1992.

Bedford's dissertation covers the period from Simpson's leaving the Thirteenth Street Presbyterian Church in New York City in late 1881 to the founding of the "two Alliances" in 1887 and their merger into The Christian and Missionary Alliance in 1897.

Brandli, James J. "Recapturing the Vision: A Study of the Vision of Albert Benjamin Simpson as Articulated in His Sermons." 2009. A dissertation submitted to fulfill academic requirements for Doctor of Ministry at Trinity International University.

McGraw, Gerald. "The Doctrine of Sanctification in the Published Writings of Albert Benjamin Simpson." PhD thesis, New York University, 1896.

Reid, Darrell. "Jesus Only: The Early Life and Presbyterian Ministry of Albert Benjamin Simpson, 1843-1881." PhD dissertation, Queen's University. 1994.

Reid's dissertation covers a relative "black hole" in the early history of Simpson, covering his birth on Prince Edward Island, the family move to Chatham, Ontario in 1847, Simpson's childhood, teenage spiritual crisis, and eventual experience of salvation. His years at Knox College, courtship of Margaret Henry, marriage and his first pastorate at the Hamilton Cooke Presbyterian Church, the move to Chestnut Street Presbyterian Church in Louisville, Kentucky, and eventual move to New York where he pastored the Thirteenth Street Presbyterian Church are covered in detail. This thesis fills in the gaps found in Thompson and Tozer's biographies of A. B. Simpson.

Elliot, David R. "Studies of Eight Canadian Fundamentalists." PhD dissertation at the University of British Colombia, Vancouver B.S., 1989.